Lectionary Worship Workbook

Series II, Cycle A
Gospel Texts

Wayne H. Keller

CSS Publishing Company, Inc., Lima, Ohio

*Dedicated to all who seek
creative and energetic worship*

Copyright © 1998 by
CSS Publishing Company, Inc.
Lima, Ohio

The original purchaser may photocopy material in this publication for use as it was intended (i.e. worship material for worship use; educational material for classroom use; dramatic material for staging or production). No additional permission is required from the publisher for such copying by the original purchaser only. Inquiries should be addressed to: Permissions, CSS Publishing Company, Inc., P.O. Box 4503, Lima, Ohio 45802-4503.

Library of Congress Cataloging-in-Publication Data

Keller, Wayne H., 1930-
   Lectionary worship workbook. Series II. Cycle A / Wayne H. Keller.
      p.   cm.
   Includes bibliographical references and index.
   ISBN 0-7880-1205-3 (pbk. : alk. paper)
   1. Public worship—Handbooks, manuals, etc. 2. Common lectionary—Handbooks, manuals, etc. I. Title.
BV25.K435   1998
264—dc21   98-6061
                                                                                                                                                                              CIP

This book is available in the following formats, listed by ISBN:
      0-7880-1205-3   Book

Table Of Contents

Preface — 5

Foreword — 5

Introduction — 6

Advent — The Season Of Expectancy — 11
   Advent 1 — 12
   Advent 2 — 15
   Advent 3 — 18
   Advent 4 — 21

Christmas — The Season Of The Nativity — 24
   Christmas Eve/Day — 25
   Christmas 1 — 27
   Christmas 2 — 30

Epiphany — The Season Of The Evangel — 33
   Epiphany Day/The Baptism Of The Lord (Epiphany 1) — 34
   Epiphany 2 — 37
   Epiphany 3 — 40
   Epiphany 4 — 43
   Epiphany 5 — 46
   Epiphany 6 — 49
   Epiphany 7 — 52
   Epiphany 8 — 55
   The Transfiguration Of The Lord — 58

Lenten — The Season Of Renewal — 61
   Ash Wednesday — 62
   Lent 1 — 63
   Lent 2 — 66
   Lent 3 — 69
   Lent 4 — 72
   Lent 5 — 75
   Passion/Palm Sunday — 78
   Holy Thursday/Maundy Thursday — 81
   Good Friday — 82

Easter — The Season Of The Resurrection — 83
   Easter Day — 84
   Bright Monday — 88
   Easter 2 — 90
   Easter 3 — 93
   Easter 4 — 96
   Easter 5 — 99
   Easter 6 — 102
   Ascension Day — 105
   Easter 7 — 108

Pentecost — The Season Of The Holy Spirit   111
    Pentecost   112
    Trinity Sunday   115
    (Proper One)   118
    (Proper Two)   118
    (Proper Three)   118
    Proper 4, Pentecost 2, Ordinary Time 9   119
    Proper 5, Pentecost 3, Ordinary Time 10   122
    Proper 6, Pentecost 4, Ordinary Time 11   125
    Proper 7, Pentecost 5, Ordinary Time 12   128
    Proper 8, Pentecost 6, Ordinary Time 13   131
    Proper 9, Pentecost 7, Ordinary Time 14   134
    Proper 10, Pentecost 8, Ordinary Time 15   137
    Proper 11, Pentecost 9, Ordinary Time 16   140
    Proper 12, Pentecost 10, Ordinary Time 17   143
    Proper 13, Pentecost 11, Ordinary Time 18   146
    Proper 14, Pentecost 12, Ordinary Time 19   149
    Proper 15, Pentecost 13, Ordinary Time 20   152
    Proper 16, Pentecost 14, Ordinary Time 21   156
    Proper 17, Pentecost 15, Ordinary Time 22   159
    Proper 18, Pentecost 16, Ordinary Time 23   162
    Proper 19, Pentecost 17, Ordinary Time 24   165
    Proper 20, Pentecost 18, Ordinary Time 25   168
    Proper 21, Pentecost 19, Ordinary Time 26   171
    Proper 22, Pentecost 20, Ordinary Time 27   174
    Proper 23, Pentecost 21, Ordinary Time 28   177
    Proper 24, Pentecost 22, Ordinary Time 29   180
    Proper 25, Pentecost 23, Ordinary Time 30   183
    All Saints' Sunday   186
    Proper 26, Pentecost 24, Ordinary Time 31   189
    Proper 27, Pentecost 25, Ordinary Time 32   192
    Proper 28, Pentecost 26, Ordinary Time 33   195
    Pentecost 27   198
    Christ The King, Proper 29   201
    Thanksgiving Eve/Day   204

Introduction To The Appendices   207

Contents Of The Appendices   207

Appendix I — Music Resources   208

Appendix II — Additional Worship Resources   209

Appendix III — Ways To Use The Senses In Worship As Celebration   211

Appendix IV — An Order Of Worship   214

Appendix V-A — Sermon Evaluation By The Congregation   218

Appendix V-B — Worship Evaluation   220

Preface

Several years ago, *Life Magazine*, and others, referred to 11:00 a.m. Sunday morning worship as the most segregated hour of the week. For many, however, Sunday worship has become the most boring hour of the week. And why not! Many view worship as a spectator sport in which congregations compete for members who pick and choose what suits their fancy. Much worship has become I-centered. "What can I get from it for me and my family?" and "If my church doesn't produce what I want, I'll go elsewhere."

For me, no spectators are allowed in worship. God calls the congregation to celebrate — sometimes silently, sometimes loudly, sometimes casually, sometimes formally — with heart, spirit, strength, mind. Worship, as celebration, leads to life as celebration, amidst joy, sadness, fear, confusion, anger. Celebration involves comforting and confronting. I consider the liturgy as the work — and the play — of the people; for worship, at its best, celebrates every dimension of life, every aspect of existence.

Wayne H. Keller

Foreword

The first time I met Wayne Keller was a shock to my lifetime Presbyterian persona. Wayne had been called to serve as interim pastor for our small congregation in Graham, Washington. We were a diverse group and many of us came to the church from various nearby suburbs, with backgrounds in many different denominations.

As the three generations of my family sat expectantly that first Sunday, we were suddenly confronted by this pastor in a white robe with Snoopy, of cartoon fame, dancing across it. This was a statement before he spoke a word and he had my attention. I realized this man was pushing me to take part in the worship experience. No longer did I have the option to attend church, sitting sedately while the pastor spoon-fed me salvation.

Wayne pulls out all the stops. He uses language veering away from the usual "churchy," reverent vernacular with *Wow, yes indeed*, and a lilting *Ta Da*! He also assures us it is okay not to be perfect and sin is **missing the mark**. The *Cotton Patch Version* of the New Testament is a favorite tool of Wayne's for communicating the Word. Wayne always wants us "to get it," and really understand what he is trying to share with us.

Music can be the choir or a contemporary song on tape, drama can be a skit or a written scene, but Wayne believes in delivering the message. The message can be thoughtful or upbeat but always imparting to the congregation connectiveness, compassion, and love. But, most of the time, it is a joyous celebration, a party, despite the ups and downs of human existence. Wayne will always be bold colors, balloons, and laughter to me. Yet, in the midst of the celebration, Wayne cautions us that "all of life is holy ground, so watch where you are stepping."

As Wayne pulls the congregation into the worship service, we become part of it in spite of ourselves and discover the adventure of life. He challenges us intellectually to think with the mind of the Christ and receive Christ's love so we can do his will in the tensions of today's world, for the theology of Wayne Keller does not deal so much with the hereafter as with the here and now.

When I listen to his sermons, I always get recharged for the coming week. The pageantry, simple language, and active participation magically come together to speak a simple "Thank you, Lord."

June Randolph
Member of the Evergreen Presbyterian Church
Graham, Washington

Introduction

"The work (and I add, the play) of the people defines worship." Yet, think how often worship becomes "the production of the pastor, with a little help from the musicians, ushers, greeters, choirs, lay assistants, custodians, church secretary." For many, the only important worship leader remains the pastor, effective or ineffective.

This workbook provides hundreds of ways for the congregation to participate, far beyond its standing on call, sitting on command, singing on cue. Effective worship requires preparation and pre-preparation, preferably eight to ten weeks in advance. Following the lectionary makes that possible. This workbook will facilitate that planning, and at the same time stimulate your own creative juices.

Before beginning specific Sunday preparation, I invite you to consider the following theological and practical concepts and awareness, which contribute to the creation of powerful and provocative celebrations.

I. Theological Concepts And Awareness

A. Soren Kierkegaard sets the worship scene. He compares worship with drama.

Drama	**Usual Worship**	**Kierkegaard's Analogy**
Audience	Congregation	God, actively engaged
Actors	Pastor, Musicians, etc.	Congregation, actively involved
Prompters	God	Pastor, etc., actively leading

In Kierkegaard's belief, God in Christ puts us on notice through the Scripture that the Holy Spirit comforts and confronts (we prefer comfort), not only during the worship hour, but in every hour of our life. Psalm 23:6, from the Hebrew language, drives home God's radical involvement with us. "Of a certainty! God's covenant grace and God's steadfast love *hotly pursue* us!" An extra-biblical source echoes the Psalmist, namely, Francis Thompson's *Hound of Heaven*, in which God pursues us as a bloodhound pursues a wanted criminal.

B. Isaiah 6:1-8 sets the biblical scene. Read the passage carefully and often. Notice the flow in Isaiah's experience: adoration, confession, thanksgiving, dedication. Corporate worship begins with God, not with us. "Holy! Holy! Holy is the Lord of Hosts!" Then, when we see God for who God is, we see ourselves for who we are. "Woe is me, I am lost; for I am a man of unclean lips; and I live among a people of unclean lips." Isaiah had the sense to begin with his own sin before confessing the sin of his people. Confession led to forgiveness and thanksgiving. "Now that this (live coal) has touched your lips, your guilt has departed and your sin is blotted out." And finally, cleansed, renewed (not perfected), he affirms his commitment. "Here am I; send me!" Of course, in between thanksgiving and dedication comes proclamation, which also belongs to the whole congregation as participants, not spectators.

II. Practical Concepts And Applications

We need to find ways to involve everyone who wants to be involved, and even those who want no one, including God, to bother them. We can know, however, that a God-event will happen *every* Sunday, *and* not to everyone; for we have no idea why people come to worship. We know only the reasons and justifications people give for *not* coming to worship. We are responsible *for* no one except ourself; we are responsible *to* everyone, including ourself. I remember reading in *Playboy* magazine years ago (for the articles, of course) a letter to the editor, written by a young man visiting in town that morning.

Despite the "openness and honesty" of *Playboy*, the man's name was withheld. Following worship, the pastor's wife invited him to come to dinner at the pastor's house. She knew that her husband would be out of town the rest of the day. They spent the afternoon engaged in sex. The author titled his letter to the editor, "Saved by Religion." Remember again, that we are responsible *for* our own behavior, not for what others do and say in the name of their religion.

A. Preparing for Worship

1. *Have sermon discussion* before and after worship. Invite six to ten people to meet with you, in advance, to discuss the Scriptures. Following worship, provide an opportunity for any and all to meet with you. Listen to what they say. Take notes. Clarify. Never preach a second sermon. You, the pastor, are there to learn from them. The people will educate you and help to strengthen your ministry.

2. *Establish the following groups:*
   a) *Prayer groups* to pray for the Spirit to empower and change lives. Different groups can be assigned for a specific amount of time.
   b) *Banner groups*, not only to develop banners for each season of the church year, but ultimately, for each Sunday. Many seniors enjoy sewing.
   c) *Artist groups*, to design bulletin covers and bulletin symbols which reflect the theme for the day. All ages can participate.
   d) *Senses groups*, to discover ways to use all of the senses in worship, not just seeing and listening, and occasionally, touching.
   e) *Drama groups*, for those who like to act. This need not take memorizing; it does take preparation. Young people especially enjoy acting. And the Scriptures command action, more than traditional reading. Encourage them to write their own dramas and to put the Scripture into their own language.
   f) *Dance groups*, to interpret the Scripture and hymns. These persons will provide a new dimension to worship.
   g) *Sign group or person*, to interpret worship for the deaf.
   h) *Evaluation groups*, to check out the results, not with a critical eye, though never discount the importance of that, but rather, to discover new possibilities to include the whole people of God and the wholeness of the people in God.

3. *The bulletin and printed order of worship* (though, occasionally, use *no* bulletin; you may be surprised by the response) represents the most obvious educational tool in the hands of the pastor and all of the worship leaders. Yet, many bulletins represent nothing more than "sanctified laundry lists," thrown together by the wind, or tossed together with no imagination or biblical guidance. In my first pastorate, the senior pastor changed each week only the hymns, Scripture, printed confession of sin, and the sermon title. Everything focused on the sermon. The remaining parts of worship served only as "the preliminaries." The people, rotely and remotely, responded as automatons, which, of course, led to spectator worship. So, if the people received nothing from the sermon, they received nothing from worship.

B. Specific Ways to Involve the Ecclesia; the Called-Out Ones; the Community of Faith, Hope, Love, Justice, Peace:

1. Change the introductory headings to reflect the season of the church year. Here are several examples:

ADVENT

The Church of Jesus the Christ
Meets Occasionally (at this address)
and Scatters Usually Around the County, State, Nation, World.
We Celebrate This Season of Expectancy,
Even Though We Already Know the Outcome.

CHRISTMAS

The Sovereign Has Come to Establish the Kingdom.
The Savior-Lord Reigns.
We Meet Weekly in Corporate Worship
(at this address)
to Celebrate the Reign of God.

EPIPHANY

The Church of Jesus the Christ
Celebrates the Good News Weekly at (your address)
during this Epiphany Season
as We Learn to Share Christ's Love
with the World of People, Animals, and Nature.

LENT

Lent, the Season of Renewal
The Community Gathers
to Examine
Its Reason for Being,
as It Prepares for the Easter-event.

EASTER

Easter — the Season of Resurrection
to Discover
Who We Are   Whose We Are
What We Do   Where We Go
in the Power of the Risen Lord.

PENTECOST

The Church of the Living Christ
Meets Occasionally (at this address)
to Celebrate the Season of Pentecost
as We Learn to Share the Good News of Christ's Love
with the World
of
Education, Recreation, Economics,
Politics, Family, Neighborhood,
and All the Rest.

2. Place a statement at the beginning and end of each order of worship which captures the theme for the day. Sometimes I spend fifteen minutes looking for the right quote. This gives people something to hang on to during the week. Many have reported saving these meditations and rereading them often.

3. Change the heading of each section of worship also with each season of the year. Notice these in the specific worships for each Sunday.

4. Never use the word "announcement." Ugh! Instead, use separate sections in the bulletin, titled, "Opportunities for the Day," "Opportunities for the Week (Weak)," "Opportunities for the Month."

5. Never, ever, use the term, "special music," unless you plan to designate every part of worship "special." Where that idea occurred, I have no idea. Much of the time, it has nothing to do with worship for that day. The Adversary must have instituted the practice. Instead, put the music where it belongs, usually as a response to one of the acts of worship.

6. Use a "Hymn of the Month" to introduce new hymns. Many older members would settle for their ten favorites (or is it five?) for every Sunday, totally eliminating music that makes sense to children and young people. Introduce some hymns and other music through the message with the children of all ages. Pastors and laypeople can get away with almost everything in the children's message — unfortunately! Present a history of the hymn in the bulletin or church newsletter. At the end of the year, perhaps at Thanksgiving time, center worship around the new hymns the congregation has learned that year.

7. Invite people to stand during the reading of the gospel, a lost or neglected tradition. At the same time, invite the actors and dancers in your congregation to establish groups that will dramatize the Scripture and other parts of worship.

8. Educate the congregation to use proper language. For example, we receive the offering; we never take a collection. We offer our gifts; we do not make a donation. We give to the mission, not to a budget; budgets are close-ended; the mission remains open-ended.

9. Put the following Sunday's Scripture, or several Sundays' Scriptures, in the bulletin and the church newsletter. A majority of the members do something other than worship on any given Sunday. Encourage the people to read the Scriptures before coming to worship and to share insights about them with each other and the pastor before, during, and after Sunday morning.

10. Because worship as celebration, drama, play is interactive, I invite the people to interrupt at any time for questions, clarification, disagreements, or affirmations. You will need to give them permission to interrupt the authority. Most of us received messages as children never to interrupt the authority for any reason, even when the authority makes no sense at all. These moments of interruptions are especially challenging and fun.

We often put special emphasis on Advent, leading to Christmas, and Lent, leading to Easter, as if somehow these hold more importance in the church's life than the other four seasons. Invite the congregation, all ages, to prepare a devotional booklet for each season. If you have sixty member or visitor families, everyone will have an opportunity to contribute. Ask the families to prepare a meditation for a specific Sunday. If you follow the lectionary, or even if you don't, use the lectionary to assign specific Sundays. Make copies available to anyone who enters your congregational life.

You will notice that I include the authors, translators, harmonizers, and dates of the hymns. I want to make us aware of the rich heritage that we receive as a gift from God and the historical church.

Worship that changes lives requires imagination, creativity, sensitivity to every age group, and good old plain hard work. This workbook will give you many ways to open yourself and your people to the leading of the Holy Spirit, because, "All of life is holy ground, so watch where you're stepping."

Wayne H. Keller

P.S. How could I forget the *Musical Instrument Group*! Invite, encourage, urge people to bring to worship whatever musical instrument they play, including the kazoo, comb, cymbal, ukulele, guitar, and so forth. Ask them to participate in all of the music throughout worship. If they play no instrument, invite them to hum or whistle. "Let everything that breathes praise the Lord!"

Advent
The Season Of Expectancy

Liturgical Color: Purple/Blue

    The church regulates the year, not by the civil or astronomical calendar, but by the events in the life of Jesus the Christ, the Son of Righteousness and Salvation. The church year, therefore, begins with Advent, the season of preparation for the celebration of the incarnation of the God/Man. Since the seventh century, the Western church has begun Advent on the Sunday closest to the Feast of Saint Andrew, ending it on the Sunday before Christmas day, a period of four weeks.

    Traditionally, purple, though now replaced by blue, is the color for Advent. These colors symbolize our need for the searching of our hearts and changing our lives as we consider the need which brought Jesus to dwell among people. Purple/blue are also the colors of royalty, suggesting the second aspect of Advent, that is, the righteous rule of Christ as King of kings and Lord of lords. For in the endless cycle of the year, Advent is both a beginning and an ending, directing meditation and worship toward the appearance of God among people in the person of Jesus of Nazareth; and following Kingdomtide, it also points us to that future coming of Christ at the end of time when his righteous rule will encompass the world.

    The custom of the Advent wreath with its four candles comes to us from Europe and gains in popularity each year. We can include the use of the candles in worship, church school, youth fellowship, and as a family activity. We can encourage such use of the Advent season in our homes; for we are brainwashed by the culture's commercialization of this season and need all the help we can get to regain and retrieve the biblical truth.

The Season Of Expectancy

Advent 1

Liturgical Color: Purple/Blue

Gospel: Matthew 24:36-44

Theme: *Watchfulness.* For what do we watch this Advent Season? Does it have anything to do with Jesus' birth? If so, how do we see and experience that event making any difference in our lives?

The Community Gathers To Celebrate Its Expectations

Invitation to the Celebration

The choir or choirs enliven the beginning of worship with Avery and Marsh's "Hey! Hey! Anybody Listening?" Ask the choir members, in advance, to bring to worship the musical instruments suggested in the hymn: drum, harp, chime, mandolin, tambourine, cymbal, fireman's bell, and even "If I had a hummingbird, I'd hum it." If these are unavailable, bring your own creative substitutes. For next week, invite the congregation to sing the chorus only; ask the people today to bring their own instruments of praise, including the kazoo or tissue paper and comb. (Order through Hope Publishing Company. See Appendix I for address.)

Declaration of Joyful Expectations Pastors and Ministers

P: Come on! I invite us to watch what we're thinking, saying, doing by watching the activity of God on behalf of God's world.

M: We have watched — sometimes. We do watch — sometimes. We will watch — sometimes. During this time, we focus our energies, resources, being, in order to hear and to respond to the old good news once again.

P: Welcome in the name of the coming, yet already present, Savior-Lord.

M: Thank you, pastor. We watch together in the name of the living Christ.

(Despite the congregational pressure, use Advent hymns during Advent; use Christmas carols during Christmas.)

The Community Faces Up To Itself

The Act of Recognizing Our Humanity Pastor and Ministers

What do you bring to the act of confession around the theme of watchfulness? Does it have anything to do with a new vision of the Savior? Before we pray this prayer together, pray it silently and let God's Spirit clean out those areas of life that we usually keep from our mate and children and parents, and yes, even from ourselves.

Ministers: Our God, we tend to minimize the importance of watchfulness and readiness. It makes so little difference, we seem to think, if we're ready or not. There is always tomorrow. We leave it to others in our household to do what we need to be doing to keep our faith alive. We alibi; we neglect; we do everything but live our faith. Through the indwelling Presence and Power of your Spirit, make us aflame with our obedience to You, no matter what the cost. Make our faith contagious, so that it will spread to others, until faith in the living Lord encircles the earth. And make us know, O Lord, that You call us daily, hourly, that the time for action is now. *(Two minutes of silence.)*

The Act of Receiving New Life   Pastor

Pastor: Please stand and look at the cross. *If* we are Christians, we know that the past is forgiven, every minute of it up to this moment. Do we believe that, not only with our mind, but with our heart? So, receive again from God the life we considered alienated and lost. Share again, and always, that life with the whole universe, the truth of God's acceptance and liberation, a message that most of the world, and too much of the church, still waits to hear. *(Now, ask the people to remain in silence for two minutes. During this time, ask them to look at their fellow church members, fellow cross-bearers, and give the sign that they believe in forgiveness — a smile, a thumb's up, raised arms. After two minutes, say, with energy)* And all the people said, "Yes, indeed; yes, indeed!"

The Community Responds To God's Watchfulness

Message with the Children of All Ages

For what are you watching? At school? At home? At play? "Watch out!" means, "Be on guard! Don't speak to strangers! Come straight home after school!" During this week, think about the things you're watching for. Write them down, and bring them with you next week.

Reading from the Newer Covenant

Invite a member of the church to read the Scripture out of sight of the worshipers. Use a microphone. Have that person practice in your presence, or in the presence of someone skilled in reading. The reading needs to be read dramatically, punctuating the theme of watchfulness.

Proclamation of the Good News

Encourage the people to respond verbally during the message. Begin by asking, "For what are you watching this Advent Season?" Give them time to respond. Continue with what you're watching for.

Stewardship Challenge

"Watch what you're giving!" Is that how we approach the offering? Or, would God be better served if we gave, not counting the cost?

Prayer after the Offering

Freely we have received; freely, though maybe reluctantly, we give of our money, time, being, because we have them to give, and because the world needs these gifts, beginning now.

Charge to the Congregation

The pessimist insists, "All roads lead nowhere." The optimist knows, "All roads lead. Know where." We know where the Advent road leads.

Response to the Blessing

Sing the chorus to "Hey! Hey! Anybody Listening?" It leads directly into next week.

Music Possibilities In Addition To Those Already Suggested

Music for Preparation (a.k.a. the Prelude): Medley of Advent Hymns. Print the hymn numbers and invite the people to sing, hum, whistle them as they prepare for worship. Or, "Come Now, Our Savior," J. S. Bach.

Choral Introit: Use these words, "Our King and Savior draws near; O come let us adore him." *(The choir director puts notes to the words, and invites the congregation to sing it after the choir.)*

Hymn of Invitation: "O Come, O Come, Emmanuel," French Processional, 15th Century.

Response to the Act of Recognizing Our Humanity: "You are the Lord, Giver of Mercy," Appalachian Folk Medley.

Response to the Proclamation: "Praise Ye The Lord Of Hosts," Saint-Saens.

Offertory: "In Dulci Jubilo," Dupré.

Doxology: "Praise God From Whom All Blessings Flow." Use different tunes for different seasons of the church year.

Hymn of Commitment: "O Word Made Flesh And Come To Dwell," Jane Parker Huber, 1981. Tune: Melita 88 88 88. (From *Joy in Singing*, Published by the Office of Women and the Joint Office of the Presbyterian Church U.S.A. See Appendix I for address.)

Music for Dismissal: Medley of Advent Hymns. (Invite the people to remain throughout the postlude, and hum, whistle, sing the hymns.)

The Season Of Expectancy

Advent 2

Liturgical Color: Purple/Blue

Gospel: Matthew 3:1-12

Theme: *Promise with Repentance.* Have you ever made a promise you failed to keep? Or has someone made you a promise and then failed to produce? Your feelings? Their feelings? What did you or the other do about it? See what God did.

The Community Gathers To Celebrate God's Promise

Invitation to the Celebration

The choir explodes with the stanzas of "Hey! Hey! Anybody Listening?" The congregation joins in the chorus only. Invite the people to use their hand instruments and to bring them again next week.

Declaration of Joyful Expectations — Pastors and Ministers

P: Well, folks, here we are again, this second week in the church year. How have you come? *(Give them an opportunity to respond; prime several in advance if you expect no immediate response to this year's interactive worships.)* So, you're ready for some new truth this week.

M: We are open to a new awareness, a new hope, a new life — all centered around and focused on God's "old" promise to us — beginning now!

P: Great news! We continue in the name of the eternal God who has promised to become one of us. So, if you're ready, wave your hands!

The Community Faces Up To Itself

The Act of Recognizing Our Humanity — Pastor

"I'll bet you ten dollars *(name your choice)* wins the Rose Bowl game." "Let's shake on that!" "I'm sorry," your friend responds, "I don't trust your word. Let's put the bet in writing." Your friend signs his name, loses the bet, and still refuses to pay. What will you do? *(Two minutes of silence.) (P.S. The biggest complaint that I hear about the confession is its quickness; no one has time to integrate it before moving to the assurance.)*

P: Lord, we make thousands of promises throughout our lifetime.
M: We have every intention of keeping them, we really do, really we do!
P: Yet, we keep breaking them over and over. And still, we promise not to break them.
M: We admit the vicious cycle that we get ourselves into.
All: Lord, we confess our wishy-washy behavior. We set out to obey you and to remain true to our word. Yet, we "crash and burn" again and again. At times, we wonder if we'll ever get our life together, if we will ever learn the lesson of obedience. We are aware of your patience and perseverance with us. We are grateful. And in your promise, we live. Thanks. *(Two minutes of silence, considering the grace involved in God's promise.)*

The Act of Receiving New Life — Pastor and Ministers

In a *New Yorker* magazine, an executive says to his employer, "I'll admit that to err is human, Reynolds, but if I forgive you, every Tom, Dick, and Harry will be here expecting forgiveness." We may neither expect forgiveness, nor deserve it, yet it is God's gift to us when we admit that we need it. I invite you to look around the sanctuary to see the rest of the people who need God's forgiveness as much as you do. *(Thirty seconds.)*

P: Christ has promised to redeem us, restore us, reconcile us to God, to one another, to ourself.

M: We know, in Scripture, of God's promise. By God's Spirit, we receive this unconditional gift, perhaps reluctantly at first because we're raised on conditional giving; but now, we receive it and live in, through, by, with God's grace.

P: And all the people, with hands raised, said, "Amen! So be it! Yes, yes, yes!"

The Community Responds To God's Promise

Message with the Children of All Ages

Remember last week's topic? *(Wait; we need not fill every moment with words.)* Tell me what you remember. Some of you promised (which is today's topic) to write down some things to share this week. I'm wondering if you did. If so, I invite you to share them now. (If they didn't, talk about the promises that we make and often break and God's promises which God makes and never breaks.)

Reading from the Older and Newer Covenant

Have someone dress as John the Baptist, someone offstage to be the voice of Isaiah, and a reader. Dramatize the Scripture. Perhaps one of the church groups could do so for a designated period of time, during Advent, for example. Yes, this requires practice; and it takes seriously the fact that the liturgy is "the work of the people."

Stewardship Challenge

God promises to remain faithful even when we become faithless. What kind of promise do we make about our stewardship before the offering *(never call it a collection)* plate arrives each Sunday?

Prayer after the Offering

(Give it variety; too many are identical week after week.) God, thanks for your promise to remain faithful, whether we give our leftovers or first fruits.

Charge to the Congregation

If it's true that God always keeps God's promise, then it matters how we live our daily life; so, I invite us to remember God's promise in our every waking moment this coming week; and by the way, it's okay not to be perfect.

Blessing

Say it slowly and deliberately, and if possible, look everyone in the eye as you speak.

Meditation

"On the basis of the eternal will of God, we have to think of every human being, even the oddest, most villainous or miserable, as one to whom Jesus Christ is a brother and God is a Father [Mother]; and we have to deal with him [her] on that assumption" (Karl Barth, source unknown; bracketed material inserted by WHK).

Music Possibilities In Addition To Those Already Suggested

Music for Preparation: Advent Hymns (see Advent 1), or "From Heaven Above," Pachelbel.

Advent Hymn of Praise: "Come, Thou Long-Expected Jesus," Charles Wesley, 1744.

Response to the Message with the Children of All Ages: "Joy Shall Come," Hebrew Melody (from *New Wine* copyright 1969. See address in Appendix I).

Response to the Proclamation: "Awake the Trumpet's Lofty Sound," Handel.

Hymn of Commitment: "God of Our Life, Through All the Circling Years," Hugh T. Kerr, 1916; alt. 1928, 1972.

Music for Dismissal: Medley of Advent Hymns (see Advent 1).

The Season Of Expectancy

Advent 3

Liturgical Color: Purple/Blue

Gospel: Matthew 11:2-11

Theme: *Wonder.* In this television age, multitudes, even in the church, even *as* the church, have lost the ability to wonder. I invite us to begin to recapture this skill and art, beginning with this worship.

The Community Gathers To Celebrate God's Wonder That Became Reality

Invitation to the Celebration

The choir begins with stanza one of "Hey! Hey! Anybody Listening?" The congregation joins in for the rest of the hymn, using all of the hand instruments that everyone has brought. If some remain without instruments, invite those people to whistle, a lost art in the sanctuary.

Declaration of Joyful Expectations Pastors and Ministers

Is everybody listening? I hope so by now. I invite us to listen and to wonder in silence for one minute. Then I will ask you to share what you've been wondering about. (If no one responds immediately, wait. Most of the time, we rush through worship, giving no one a chance to digest anything. Still, after two minutes, if no one shares, offer your own wonderings, beginning with, "I wonder why none of you responded?")

P: We know that you waited, Lord, until the time was right to send Jesus.
M: Thank you. We wonder why we're so insistent on setting your agenda.
P: We do know why, we just don't want to admit that we want to be in control — of mate, children, parents, life, You.
Repeat after me: Lord, I *(your name)* promise, this week, to take ten minutes a day to wonder, to let you be in control of my wonderings.

(Despite the congregational pressure, use Advent hymns during Advent; use Christmas carols during Christmas.)

Hymn of Advent

Have you given in yet to the pressures of truly sincere people to sing Christmas carols? I hope not.

The Community Faces Up To Itself

The Act of Recognizing Our Humanity

J. B. languished in jail wondering when this Jesus would mobilize his people and attack the Romans. (Well, he might have been thinking that.) Nothing was working out as he expected because he had his own agenda and forgot to check on God's agenda. In what ways do we resemble J. B.? Think of the things about which we wonder: Why do the innocent suffer? Why am I not rich and famous? Why does my income run out before the end of the month? In silence, consider this theme. Write down your responses. I will give you an opportunity to respond in two minutes. *(Be sure to wait two full minutes.)* Invite a few to respond. Remain calm if no one does. Interactive worship takes time to get used to. Set the example by sharing your own wonderings.

The Act of Receiving New Life

Remember the hymn which begins, "I wonder as I wander ..."? I invite us today to make our wanderings full of healthy wonderings. Through God's Spirit, we can transform our unhealthy wonderings — that is, "I wonder what life would be if I had married someone else ... if I had been born in a different place at a different time to different parents ... if I had had no children, or children later, or children earlier ... if only I had gone to college ..." to healthy wonderings, "I wonder how I can change the world around me by seeing people, animals, the environment, through the eyes of God?" In silence, for two minutes, write down your healthy wonderings. Invite several people to respond at the appropriate time.

Response

"Day By Day" (words and music by Stephen Schwartz; copyright by Valendo Music, Inc., and New Cadenza Music Corp., 1700 Broadway, New York, N.Y. 10019, from the production *Godspell*).

The Community Responds To God's Wondering

Message with the Children of All Ages

I'd like to know what you're wondering about Christmas. (Probably, some wonder what they will get. Have them share their guesses.) Do you ever wonder about other things? *(Give them time to respond.)* Maybe they're wondering about friendships, school, parents, vacation, the future. Tell them about J. B., how he announced the coming of the Messiah, Jesus, and how, now, he's wondering, "If this Jesus is the one God had sent to bring peace to the world, why didn't he, John, see the results? Maybe we should look for someone else." As part of the message, acknowledge that doubting is okay for Christians. God accepts us, even when we doubt and wonder about who Jesus is and why he came.

Reading from the Newer Covenant

Use your drama group. Characters will include J. B., a small band of disciples, and Jesus. Follow the dialogue in the text. Practice.

Proclamation of the Good News

Invite the people to interrupt at any time if they are confused about the message. (You may need to give them permission many times before they respond. My wife needed only one invitation. She comes from a non-church background, minus "churchly inhibitions." Her willingness to risk encouraged others to do so.)

Stewardship Challenge

When you put money in the offering plate, do you ever wonder what others give and why? Do you think that they're thinking the same about you? Do you envy what they give, or what you think they give? Do you get angry because you think that they could give more if only they were more dedicated than you? What is your motivation for placing your money in the offering plate?

Prayer after the Offering

By your Spirit, Lord, keep on cleaning up my motives for my "churchly" stewardship.

Charge to the Congregation

No matter what we wonder about God's plan, God's timetable, as people of faith, hope, love, God calls, invites, urges us to share these qualities, not only with our fellow church members but also with the neighbor down the street, or across the desk, or in need, whatever form it takes; with whom we go bowling or fishing, play cards, have barbecues, attend ball games; with whom we share just about everything else.

Meditation

To those who wish to travel with him, no matter how reluctantly, no matter how cautiously, no matter how discreetly, Jesus says, "Give up your Linus blanket — NOW!"

Music Possibilities In Addition To Those Already Suggested

Music for Preparation: Medley of Advent Hymns (see Advent 1) or, "Come, Now, Savior of Our Race," Bach.

Advent Hymn of Praise: "Lift Up Your Heads, O Mighty Gates," George Weissel, 1642. Translated by Catherine Winkworth; 1855, alt.

Response to the Proclamation: "I Wonder as I Wander," Author unknown.

Offertory: Music to Psalm 146.

Hymn of Commitment: "O Day of God, Draw Nigh," R. B. Y. Scott, 1937, 1939; alt. 1972.

Music for Dismissal: Medley of Advent Hymns (see Advent 1).

The Season Of Expectancy

Advent 4

Liturgical Color: Purple/Blue

Gospel: Matthew 1:18-25

Theme: *Fulfillment.* "The thing we've got to guard against is taking God's grace for granted, just because God has granted us God's grace. Grace is not cheap. It is free; it is not cheap" (Ted Gill).

The Community Gathers To Celebrate God's Promise Of Fulfillment

Invitation to the Celebration

The choir, congregation, and all the musical instruments combine to sing praises. Make this a powerful beginning of worship. Sing it several times if appropriate. What else but "Hey! Hey! Anybody Listening?"

Declaration of Joyful Expectations   Pastors and Ministers

If we are failing to listen by now, we may never hear the Good News. Here it is once again: "God loved the world, the world, even that part of the world we hate, ignore, reject; God loves even *that* part of the world also to which God sent the unique, one-of-a-kind son." Wow! Do we believe that? Do we put our trust in that kind of a God? And all the people said ...

P: I invite us to celebrate the Presence of God in and for the world.
M: That's what we've come here to do.
P: I invite us to celebrate the Power of God in and for the world.
M: That's what we've come here to do.
P: I invite us to celebrate the Purpose of God in and for the world.
M: That's what we've come here to do.
P: I invite us to celebrate the Person of God in and for the world.
M: You have our word on our celebrating Good News of the newborn King.

Hymns and Carols

If you do use Christmas carols, at least begin worship with an Advent hymn, such as "O Come, O Come, Emmanuel," to lead into the birth of Jesus.

The Community Faces Up To Itself

The Act of Recognizing Our Humanity

(Before entering the pulpit today, consider what you think that the people expect in worship. Probably most want to hear comforting, not confronting, messages. They need to hear the whole gospel.) I invite us to turn back the clock to the 1950s, at the time when cheap grace infiltrated American Christianity. *Time* magazine did an article on what it called the "religious corn" songs, one of which was "I Believe." The song sweetly promises us that "He'll (God was always a "He" in those days) always say, 'I forgive.' " Of course, God forgives. Forgiveness comes at a price. We Protestants have been less than honest when we criticize our Roman Catholic friends for misusing the confessional booth. "All they have to do is go into the booth, get forgiveness, and go out and do the same things over and over." That sounds no different from what we Protestants do. Maybe we're jealous of their system. For a few minutes, I invite us to go into our own private confessional booths. Let the Spirit of God speak to us. What obvious, and not so obvious, sin do we need to bring to God's attention, and ours? Begin this Advent to make a diary of what you are discovering about yourself. *(Silence for three minutes.)*

Response

"God Be In My Head" (music by John Anderson, in *New Wine*, published by the Board of Education of the Southern California-Arizona Conference of the United Methodist Church. See Appendix 1 for address information).

The Act of Receiving New Life   Pastor and Ministers

Sam Miller, in his book *The Life of the Church,* says, "We have to accept the fact that we are acceptable in God's sight ... God's grace accepts us even though we are sinners; and God accepts us as if we were not sinners." Repeat two or three times, because many, even longtime church members, are still trying to work their way into the Kingdom. We deserve death. But God's grace acquits us, not because we are innocent, but because we are guilty. And when we hear this good news, the acquittal of the guilty, we cannot just sit there as bumps on a log, as if we were reciting a quaint nursery rhyme, "Mary had a little lamb ... isn't that nice. I believe in the forgiveness of sin ... isn't that nice." This is good news, folks, the best news that the world has ever received. Rejoice and be glad! Stand and shout, "Thank you, Lord!" Offer your own praise word!

P: We are now present, fully present, Lord. Thanks for receiving us!
M: We are here because You have called us, forgiven us, energized us. We are new persons, who have received life in him who is the Lord of life and death.
P: Giver of life, thank You for healing us, for freeing us to be real.
M: Holy Spirit, keep on speaking to us. Insist that we keep on listening. Fill us this moment. So be it, Lord; so be it!

Response

"Doxology" (by Richard Avery and Donald Marsh; Hope Publishing Company. See Appendix 1 for ordering information).

The Community Responds To God's Promise Of Fulfillment

Message with the Children of All Ages

Do any of you have difficulty giving gifts for any occasion? What do you like to give? I have an acquaintance who says, "Give guilt, the gift that keeps on giving." I doubt that most of us need any more of that. Now, do any of you have difficulty receiving gifts? If you don't, I'll bet that some of your parents do. I know of people, including myself, that when someone pays them a compliment, they say, "I could have done better"; or, "If you really knew me, you wouldn't say that"; or, "I know people who do much more than I." Any of you do that? Ask your parents if they ever respond that way. Christianity is a strange thing. It begins, and continues, with an act, with many acts of receiving. If we fail to receive God's love first, it's impossible to share it with others. So, this week, I want you to think about all the gifts that you receive every day, including the air we breathe, the water we drink, the friends we have.

Reading from the Newer Covenant

If you want to stretch the congregation's imagination and have fun at the same time, begin the Scripture with the reading of Matthew's genealogy. To do this, you will need to have Doug Adams' version. Each name is followed by one of these responses: Applause and cheers, boo, hiss, moan, huh. Each response is put on a large piece of cardboard for all the people to see clearly. (You can order this idea from Doug at the Pacific School of Religion, 1798 Scenic Avenue, Berkeley, CA 94709; 510-848-0528; Fax: 510-845-8949.) The congregation will never again be the same!

Read the assigned Scripture from the *Cotton Patch Version* by Clarence Jordan. I suggest this because the original versions have become so acculturated that people may miss the incomparable message. An updated version of the *Cotton Patch* is now available. Association Press of New York published the original.

Proclamation of the Good News

For the brave, consider the topic, "Christmas is not for the children." (If you want my version, send S.A.S.E. to author.)

Stewardship Challenge

What are you willing to receive, from God, from the world, from each other before you give? It may be more blessed to give than receive; it is more difficult to receive than give. Our faith always begins with an act of receiving.

Prayer

Lord, teach us how to receive, so that we will give for the right reasons.

Charge to the Congregation

We receive far more than we give. We give in response to what we already have received. It all begins with our recognition that "justification (that is, made right, whole, in a complete relationship with God) by the law would be the acquittal of the innocent; justification by grace (God's unconditional acceptance) is an acquittal of the guilty." So rejoice, rejoice, rejoice. And all the people said, WOW! THANKS!

Meditation

"Leave the door open; he/she may be afraid to knock." How many times, in how many ways, did God knock before we finally opened the door?

Music Possibilities In Addition To Those Already Suggested

Music for Preparation: Medley of Advent Hymns (see Advent 1).

Hymn of Praise: "O Come, O Come, Emmanuel" (or have you given in to the pressure of singing Christmas carols?).

Choral Introit: (Soloist or Choir) "A Voice in the Wilderness," by John Prindle Scott.

Older Testament Lesson: A musical version of Psalm 24.

Response to the Good News: "Jesu, Joy of Man's Desiring," Bach.

Offertory: "Lo, How a Rose," Brahms.

Advent Hymn of Commitment: "Watchman, Tell Us of the Night," John Browning, 1825; alt. 1972.

Music for Dismissal: Medley of Advent Hymns (see Advent 1).

Consider this: As you move through the church year, point out the different times, places, and authors of the music. "I wish that we would sing the old songs," usually means that "I want to sing only the ones that I know." Use worship to educate the people about our rich heritage from every age. Now and then, print a half sheet for the bulletin or newsletter giving a history of the hymn or other music. If the clergy fail to educate the people, who will do it?

Christmas
The Season Of The Nativity

Liturgical Color: White
(December 25—January 6)

"The person who has seen me has seen the Father ..." (John 14:9).

The most popular of the church festivals is the season of Christmas. The name itself, a contraction of the phrase, "Christ Mass," became general around the twelfth century, although other earlier designations, such as the Feast of the Nativity, did appear.

It may contain one or two Sundays, depending on the day of the week on which Christmas falls. Its message focuses on the word "incarnation," which comes from the Latin word *caré* (flesh) and *Immanuel* (God with us).

As a specific festival, Christmas was unknown in the church for the first two centuries of the Christian era. This occurred because, during the spread of Christianity, the church emphasized the ministry and mission of Christ climaxed by his death and resurrection. In addition, during those early years, Christians regarded birthday celebrations as pagan. In reality, however, Christmas developed from a pagan festival celebrating the birth of the sun-god. On the first day of winter, the shortest day of the year, the sun-god was said to have had a "rebirth." From that day on, the length of the sun's appearance increases each day. In our times, the day falls on December 21. However, in the fourth century, it occurred on December 25. At that time, Julius I (Bishop of Rome, 337-352 A.D.) was Pope. Saint Chrysostom reported that Julius was probably responsible for establishing December 25 as Jesus' birthday.

We celebrate Jesus' birth, along with his death and resurrection, to focus on the whole gospel of God's grace and justice. William Temple once said that "God is the perfect union of love and power." We do an injustice to the good news if we emphasize one quality over the other.

The Season Of The Nativity

Christmas Eve/Day

Liturgical Color: White

Gospel: Luke 2:1-20

Theme: *Birth.* "God walking on earth is more impressive than our walking on the moon" (author unknown).

The Community Awaits God's Coming
"For whom are we waiting, anyway?"

Plan for a family to light the Advent candles.

Invitation to the Celebration
Use one more time, "Hey! Hey! Anybody Listening?" Encourage visitors to hum or whistle. Invite those who have been coming during Advent to walk around the sanctuary greeting one another as they sing. Following the pastoral invitation, sing an Advent hymn. Offer a prayer of praise for the coming, yet present, Messiah. To conclude the Advent portion of worship, read Isaiah 40:1-8, from the *J. B. Phillips* translation.

The Community Celebrates Christ's Birth
"God so loves the world that God gave the only forgotten son. Remember?"

Invite several readers, with whom you or someone will practice. Use a variety of musicians and musical instruments. Use different versions of Scripture. (My personal favorites are the *Phillips* and *Cotton Patch* translations.)

Consider the following order:

Congregation: Carol: "Watchman, Tell Us of the Night"

Scripture: Micah 5:2-4. *(Have the readers scattered throughout the sanctuary.)*

Choir with violinist: "Lo, How a Rose" Michael Praetorius.

Scripture: Luke 2:16.

Congregation: Carol: "O Little Town of Bethlehem" stanzas 1, 2

Scripture: Luke 2:1-7.

Children's Carol: *(sung by children or children's choir)* "Away in a Manger"

Scripture: Luke 2:8-9.

Choir and Instruments: "As Lately We Watched" Austrian Carol

Scripture: Luke 2:10-14.

Congregation: Carol: "Angels from the Realm of Glory"

Scripture: Luke 2:21-41, selected verses.

Congregation: Carols: "It Came Upon a Midnight Clear" stanzas 1, 2; "Born in the Night, Mary's Child"; and "On This Day, Earth Shall Ring"

Pastor: *(Read from the Newer Covenant)* 2 Corinthians 9:6 to the end

Meditation: "The Incomparable Gift" 2 Corinthians 9:15
Build the meditation around this: Years ago, a well-known distillery advertised its most famous bourbon as "the gift incomparable." Really now!

Prayer Response to the Meditation: Ahead of time, ask several people to pray.

Choir and Instruments with the Prayer: "For To Us A Child is Born"

The Community Responds To Christ's Presence
"Have we chosen to call ourselves after Christ's name and refused to follow after his life?"

Ceremony Of Candle-Lighting
Check with the legal authorities about candle-lighting in your area. If you have everyone light candles, give explicit directions and cautions.

During the lighting, have a soloist sing "O Holy Night." Following the singing and lighting of candles, have the people remain in silence for two minutes. Follow this with sentence prayers by the people.

Carols
"What Child Is This?"; "Silent Night"; "Joy to the World"

Charge to the Congregation
The birth of Jesus holds no eternal promise without his death, resurrection, presence; for the Spirit of God draws us toward his total ministry and mission. So, the question is this: What are we doing with the one who is called Jesus the Savior and Christ the Lord? What will we do with Jesus the Christ, Immanuel, God with us, the Wonderful Counselor, the Mighty God, the Everlasting Father, the Prince of Peace? We will not escape answering those questions in word and deed, in thought and action, by decision or default.

Carol
"Joy to the World," using all the choirs, the instruments, including the hand instruments and the congregation, with energy, enthusiasm!

Meditation
"The person who has no Christmas in his/her heart will never find Christmas under a tree." For, "Gratitude is the memory of the heart."

The Season Of The Nativity

Christmas 1

Liturgical Color: White

Gospel: Matthew 2:13-23

Theme: *Birth and Escape.* We free Christ from the perversions of Christmas, not by trying to take him out of our Christmas celebrations, but by our seeing the whole story, which includes the massacre of the innocents. We may want one without the other; Christ will have none of that.

The Community Acknowledges God's Presence

As people arrive, have several people with large placards in various parts of the sanctuary. These signs say "Silence," or "Quiet, please." By the time worship begins, the only visible sound will be people's breathing.

When all have arrived and latecomers have been seated, the pastor begins. "Welcome to this celebration of the Savior's birth, this ___ day of Christmas when my true love gave to me _____." *(Pause for one minute.)*

The pastor continues: "Take a few moments to catch your breath following the preparations for Christmas." *(Pause.)* Then, slowly and deliberately, ask the following questions:
1. "Have any of you vowed never again to allow yourself to get so caught up in details that you had no time to prepare for the actual 'reason for the season'?" *(Pause; ask for a show of hands.)*
2. "What Christmas leftovers do you bring to this worship: joys, frustrations, sadness, anger?" *(Pause; ask people to respond. You may want to ask, ahead of time, several people to respond.)*
3. "Who of us made the connection between Jesus' birth and what happened to him and his family the next two years? Our danger is to sugarcoat his birth and to ignore the next stage of his life. He became a refugee, hiding from the authorities."

Introduce today's gospel lesson, either directly from the Greek New Testament, or one of the newer translations. *(Make certain to use a translation, rather than a paraphrase; my personal preference is the* Cotton Patch *translation.)*

The Community Celebrates Christ's Birth

Sing several of the Christmas carols. Conclude with "We Three Kings of Orient Are." Ask three men to sing solos to stanzas 2, 3, 4.

The Community Looks Beyond Jesus' Birth

Soloist to sing "Masters of War" by Bob Dylan.

Pastor to read, slowly and deliberately, the gospel lesson again. Invite the people to write down their thoughts of what happened to Jesus in light of Dylan's song. Give them some time. Then ask if any would be willing to share their thoughts. If they are hesitant, do not rush in with your ideas. After two minutes, if no one has responded, then offer your own meditation.

The Community Examines Itself

Introduction to Our Self-Examinations Pastors and Ministers

P: I say it and you feel it in your hearts: You and I, behind "Merry Christmas" smiles, are afraid to be alone. You and I, behind the presents we give, are reluctant to love. You and I, behind our friendly words, are unwilling to stand beside another. You and I, behind our hymns and prayers, are afraid to stand before God. I say it and we feel it in our hearts.

M: Lord, have mercy on us; please have mercy on us.

P: I invite us to pray; pray only the parts of the prayer that touch you.

All: God, in the maze of the mass media of our day, we have all but lost our true identity. Succumbing to the pressures to conform, we have forgotten, or never learned, how to be ourselves in the light of your calling. We have sought to escape the birth-pangs of selfhood, by seizing ready-made actions and responses of others. This betrayal of the self has left us "hollow persons." Forgive us when we fail to live up to our high calling, and reveal to us a future that transcends the sin of the past. Grant that we come to know your liberating word that became incarnate in him who is the living word. Let it be.

Possible Results of Our Self-Examination Pastor

In Christ, the Savior, we can, we do experience forgiveness, not the slushy forgiveness of our culture, but the transforming forgiveness of our Christ. To us is born a Savior who is Christ the Lord; and to us is born, this moment, the possibility of life in him. We need no longer yearn for God as though God were absent. Our healing no longer means a search, but a surrender to him who is always and everywhere present in Spirit. I invite us to sing that prayer which is most appropriately the prayer of the faith community.

The congregation sings Malotte's version of the Lord's Prayer.

The Community Hears And Proclaims God's Truth

Message with the Children of All Ages

Tell the story of today's gospel lesson with the emphasis on what happened to Jesus and his family to escape death. Children often hear only the sweetness and light of Jesus' birth, and nothing more. Find a contemporary story of a refugee child in today's world. They need to become sensitive to the world's needs, beginning now.

Proclamation of the Good News

Ask the people if they were raised on the comforting words of Jesus' birth or the confronting words. *(Raise hands.)* Now, have we experienced Christmas any differently this year? Consider focusing the message on these words of Robert McAfee Brown: "It's easy to gush over 'the baby Jesus,' and what a sweet picture the stable scene makes on a Christmas card with cute angels flying overhead. We must not forget that the baby Jesus, whom everyone helps to adore, will grow up to be the man everyone helps to crucify."

At the end of the message, ask again, with a show of hands, which they prefer, comforting or confronting? Any particular reason? Wait for an answer.

Stewardship Challenge

A *Saturday Review* cartoon has a family enmeshed in the aftermath of opening presents which are strewn all over the living room floor. The wife admires her fur coat; one of the children is watching the new television, while two other children are playing with their new toys. The husband stands in the middle of this stuff, and with champagne glass in hand, says, "That's what makes America great — a scene like this!" I want to assure you today, that is not what makes America great. Let us present to God what does make America great, an openness to the leading of God.

Charge to the Congregation

Christmas is about presenting and responding to the whole Christ, not simply and only that which comforts us. This Jesus, who became the Christ of the Cross and empty tomb, lives among us, in us, and through us. He calls us to comfort one another when needed, and to confront one another when necessary, not in our own power but his. And all the people said, "Right on!"

Meditation

W. J. Cameron has said that "there has been only one Christmas (the rest are anniversaries) and it is not over yet." Because "either Christmas is forever or for never; either Christmas is more than one day, or it is not even one day; either Christmas is for everyone or it's for no one!" (WHK).

Music Possibilities In Addition To Those Already Suggested

Music for Preparation: Medley of Christmas carols, or "Jesu Bambino," Pietro Yon.

Hymns of Praise: Select several; the people will rejoice that Christmas finally has arrived, and that their pastor now gives them permission to sing the carols!

Response to the Act of Receiving New Life: "Pardoned Through Redeeming Grace," Edward Osler, 1836; alt. 1972.

Prayer Response following the Sermon: (Choir) "With Joyful Mirth," Pooler.

Offertory: "Greensleeves," Vaughan Williams.

Hymn of Commitment: More carols. Point out that, in addition to God's love and mercy, it also includes God's justice and holiness. The church is in the business of bringing justice to the least, last, lost, and lowest members of society.

Music for Dismissal: Medley of Christmas carols. Invite the congregation to stay and sing, hum, whistle, rejoice.

The Season Of The Nativity

Christmas 2

Liturgical Color: White

Gospel: John 1:(1-9) 10-18

Theme: *Birth of Jesus and Birth of the New Year.* "To believe in God means that we believe in surprises." When God became one of us, is that still a surprise to us? If not, what have we done to take the surprise out of it?

The Community Acknowledges God's Presence

Invitation to the Celebration

In the name of the newborn one, welcome to the ____ day of Christmas, when my true love gave to me _____. Yes, folks, it's still Christmas, despite the fact that the mass media is preparing us for the next buying frenzy, called *(you fill in the response)*. Welcome to the second Sunday of Christmas, and to the first Sunday of the New Year. We will consider both events today.

Pastor continues: For a few moments in silence, focus your attention on the Cross. *(One minute.)*

1. How do you compare your actual preparation and celebration with the central symbol of our faith, the empty Cross? *(Silence.)* Would anyone take the risk of sharing your thoughts? *(Silence. Remain calm if no one responds; people will respond internally, one way or the other, if not externally.)*
2. As we enter into this new year, what new decisions are you willing to make to keep the Cross central in your activities? Because, "all of life is holy ground, so watch where you're stepping." (I take credit for this quote.) *(Again, silence. Then, ask the people to share. If no one responds, offer your own decision.)*

Pastor continues: Now, are you ready to celebrate the good news?

M: Yes, and no! Yes, we want to grow in our faith. No, we are fearful that we will not succeed.
P: The word "succeed" is a non-biblical word. The words "acceptance, confession, pardon, thanksgiving, commitment, beginning again" — these are. It's okay not to be perfect.
M: What a relief! We begin this new year, and each day of the new year, with the promise of God's Presence and Power directing our lives.

Response

With energy, believing that God wants our salvation and commitment more than we do: "Joy to the World!" Use all of the musical instruments available. Ask those who choose, to whistle, a lost art in worship. Remember, "Make a joyful noise to the Lord." God chose, at least here, not to define what that means.

The Community Examines Itself

The Act of Recognizing Our Humanity

On New Year's Day, how many of us made New Year's resolutions? Care to tell us what they were? *(You may want to give one of your own.)* By now, how many of us have broken them? Care to tell us? *(You may want to give one of your broken ones, if not too embarrassing.)* The confession provides our opportunity to begin again. So, I invite us to pray this prayer, slowly and deliberately, in silence. *(Ask a musician — organist, pianist, flautist — to play during the silence.)*

Holy God, we confess that we have tried to live our lives within the narrow, limited dimensions of our own wisdom and strength. We are painfully aware of our inadequacies: Our love is shallow and selfish; our feelings are often distorted and easily hurt; our patience has a short fuse, and our dispositions often reflect our inner tensions; our disappointment with life and people is reflected in our attitudes; our anxiety over society and world conditions exposes our lack of hope; and our fearful caution reveals how little we trust You. Therefore, we often order our lives around our own abilities and skills and miss the adventure of life that You have prepared for us. We confess to You all of the things that we dared not attempt — the courageous deeds we considered but were afraid that we could not do; the gracious thoughts we had but never expressed; the forgiveness we felt, but never communicated. Forgive us, Lord, for forgetting that You are able to do in and through us what we could never do by ourselves, and then, settling for a life which is a mere shadow of what You had prepared for us. Now, in the quiet of this time of confession, which we hope is honest — only time will tell — plant in us the vivid picture of what you are able to do with lives such as ours, and give us the gift of a new excitement about living life by Your triumphant adequacy.

The Act of Receiving New Life

What difference will this act of confession make in your life? Write down one difference. *(One minute of silence.)*

Response

"I'll Never Be the Same" (words and music by Ruth S. Sandberg, from *New Wine*. See Appendix 1 for the address).

The Community Hears And Proclaims God's Truth

Message with the Children of All Ages

Develop the message around the theme of promises made and promises broken. What do the children do, and what do their parents do, and what does God do? Any similarities and differences?

Reading from the Newer Covenant

Read from different places in the sanctuary. Make certain that everyone can hear, especially if laypeople read.

Proclamation of the Good News

"Battle on a Small Planet" Filmstrip. (This was produced long ago by Richard Gilbert for the Division of Evangelism, United Presbyterian Church, U.S.A. You can check its availability through the Presbyterian Church, U.S.A, 100 Witherspoon St., Louisville, KY 40212-1396. I have one copy. Please send author $10 for borrowing it for a onetime use.)

Stewardship Challenge

What difference does our membership in, with, as the ecclesia, locally, nationally, internationally, make in our lives, toward family, neighbors, enemies, world? And, what happens to us, with us, and what do we do if our commitment to Christ and the church changes? Let the people digest those questions before receiving the offering.

Charge to the Congregation

When the shepherds arrive at the manger, W. H. Auden has them say, "O here and how, our endless journey begins."

Meditation

"A Christian is an 'alleluia' from head to foot" (Saint Augustine).

Music Possibilities In Addition To Those Already Suggested

Music for Preparation: Medley of Christmas carols (see Christmas 1).

Hymns of Praise: Again, select several. Christmas season is the time to sing carols, rather than allowing the mass media to set the Christmas agenda, beginning back there in July.

Hymn of Commitment: "Lord of the Dance," Shaker tune. Sydney Carter, 1963. Teach this powerful hymn to the congregation; it incorporates the entire life and ministry of Jesus. Ask someone, well in advance, to present a liturgical dance of this hymn as the people sing it.

Consider this: Select music from your own tradition, denomination, and locale which will give a powerful ending to the Christmas season.

Epiphany
The Season Of The Evangel

Liturgical Color: Green
(January 6 to the Beginning of Lent)

The Epiphany season varies in length, depending on the date of Easter, and continues to Ash Wednesday. The difference, created in the length of the year, is compensated for in the Pentecost season.

Epiphany, the oldest festival of the church year, originally a pagan festival to the sun-god, was taken over by the church and packed with new meaning. The pagan festival celebrated the birth of Aeon in the night between January 5th and 6th. From that day, the sun appeared longer each day. Eventually, due to errors in measuring time, the first day of winter shifted to an earlier date; January 6 was retained as the date for this festival.

By the fourth century, the first day of winter occurred on December 25, and a new pagan sun-festival was instituted. Christmas later replaced this latter festival. Both Christmas and Epiphany thus originated from a sun-festival held on the first day of winter. The first day of winter now normally occurs on December 21, but the festivals emerging from previous winter solstices remain as they were.

The word "epiphany" means "to show." In its root form, the word often was used to describe the dawn and the appearances of the gods to people. The word "manifestation" also describes Epiphany, and refers to the demonstration of the Glory of God's sending Jesus the Christ into the world. Until the institution of Christmas in the fourth century, both the birth and baptism of Jesus were commemorated on Epiphany. With the celebration of Jesus' birth at Christmas, the Eastern Church (Byzantine) restricted Epiphany to the celebration of Jesus' baptism. In the Western Church (Rome), however, Epiphany became associated with the coming of the Wise Men. Because the Wise Men were not Jews, the importance of Epiphany's message deals with the revealing of Christ to the Gentiles. Therefore, the Epiphany season has become a time for emphasis on the church's missionary task.

Two symbols which focus on Epiphany are the Cross and Crown. The Crown represents the Wise Men who came to Jesus. Also the Crown proclaims the fact that Christ is King, not only of Israel, but of all who put their trust in him for new and eternal life.

The Season Of The Evangel

Epiphany Day/The Baptism Of The Lord (Epiphany 1)

Liturgical Color: Green

Gospel: Matthew 2:1-12 (3:13-17)

Theme: *Visit of the Magi to Jesus; Herod's "Antipathy" toward Jesus; John's Baptism of Jesus.* "The way from God to a human heart is through a human heart" (Samuel D. Gordon).

Adoration And Praise

Invitation to the Celebration
   (Throughout Epiphany, invite people to wear green.) In the name of God, the Evangel, who invites, calls us to be evangels, welcome to the first Sunday in Epiphany, the least-known and most neglected season of the church year. Who knows what Epiphany means? *(Wait. Tell them.)* Who knows how long it lasts? *(Wait. Tell them.)* Who knows what season follows? *(Wait. Tell them.)* In this season, the gospel becomes universal. It begins with the coming of the Wise Men, so we can now sing "We Three Kings of Orient Are." However, it also includes the massacre of the innocents, the slaughter of all boys two years and under, because Herod could tolerate no one challenging his power. And, finally, on this Sunday's event, Jesus' ministry begins with his baptism.

P: Let's celebrate God's Presence and Power! Are you ready? Are you willing?
M: Yes, we are! *(Say that only if you mean it.)* We come to worship to be challenged intellectually; to think with the mind of Christ; to receive his love for emotional strength; and to gain courage to do his will in the tensions of our time.
P: We are God's people, called and appointed to live by God's power and for God's glory.
M: We have come to hear again what this means, and to receive the energy we need to be faithful.
P: God is able to provide beyond our expectations. Therefore, surprised by joy and amazed by grace, let's celebrate with our whole being!

Confession And Forgiveness

The Act of Recognizing Our Humanity
   Think about the people and events that brought us here today. How often were we invited, when we said, "No, maybe, later." How many evangels did God place in our lives before we said, "Yes"? Take two minutes to write them in your journal. Then, remind the people once again that God calls us in whatever way God chooses to face us with the good news, which in the beginning may sound like bad news; or else, why would we keep rejecting it? Focus here on the times and ways that we said, "No." Bring your "no" responses to God for examination and forgiveness. The Evangel seeks our YES. Give the people time to think. After several minutes, ask if any would share their insights.

The Act of Receiving New Life
   Now, I invite us to look at our lives once again. How did we come to the point of saying "yes," no matter how reluctantly at first? Identify the evangels, by name, to whom we finally listened and responded. Write down their names. *(Again, give the congregation sufficient time. I have seen pastors run through*

this act of worship as if they were chasing a fire engine.) Then, ask the people to share, not specific names of their evangels, but titles, such as teacher, neighbor, church member, pastor, and so forth. Following each, invite all to respond. And all the people said, "Thank you, Lord!"

Listening And Proclaiming

Message with the Children of All Ages

If you have baptism this Sunday, and what better way to celebrate the Evangel, invite the children to sit in the chancel. Some will have been baptized; some not. Teach the meaning of the sacrament. During the message, sprinkle water over the children and the rest of the congregation. Ask those who have been baptized to put their hands on their heads and say, "I am baptized!" Invite those who have not been baptized to say, with hands on heads, "I am a child of God!"

Reading from the Newer Covenant

Always give background to the Scripture. Use your drama group, or ask several people in advance, to read the Scripture as a dialogue. (It was that originally.) You will need a reader, Herod, priest and scribe, an angel, a prophet. My belief is that most people tune out during the reading and want to get on with the sermon. Our people are biblically illiterate and need all the encouragement they can get to make the Bible come alive. They need to hear the entire message, its joy and pain, from the Wise Men, the massacre of the children, to Jesus' baptism.

Proclamation of the Good News

1. Put the coming of the Wise Men into proper perspective, two years after Jesus' birth. Ask a member of the church, well in advance, to learn some facts about the men, and to present those facts at the beginning of the sermon.

2. The massacre of the children. (Many of us want the sweet, pleasant, cultural accoutrements, rather than first century reality.) For one of the most powerful presentations, read "Of Mangers and Massacres," by Howard Friend, in the November/December 1996 edition of *The Other Side* magazine. (Order by calling 1-800-700-9280.)

3. Refer to the evangels who have reached out to us, even when we had no idea they were angels and evangels unaware.

4. To whom will you reach out this week? Ask the congregation to name one person, silently, to whom each will minister as an angel/evangel this week.

Response

"See, and Come Running" (by Dick Avery and Don Marsh, see Appendix I for the address).

Stewardship Challenge

Throughout Epiphany, the offering will consist of two parts: the first part, receiving; the second part, giving.

1. Prepare three-inch stars on green paper. On each star place a word that describes a quality of life. For example, awe, choice, daring, exuberance, and so forth. (I have lost the source of this idea; I recall that it appeared in the Presbyterian (U.S.A.) magazine some years ago. You may track it down by writing the Louisville office. See Christmas 2 for the address.) Place the stars so that no one can see what's printed. Pass around an offering plate each Sunday. Each person gets only one star during Epiphany. Suggest that the star each gets may be a quality each has or which each needs to develop. Invite one or two people each week to share an event or experience around his or her star.

2. "The test of discipleship is how much we are at odds with the world, not our degree of adjustment to it," which, by the way, is the problem with much counseling (Kenneth Clark).

Hymn of Commitment

"Nobody Said It Was Going to Be Easy" (by Avery and Marsh, from *The Second Avery and Marsh Songbook*. Order from Hope Publishing Company. See address in Appendix I).

Charge to the Congregation

O God, if not us, who; if not here, where; if not now, when? And the fact is that God calls us, here, now, sends us out, here, now, in the name of God the Creator, Liberator, Sustainer, Energizer to share good news.

Blessing

Ask the people to raise their hands, to look at one another, and to offer these words, slowly: "The Lord bless *(you)*, this day and every day."

Meditation

John 3:16, paraphrase: "The heart of Christianity is not concern for the soul, but concern for the world."

Music Possibilities In Addition To Those Already Suggested

Music for Preparation and Dismissal throughout the Entire Season of Epiphany: Medley of Epiphany Hymns. Because this remains the most neglected season of the church year, we need to do an extraordinary job of teaching the people what it means. Ask the people to turn to the Epiphany section of the hymnbook before they begin to sing. Describe to them what the season means, and the various events of the season.

Other Hymns: "Jesus Shall Reign," Isaac Watts, 1719, based on Psalm 72. "No Longer Strangers," Richard Avery and Don Marsh, from *The Second Avery and Marsh Songbook*. (Order from Hope Publishing Company, see Appendix I for address.) "Good News Is Ours to Tell," Jane Parker Huber 1978. (Order from The Joint Office of Worship, 1044 Alta Vista Road, Louisville, Kentucky 40205.) "O God, This Child from You Did Come," Frank Brooks, Jr., 1972. "Fairest Lord Jesus," Silesian Folk Medley.

Response to the Proclamation: (if you emphasize Jesus' baptism) "Passed Thru the Waters," Avery and Marsh, copyright 1971, *Avery and Marsh Songbook*. (Order from Hope Publishing Company. See address in Appendix I.)

Response to the Scripture Reading: "Thou Art Jesus, Savior and Lord," Schuetz.

Offertory: "The Lord Is My Shepherd," any version.

The Season Of The Evangel

Epiphany 2

Liturgical Color: Green

Gospel: John 1:29-42

Theme: *The Lamb of God and the Calling of Several Disciples.* Some never get excited over Christianity. The truth is, we cannot get excited over something we do not have. When we know that God has called us to become new persons, our excitement knows no bounds.

Adoration And Praise

Invitation to the Celebration
(In advance, ask five or six people if you can use their names in the call to worship.) Remember the tobacco radio ad, "Call for Phillip Morris!"? Piggyback on this idea from the balcony, rear of the sanctuary, or on a megaphone. "Call for *(name each person)*." After finishing, offer one minute of silence, after asking, "How many of you received God's call as obviously as that?" *(Show of hands.)* Now, silently, consider how you did receive God's call. Was it somewhere between the call of Peter and Paul?

P: Lord, we know that you call us to be your persons in many ways.
M: Thanks for not expecting us to hear and to respond in the same way.
P: In this worship, give us your spirit to review and to renew our call.
M: We're waiting, with anticipation, to hear from you. Indeed we are! So, open our ears, and then, our voices, for the sake of the good news.

Response
"Be Thou My Vision."

Confession And Forgiveness

The Act of Recognizing Our Humanity
I invite us to examine our call to become Christ's person in light of the call that came to the biblical people. So, pick your favorite biblical character. As homework this week, find out as much as you can about him/her. Note their warts and wonders, strengths and weaknesses, denials and obediences. Notice how similar and different you are from that person. As a result of your study and your comparison, what do you decide about yourself? And how will that decision affect your confession of sin next week and from then on? Take a few minutes to choose your biblical person.

Response
"When I Had Not Yet Learned of Jesus" (Yoosun Lee, 1967; paraphrase c.1990, Jane Parker Huber; Westminster/John Knox Press).

The Act of Receiving New Life
Unfortunately, we have allowed ourselves to make heroes and heroines of the biblical people. As a result, many, inside and outside of the church, consider themselves inferior, inaccessible to God. Away with such rubbish! God receives a broken and contrite life. No sin keeps us from God, except one: Sin against Holy Spirit, which means that we keep saying "no" forever. And even if we do, God keeps

pursuing us anyway. *(Invite people to read **The Hound of Heaven**, by Francis Thompson; make copies available.)*

P: The word of Christ is good news.

M: Our humanity has been received. We can be ourselves.

P: The past is forgiven — all of it, up to this second! The future is before us — all of it, beyond this second!

M: We live with courage and with a deep concern for people of all conditions and cultures.

P: I invite us to give thanks, and to embrace our lives.

M: Indeed we do! Be it so!

Response

"Fill My Cup, Lord." Soloist sings stanzas; people sing the chorus. (Words/music by Richard Blanchard; arranged by Eugene Clark; copyright assigned to Sacred Songs, Division of Word, Inc.; found in *Folk Encounter*, Hope Publishing Company. See Appendix I for address.)

Listening And Proclaiming

Message with the Children of All Ages

When your mother or dad or teacher calls you, what do they want you to do? *(Give examples.)* "Time for dinner!" "Come in out of the cold!" *(Let them respond.)* How do you suppose Jesus calls you? Any ideas? *(Take your time. If no response, ask one of the older children who did not come forward. You may want to prepare this person in advance. Share your own call, only do so briefly. Point out the many ways that God calls people.)*

Reading from the Newer Covenant

Drama group to act out the scene; or develop the scripture into a litany. Or, for the extra-creative, prepare a contemporary version of the scripture; or use the *Cotton Patch* version by Clarence Jordan (Association Press, New York).

Proclamation of the Good News

If you have good rapport with your congregation, speak on the theme, "How I Became a Christian." Be certain to identify your doubts, questions, frustrations, resistances, as well as the joys of the struggle.

Stewardship Challenge

1. Hand out the stars to those who have not yet received one.
2. In advance, ask two people who received stars last week to share their experience. Continue to do this until the last Sunday of Epiphany.

Hymn of Commitment

(The result of the call) "Here I Am, Lord" (by Daniel Schutte, published by North American Liturgy Resources, found in *The Presbyterian Hymnal*, Presbyterian Church — U.S.A.).

Charge to the Congregation

We are called, not to be another Christ, not to imitate Christ, but to obey Christ. Personally, I am not interested in listening to people say, "But what would Christ do?" Who cares what Christ would do? Besides, he's already done what he would do. What are *you* supposed to do? Stop blaming it all on Christ. Start addressing yourself, in his name, to his world (from *Listen Pilgrim*, slightly revised).

Meditation

"If one-tenth of the things we say we believe as Christians are true, then we ought to be ten times as excited as we are" (William James).

Music Possibilities In Addition To Those Already Suggested

Music for Preparation: Medley of Epiphany hymns. (See Epiphany 1.) Or, "Adagio," Sonata in E-flat, Bach.

Hymn of Praise: "Brightest and Best of the Sons (Ones) of the Morning," Reginald Heber, 1811; alt. 1972.

Older Testament: Use the hymn, "O Sing a New Song to the Lord," Pry's Welsh Psalter, 1621; or have the choir sing a version of Psalm 96.

Response to the Message with the Children: "A New Wind Blowin'," words/music by David Yantis, copyright 1969, from *New Wine, Songs for Celebration*. (See Appendix I for address.)

Offertory: "Rejoice, My Soul," Karg-Elert.

Hymn of Commitment: "The Great Creator of the Worlds," from Epistle to Diogenetus, second or third century; para. by F. Bland Tucker, 1939, 1972.

Music for Dismissal: Medley of Epiphany hymns. Coordinate them with the theme of the day.

The Season Of The Evangel

Epiphany 3

Liturgical Color: Green

Gospel: Matthew 4:12-23

Theme: *Jesus Begins His Ministry and Calls Some Disciples.* "The Word divides a crowd into individuals" (Soren Kierkegaard). "The church cannot avoid involvement; it can only indicate if it is on the side of freedom or repression" (Eugene L. Smith).

Adoration And Praise

Invitation to the Celebration
Begin with words similar to these: "You are all sinners in the hands of an angry God. So repent, or go to hell. That's what the Bible says, and that's what you need to believe, or else...." How would you like to hear that every week? Or even, once a year? People throughout much of church history have heard precisely that. Jonathan Edwards had people groaning and sitting on the edge of their pews crying out, "God, have mercy on me!" as he preached his famous sermon, "Sinners in the Hands of an Angry God!" Though the method of proclaiming repentance has changed in the contemporary church, the message still rings forth, "Repent, for the Kingdom of Heaven has come near."

Response
"Praise Ye (You) the Lord, the Almighty" (Joachim Neander, 1680). *(Encourage people to stroll around the sanctuary as they sing.)*

P: Who are you to have come here?
M: We are forgiven repenters.
P: What is it to be a forgiven repenter?
M: It is to acknowledge our brokenness, I-centeredness, rebellion, and to have received God's amazing forgiveness.
P: Why have you come?
M: We have come out of gratitude to offer our thanks to the One who receives us unconditionally, in order that we will more effectively witness to and for God.
All: Let's do just that! And all the people said ...

Prayer of Praise *(printed)*
Eternal and loving God, we praise you, whose name is love, whose nature is compassion, whose presence is joy, whose word is truth, whose spirit is goodness, whose holiness is beauty, whose will is peace, whose service is perfect freedom, and in knowledge of whom stands for the results of our repentance, life eternal with You (author unknown).

Confession And Forgiveness

The Act of Recognizing Our Humanity
Ask someone to read, from the rear of the sanctuary, and with much energy, the words of Paul. As he/she reads, ask the people to be aware of what they are thinking and feeling, and to ask, "What do these words have to do with me? Today? Now? Here in worship? Beyond worship?" From the *Cotton Patch* version (sexist language omitted): "There isn't a pure person anywhere. Nor one who is fully sensitive.

Nor one who really sets his/her heart on God. All kicked over the traces and became worthless. There isn't one worth his/her salt, not a single, solitary one." No wonder Jesus called/calls us to repent! What a contrast with a *Ladies' Home Journal* poll taken years ago. Of those Americans polled, 95 percent admitted that they prayed. Only five percent felt the need for confession. Does that seem strange to you? If so, why? Write down your response. *(Three minutes of silence.)* Then, ask if anyone would take the risk of sharing his/her thoughts. If not, how about yours?

Response

"Jesus the Man" (Confession) (words and music by Dave Farley, from *New Wine*. See Appendix I for address).

The Act of Receiving New Life

To know that repentance means not "to be sorry again" or "feel guilty," but rather, "change your mind, change your way of thinking and living," then we will receive and live in the good news that we are put in a new relationship with God. Confession comes, not from the skimmed milk of our external goodness, but from the thick cream of our interior brokenness and alienation. God's presence empowers us to "change our minds." How do you see that happening this week? Write it down.

P: To be "in Christ" is to know that we are forgiven.
M: Christ, by offering us forgiveness, leads us to a new understanding of who we are and where our lives are headed.
P: I invite us to remember his way of freedom, hope, and responsibility, that is, our response to God's ability.
M: We rejoice in new life!

Listening And Proclaiming

Message with the Children of All Ages

In advance, ask a family, which is willing to take a big risk, to share an example of how it worked through a painful, broken experience between parents and children. Identify how the family members felt before and after the event. Use this example, in review, at the beginning of the proclamation.

Stewardship Challenge

1. Hand out stars to those who have not yet received one.
2. Ask two people, in advance, to share their experience about the message on their stars.

Charge to the Congregation

Repentance results in new, not perfect, activity. How will your life be different this week because you worshiped today? As you consider your "about-face" (one way to define repentance), what form and content will that about-face take? As you leave the sanctuary today? Go to school or work tomorrow? Play racquetball or tennis or whatever this week? As you relate to your family, neighbor, enemy from now on?

Meditation

A changed mind leads to changed behavior; a changed behavior leads to a changed mind. "It is easier to act your way into a new way of feeling, than to feel your way into a new way of acting" (author unknown).

Music Possibilities In Addition To Those Already Suggested

Music for Preparation: Medley of Epiphany hymns or "Fugue in C-major," Buxtehude.

Choral Introit: "Rejoice You Pure in Heart," stanza 1. Edward H. Plumptre, 1865; alt. refrain added, 1883.

Hymn of Praise: "Christ, Whose Glory Fills the Skies," Charles Wesley.

Response to the Newer Covenant: "Be Thou Not Still," Foltz.

Response to the Proclamation: "Dear Lord and Father of Mankind" (point out the sexist language), John Greenleaf Whittier, 1872. This hymn was part of a larger text in which Whittier revealed his dislike of outward ceremony and in which he emphasized the need for the quiet indwelling of Christ's presence in people's lives.

Offertory: "Our Father Who Art in Heaven," Bach; or "Praise Be to God in the Highest," Zachau.

Hymn of Commitment: "Christ Is the World's True Light," George Wallace Briggs, 1931; alt. 1972.

Choral Response to the Benediction: "Amen Chorus" from "Lilies of the Field."

Music for Dismissal: Medley of Epiphany hymns, or "Credo," Haydn.

The Season Of The Evangel

Epiphany 4

Liturgical Color: Green

Gospel: Matthew 5:1-12

Theme: *The Beatitudes.* "Don't worry; be happy!" Isn't that what all of us want, if not as Christians, then surely as citizens of America?

Adoration And Praise

Invitation to the Celebration
In advance ask three people to introduce worship by describing what they perceive the world considers "happiness." Then, the pastor says, "Well, isn't everybody happy? Isn't happiness the goal of everyone, every Christian? Isn't life to go up and up when we say 'yes' to Christ? When the Son shines in our lives, then the sun shines over all of life — well, doesn't it? Today, in the name of Jesus who spoke the Beatitudes, we explore the meaning of happiness. Our beginning clue is this: The Bible's understanding of happiness contrasts radically with the approach that many of us use to find happiness." (R.S. = Right Side; L.S. - Left Side),

P: Make a happy, no, make that a joyful celebration to the Lord, all of you. Serve the Lord with happiness, no, make that gladness!
M: We come into God's presence, some of us happy, some of us sad, some of us angry; and all of us come with joy!
P: Know that the Lord is God!
R.S.: God made us, and we are God's people, no matter how we feel.
L.S.: We, too, are God's people, no matter how we feel!
R.S.: We enter God's gates with thanksgiving, and God's courts with praise!
L.S.: We give thanks to God; we praise God's name!
All: For the Lord is good; God's strength endures forever, and God's faithfulness to all generations! Amen to that! It's a fact! *(Repeat this last response until the people give it some energy and enthusiasm.)*

Confession And Forgiveness

The Act of Recognizing Our Humanity
Read slowly, and deliberately J. B. Phillips' "Beatitudes of Modern Man (Persons)" from his book *Is God At Home?* (copyright 1957 by Abingdon Press). Have the organist, pianist, guitarist play a "happy song" during the reading, perhaps "Don't Worry; Be Happy." Offer two minutes of silence for the people to absorb the reading.

The Act of Receiving New Life
Happiness in the dictionary means "lucky, fortunate; having, showing, or causing great pleasure or joy; suitable and clever." Happiness in the Beatitudes means "how satisfied, how complete, how fulfilled are those who ..." What satisfies, completes, fulfills us? Consider joy for happiness. At this point, ask the congregation if any need clarification. Give several minutes of silence if no one responds; they may process the information internally during worship, and externalize it only later.

Response

"Happy the Man" (change "man" to "one" as you sing). (Words and music by Sebastian Temple, copyright 1967. Franciscan Communications Center, Los Angeles, CA.)

Listening And Proclaiming

Message with the Children of All Ages

Ask them what makes them happy. Did they receive any Christmas gifts which did that for them? Maybe you have had the Christmas morning experience that I did. My son ripped through his gifts, tossing paper and ribbons all over the living room. When he finished, he said, "Is that all there is?" Perhaps you will want to integrate a conversation between Charlie Brown and Lucy. Charlie says, "Does it really make you happy to tear me down, Lucy? Does it really make you happy to know that all your insults are hurting me?" Lucy turns to him, with a smirk on her face, and says, "Do I *look* happy?" Charlie, sadly, responds, "I couldn't deny it." Apply these ideas that best fit your situation.

Reading from the Newer Covenant

Use Clarence Jordan's *Cotton Patch* version of the Beatitudes. Have someone play quietly in the background, "Don't Worry; Be Happy" (Association Press/New York).

Proclamation of the Good News

Consider the sermon theme, "Happiness Doesn't Come in Pills." In the April 7, 1957, issue of *Quote* magazine, a Harvard psychologist predicted that eventually pills will control all of our emotions; in honor of this prediction, the editors of *Quote* compiled a poem about pills. Here is the first verse: "A pill will rid my soul of hate. My pistol now is notchy. I'll think that everyone is great, And beam like Liberace." (If you want the poem and/or sermon, please send $1.00 and SASE to author.)

Stewardship Challenge

1. Hand out Epiphany stars only to those who have not yet received them.
2. Ask two people, in advance, to share their experience about the message on their stars.

Charge to the Congregation

Has your understanding of happiness changed during worship? In what way? Give people an opportunity to respond. Never rush through worship. People need time to integrate new ideas and images. I hope that you know by now that "the pursuit of happiness is a most ridiculous phrase; if you pursue happiness, you will never find it" (C. P. Snow).

Meditation

"Happiness is not a state to arrive at, but a manner of traveling" (Margaret Lee Runbeck).

Music Possibilities In Addition To Those Already Suggested

Music for Preparation: Medley of Epiphany hymns, or "Adagio" (Sonata II), by Mendelssohn.

Hymn of Praise: "Rejoice and Be Merry," Old Scotch gallery book.

Response to the Prayer of Praise: "Happiness Is thy Lord," words and music by Ira F. Stanphill, copyright 1968 by Singspiration, Inc.

Response to the Proclamation: Select a "joy" anthem from your choir's repertoire; "All My Heart Today Rejoices," by Paul Gerhardt, 1653.

Offertory: "Antiphon," by Dupré.

Hymn of Commitment: "Joy to the World" by Isaac Watts, 1719.

Music for Dismissal: Medley of Epiphany hymns, or "Fanfare" by Dubois.

The Season Of The Evangel

Epiphany 5

Liturgical Color: Green

Gospel: Matthew 5:13-20

Theme: *Salt, Light, Righteousness.* "The one thing that Christianity cannot be is moderately important" (C. S. Lewis).

Adoration And Praise

Invitation to the Celebration

Enter from the back of the sanctuary and scatter salt over the people as you come down the aisle. Ask ushers or others to assist so that every part of the congregation is covered. If you think this idea is too radical, take a powerful flashlight into the pulpit, and point it at the congregation, as you repeat again and again, "You are the light of the world." Then, did you folks know that you are the salt of the earth and the light of the world, according, not to Garp, but to Jesus? Please raise your hand if you knew that. If you failed to know that, write your reason in your diary; or if you want to take a risk at the beginning of worship, tell us. We would like to know you better. And I promise you that I will make no judgment about your life. What I will do is affirm your courage. *(Wait for one minute.)*

Notice the promise in the pastor/ministers response:

P: Come on! Celebrate the God who is Creator, Liberator, Sustainer, Energizer of the ones who call themselves salt and light, the new creation.

M: We do come to celebrate our saltiness and light. We are God's people, new persons in the new creation, made possible not by our righteous efforts, but by the death and resurrection of the Christ. We come to affirm that the old has passed away, and behold, the new has come.

P: Christ is Lord; Christ is Author of salt and light.

M: And we are new persons through him. We offer the world our salt and light. As transformed, renewed, released people, we celebrate with praise and enthusiasm!

Response

"You are the Salt of the Earth" (Avery and Marsh, *The Second Avery and Marsh Songbook.* See Appendix I for the address).

Confession And Forgiveness

The Act of Recognizing Our Humanity

I'm going to read Matthew 5:19-20. I will read slowly and deliberately. Please note on paper your feelings and thoughts. Then, are any of you willing to share them with us? Yes, I know that it's risky; but remember that the liturgy is "the work of the people." *(Wait a few more moments.)* Take the risk of sharing your own feelings and thoughts. Present the hopelessness leading up to this corporate prayer: "Almighty God, We confess that we have done some awful things to others and to ourselves and to you. But they are our problems. We confess the awful things we have done in order once again to be able to look each other in the eye. We confess the awful things we have done, and ask for courage to face the consequences, as forgiven men and women who take forgiveness seriously. We confess that we have lived by the sweat of our brothers' and sisters' and children's (very young children's) brows. At times we have treated our fellow humans as dogs. We have presumed to tell other countries how they shall live, and for what they must die. And we do all of this, while at the same time, claiming to be your salt and light in a desperate world. Have mercy on us, Lord. We need it badly."[1] *(Give the people two minutes to digest the prayer.)*

The Act of Receiving New Life

People of God, remember that salt and light are gifts from God. We do not earn them. They are gifts waiting for our reception of them. What do I need to say to you in this precious present moment to have you receive these gifts? Are you aware that God is waiting for you to receive them? If not, what is blocking you from receiving the greatest gift ever offered to this, or any, world?

Ministers' response: God, we open our hearts to you. We are ready to receive you and your gifts of salt and light. Thank you. And thank you for cleansing us from any and all self-righteousness that keeps us from being the salt and light which the world needs to see and experience. We are ready for your truth. We are ready to begin again.

Response

"A New Creature" (words and music by John F. Wilson, found in *Folk Encounter*. See Appendix I for address).

Listening And Proclaiming

Message with the Children of All Ages

Develop the message around salt and light, and what those can mean in the lives of children as they play, attend school, visit friends, and participate in their family.

Reading from the Newer Covenant

When you come to the part about light, turn the flashlight on the congregation. When you read verses 17 to 20, turn the light on yourself.

Proclamation of the Good News

From a Simeon Stylites article in the *Christian Century* magazine years ago, Simeon began this way: In the years preceding the formation of the United Church of Canada, a questionnaire was sent to clergy in western Canada asking about conditions there. One question was, "What are the chief obstacles to religion in your community?" One pastor replied, with much feeling, "The chief obstacles to true religion in our community are whisky and the Methodists." That probably could be said for other denominations as well.

Stewardship Challenge

1. Hand out the Epiphany stars only to those who have not yet received them.
2. Ask two people, in advance, to share their experience about the message on their stars.

Charge to the Congregation

As salt and light, a Christian is an affirmation of the Lordship of Christ; and a denier of the lordship of Caesar, no matter what form Caesar takes. A Christian, as salt and light, is a practitioner of human justice.

Meditation

"Christ is not valued at all unless Christ is valued above all" (Saint Augustine).

Music Possibilities In Addition To Those Already Suggested

Music for Preparation: Medley of Epiphany hymns or "Vision" by Rheinberger.

Hymn of Praise: "Praise the Lord, God's Glories Show," Henry Francis Lyte, 1834; alt. 1972.

Response to the Message with the Children: "I Am the Light of the World," Howard Thurman/Jim Strathdee, copyright 1969.

Response to the Proclamation: "Awake, My Heart," Jane M. Marshall.

Offertory: "Quiet Prelude," Jacobi.

Hymn of Commitment: "Be Thou My Vision," Traditional Irish Melody; trans. by Mary Byrne, 1905; versified by Eleason Hull, 1912; alt.

Response to the Benediction: Chorus only, "I Am the Light of the World." Invite the people to sing several times, and as they leave the sanctuary. (Found in *New Wine, Songs for Celebration*. See Appendix I for address.)

Music for Dismissal: Medley of Epiphany hymns.

---

1. Written by Peter Fribley, Pittsburgh Theological Seminary, Pittsburgh, Pennsylvania, slightly revised. Permission to use given by Peter Fribley, Presbyterian pastor, currently (May 1997) a Lecturer in Religious Studies with Edgewood College, Madison, Wisconsin.

The Season Of The Evangel

Epiphany 6

Liturgical Color: Green

Gospel: Matthew 5:21-37

Theme: *Anger, Adultery, Divorce, Oaths.* "O what a tangled web we weave, when first we practice to deceive" (Sir Walter Scott). "The worst blasphemy is not profanity, but lip-service" (Elton Trueblood).

Adoration And Praise

Invitation to the Celebration
   Paraphrase these words of Harvey Cox, *The Feast of Fools*: "What Christianity permits to happen in church buildings is important mainly as a clue to what it encourages in the culture. An antifestive church drives the dancers not only out of the temple, but out of the streets and houses, too, if it has the power. Likewise, the church that encourages the affirmation of the body within the sacred precinct itself may lend its support to less repressive social orders."[1] Our task, today, is to distinguish between healthy and unhealthy ways that we use our body-parts.

P: God is not dead!
M: God is alive!
P: God lives in the world, our world!
M: God lives in our hearts, minds, emotions, wills. So, with what shall we come before the Lord of life?
P: New eyes, new ears, new tongues, new hands, new hearts.
M: What do you mean, pastor?
P: New eyes to see our neighbors', including our enemies', needs; new ears to hear what people are saying, including those we would rather not hear; new tongues to speak the words of love and justice; new hands to give and not count the cost; new hearts to offer for God to use whenever God decides.
M: We come with new eyes, new ears, new tongues, new hands, new hearts. So be it for sure!

Prayer of Praise
   Eternal and present God, fill our lives with your love this hour, so that all which is non-love can be scoured out, and we can feel clean, strong, and sufficient to meet whatever faces us. Help us, not to conform to this world, but to be transformed by your Spirit. Let it be so, beginning now!

Confession And Forgiveness

The Act of Recognizing Our Humanity
   Prior to worship, make four placards large enough for the congregation to read.
   1. Murder on one side; anger on the other. Which do you need to confess? Give time for people to respond silently. Somewhere during the silence, say, "Cars do not run down nearly so many people as do people who are angry."
   2. Adultery on one side; lust on the other side. Which do you need to confess? Again, offer silence. Somewhere during the silence, say, "What form does our lust take? Wanting somebody else's mate, or children; as for example, 'Why couldn't you be like so and so?' "

3. Divorce on one side; loveless marriage on the other. Which do you need to confess? Give time for reflection. Somewhere during the silence say, "I want intimacy with my mate more than anything else in the world; now, how do I go about playing games in order to avoid the intimacy I say that I so desperately want?"
4. Swearing on one side; "yes" and "no" on the other. Which do you need to confess? Give time. Somewhere during the silence say, "How do I soften my obedience, not by my using four-letter words, but rather, by paying only lip-service to my Lord, family, friends, employer, teacher, and so forth?" Use members of the congregation to hold up the signs; make sure that everyone can see them. Give time for silence.

The Act of Receiving New Life

To confess means "to cut it out," that is, to cut out of our lives those things that get us into trouble. This is not a "do not" faith. Jesus is telling us a new and wholesome way to live. Christ's spirit gives us the energy to do so.

Ministers: Thank you, Lord, for offering us a way out of a "thou shall not faith." Thank you! Thank you! Thank you! In the name of the living God who accepts us unconditionally, and who waits for us to accept God's gift unconditionally.

Response

"Dear Lord and Father of Mankind," stanza 1 only. Sing it as a round three times.

Listening And Proclaiming

Message with the Children of All Ages

Focus on anger. Point out how much better children handle anger than many of us adults. Ask ahead of time how one of the children dealt with anger, and what happened. In one instance, the two angry people worked it out; in the other relationship, perhaps they did not, and still remain separated today. These messages need not have fairy-tale endings; they do need to be realistic and hopeful.

Reading from the Newer Covenant

Invite and practice with four people to read the four sections of Scripture from different parts of the sanctuary. Have someone hold the placards during the reading, and switch from one sign to the other during the reading. Make certain that everyone can see and hear.

Proclamation of the Good News

Many church members maintain a legalistic, what I call a "Protestant purgatory," approach to Christianity. They, despite all evidence to the contrary, are still trying to work, climb, their way to heaven, especially when they hear today's "do not" messages. Many of our people never get beyond their guilt to get to God's grace. Show them how grace can empower them to confront these issues.

Stewardship Challenge

1. Hand out the Epiphany stars only to those who have not yet received them.
2. Ask two people, in advance, to share their experience about the message on their stars.

Charge to the Congregation

In the evening of life, only one question will be asked: "How well have you loved?" If someone turned to you at this moment, and asked you that question, how would you answer it? *(One minute of silence before the benediction.)*

Benediction

Use this approach on occasions: Speak a line of the benediction, and then ask the people to raise their hands and speak it to their fellow worshipers.

Meditation

God sends no one away empty, except those who are full of themselves.

Music Possibilities In Addition To Those Already Suggested

Music for Preparation: Medley of Epiphany hymns, or "What God Ordains" by Pachelbel.

Hymn of Praise: "Praise the Lord! You Heavens Adore Him," Anon. Setting of Schiller's "Hymn to Joy," Berlin, 1799.

Response to the Scripture Reading and/or the Children's Message: "Seek and Ye (You) Shall Find," Kentucky-Tennessee Gospel Song. Found in *New Wine*. (See Appendix I for address.)

Response to the Proclamation: "O Clap Your Hands," Vaughan Williams.

Offertory: "Aria," Franck.

Hymn of Commitment: "God of Grace and God of Glory," Harry Emerson Fosdick, 1930; alt. 1972.

Music for Dismissal: Medley of Epiphany hymns, or "God of Grace and God of Glory." It's okay to repeat parts of worship. Most of the congregation watches television reruns.

---

1. From *The Feast of Fools*, by Harvey Cox; copyright 1969 by Harvey Cox. Reprinted by permission of Harvard University Press.

The Season Of The Evangel

Epiphany 7

Liturgical Color: Green

Gospel: Matthew 5:38-48

Theme: *Concerning Retaliation and Loving Enemies.* "The way from God to a human heart is through a human heart" (Samuel D. Gordon).

Adoration And Praise

Invitation to the Celebration

(Early in the week, ask four people to introduce worship by sharing new or renewed insights about what they have learned this Epiphany season. Include a preteen, a teenager, a young adult, and an older adult. Invite two males and two females. Ask them to speak no more than one minute apiece.) Begin worship with words similar to these: Welcome to the seventh Sunday in Epiphany, the season of the evangel, the recognition that the Christ has come for the whole world, not just our little corner of it. We continue by hearing from four people in the congregation what they have learned or relearned during these weeks of Epiphany. Following each presentation, I invite us to respond with these words: "Praise God for new insights and renewed commitments. Cheers to God and to *(name of person)*. So be it!"

Response

"Let's Go!" (by Avery and Marsh, from *Alive and Singing*. See Appendix I for address). You may want to use this either before or after the four presentations; or use the first three stanzas before and the fourth one after.

Confession And Forgiveness

The Act of Recognizing Our Humanity

Snoopy sits shivering in the snow. Charlie Brown says to Linus, "Snoopy looks kind of cold, doesn't he?" Linus responds, "I'll say he does ... Maybe we'd better go over and comfort him...." So they walk over to Snoopy, look him in the eyes, and greet him. "Be of good cheer, Snoopy ... Yes, be of good cheer...." And then, both of them walk away, leaving Snoopy sitting in the snow with a big question mark. As evangels of the Evangel, whom have we left sitting in the snow this week, our children who need our presence, a mate going through an illness, a conscience dulled by our busyness? For several moments of silence, consider those persons whom God has placed in our lives, but to whom we were too preoccupied to give our attention. At the end of the silence, ask the people to respond, verbally, with these words, "Lord, have mercy on me ..." and then, in silence, ask the people to give the name of the person whom they ignored, or sidestepped, or forgot.

The Act of Receiving New Life

God gives us multitudes of opportunities, yes, even missed opportunities, to respond again. Perhaps only fear keeps us from doing so. Yet, God has announced the greatest news this world has ever received. God asks few of us to stand on street corners as evangels. God has placed persons in our lives who need to see the good news spoken and lived through us. This coming week, I invite us to have a new or awakened sensitivity to the people around us, those whom we call friends and those whom we call enemies. Seek out someone who needs to know that God loves him/her. We are God's evangel to let people know the good news. What a privilege and joy, and probably some fear, to know that God has called us to such a noble task!

P: The Good News of the gospel tells us, in no uncertain terms, that the past is finished and gone. God accepts all of its pain and brokenness.

M: In Jesus the Christ, we are a new creation set free from the weight of sin, whatever form it takes.

P: In Jesus the Christ, we are a new creation; so I invite us to live as those who know to whom they belong.

M: We will live as a community of faith, hope, love, embracing new beginnings with courage, compassion, obedience, and commitment, because of God's amazing love and faithfulness to us. Let it be so!

Response

"Amazing Grace." For those who choose, change "wretch" to "someone."

Listening And Proclaiming

Message with the Children of All Ages

Ask the children what they think the Scripture means. Instead of reading the whole text, select the essence of Jesus' words. Affirm them for their responses. Ask if any have experienced the truth of the lesson; and if so, how did they respond? Share one of your own examples. And point out that children often do better than adults about not striking back and loving those who aren't lovable.

Reading from the Newer Covenant

Have two people read the Scripture, one to take the part of Jesus and the other to read the section from the older Covenant. Following the reading, ask the congregation for its response. What did the people hear; and do they really believe that Jesus' words are practical, or even possible?

Proclamation of the Good News

For part of the message, focus on the last line, "Be perfect as your Heavenly Father is perfect." Many have no understanding of what it means and become discouraged that, because they are imperfect, they will never make it into the presence of God. In an article (source lost) the author says that God is perfect because God is God, and therefore can be trusted always, to be true to His/Her identity. "For us to be perfect," the author says, "as God is perfect is to be true to our role as human beings. We sin when we step outside of our proper relational role, when we try to play god for others, or when we become as animals, tearing and devouring each other ... mortality in the sight of the gospel is being true to relationships, not adhering to an external code." Of course, we will fail. Perhaps the word "complete" would help some people to understand. "Be complete as your Heavenly Father is complete."

Stewardship Challenge

1. Hand out the Epiphany stars only to those who have not yet received them.
2. Ask two people, in advance, to share their experience about the message on their stars.

Charge to the Congregation

Use the same question as last week. In the evening of life, only one question will be asked: "How well have you loved?" So, what is the most important thing that you, as a Christian, want to say to your neighbor from whom you are alienated, to your boss, to your pastor, to your spouse or best friend, to your children, to yourself? If you can't or won't say verbally, will you write a letter? Look at your responses. In what category do your answers fall? He/she is a sinner? He/she is a person whom God loves, even though I may not?

Benediction

Before the words of the benediction, ask the people to look around the sanctuary. Ask, whom do you see? Whom do you avoid looking at? I invite you, this week, to be an evangel to those whom you avoid.

Response

"Glory be to God on High! Alleluia! *(Repeat)* Father, Son, and Holy Ghost! Alleluia!" *(Repeat, until they get enthusiastic.)*

Meditation

A young Christian was considering overseas missions as a life work. He was asked to open a new field in a distant land. He hesitated, "I just can't bring myself to go out there alone." "Would you go there," he was asked, "with a man such as David Livingstone?" "Yes, I'd be glad to." "Then why not go with Christ?" (Wesleyan Methodist). We all go everywhere with Christ.

Music Possibilities In Addition To Those Already Suggested

Music for Preparation: Medley of Epiphany hymns, or "Agnus Dei" by Bach.

Hymn of Praise: "Praise to the Lord, the Almighty," Joachim Neander, 1680; Catherine Winkworth, trans., 1863, alt.

Response to the Prayer of Praise: "Now Let Every Tongue Adore Thee," J. S. Bach.

Response to the Act of Receiving New Life: "The King of Love My Shepherd Is," Ancient Irish Melody.

Response to the Message with the Children: "Have Thine Own Way, Lord," Adelaide A. Pollard.

Offertory: "Pastorale" by Purvis.

Hymn of Commitment: "Immortal, Invisible, God Only Wise," Welsh Folk Song. Walter Chalmers Smith, 1867, 1884, alt.

Music for Dismissal: Medley of Epiphany hymns, or "Con Spirito" by Handel.

The Season Of The Evangel

Epiphany 8

Liturgical Color: Green

Gospel: Matthew 6:24-34

Theme: *Serving Two Masters with Anxiety.* "The measure of a person is not according to the number of his/her servants, but according to the number of people whom he/she serves" (Eugene Overton).

Adoration And Praise

Invitation to the Celebration

In the name of the Evangel, who calls us to be evangels, welcome to this last Sunday in Epiphany. *(Use this if Epiphany lasts less than eight weeks.)* Take one minute to write down the most important truth you learned during this season. *(Wait one minute.)* Is anyone willing to share? If no one is, share the most important truth that you have learned.

P: *(Take out your flashlight and shine it on the congregation as you say)* "You and you and you *(shine it on everyone)* are the light of the world! *(Keep shining it.)* Let your light so shine that people may see your good works and glorify your eternal God."

M: Christ has called us to live the abundant, courageous life, and to expose to people everywhere the adventure of living in fellowship with God and each other.

P: Christ is at work in you, both to will and to ask for his good pleasure.

M: We come to worship to discover more completely how to cooperate with God's Spirit in us in the world.

P: God knows both our need and our potential. God will heal the one and lift us to the other. God will not let us go. We belong to God; we are God's people.

M: We celebrate with praise, adoration, courage, joy, and *(shout out your personal appreciation)*.

Response

"Great Are Your Mercies, O My Maker" (Chinese Folk Song, Tzu-chen Chao, 1931; trans. Frank W. Price, 1953).

Prayer of Praise

"O God, overcome our reluctance to worship by overwhelming us with the Spirit's presence. Push aside any personal agendas we may have brought to this hour. Complement our preparation for worship, by mystical dimensions, which only you can add" (Walter Smith, Jr.).

Confession And Forgiveness

The Act of Recognizing Our Humanity

In the drama, *The Mask of Angels,* one of the characters says, "It's so long since I've felt like a live human being." I invite us to examine ourselves silently for a few moments. New relationships, both legitimate and illicit ones, excite us in the beginning. If they turn sour, why? What did we do? Think about the possibility that we were trying to serve two masters, literally, to live two lives, one for public appearance, one kept secret. What are we willing to do about the unhealthy ones; what are we willing to let God do with us? After several moments of silence, invite the people to pray this prayer: Lord, forgive us for thinking that we can have more than one master. Forgive us for the psychological games we think we can play without doing harm to our family and friends. Forgive us for our anxiety, brought on by our own behavior, which fails to trust you and each other. Forgive us for thinking more of what we can get than what we can give; so often judging others and not ourselves, trusting more in our possessions and performance than in your promises, desiring to use and to please others more than obeying you. Please pardon our unworthy deeds and desires, our wrong acts and attitudes, our foolish fears and failures which have not honored Christ our Lord, who knows all about us and still loves us. In his name, impart his peace and power, that we may live in the freedom and joy of the people of Christ. And all the people said.... *(One minute of silence.)*

The Act of Receiving New Life
The clue to our receiving new life is for us to take responsibility for our own behavior, thoughts, feelings, words, actions. No more scapegoating, justifying, rationalizing. As we take responsibility, our anxiety diminishes and may even disappear. Note in your journal how that happened in the past, and how it might happen in the future.

Response
"Dear Lord and Father of Mankind." Someone has changed the first line to read, "Dear Mother-Father of us all."

Listening And Proclaiming

Message with the Children of All Ages
Tell me some things that you worry about. *(Give them an opportunity to offer several.)* What do you do when you worry? Share with them your own agenda about worry. Snoopy has a solution. He's watching a bug, and says, "That little bug lives in a world all his own. He doesn't know anything about atmospheric testing, strikes, farm problems, medical care, education, or income tax. All he has to worry about is eating and getting stepped on. That's the secret ... Reduce your worries to a minimum!" That is Snoopy's answer. What is yours? *(Wait.)* If no response, assure them that no matter what is happening to them, Jesus promises his presence. Sometimes, his presence comes in the form of parents, teachers, neighbors, friends, classmates. We are not alone.

Response
"God Is My Strong Salvation." Ask the children to return to their seats; ask the parents, or the people who brought them, to take a few moments to explain what the hymn means.

Reading from the Newer Covenant
1. Ask two people, in advance, to stand in the middle of the chancel and do a tug-of-war with a strong rope; and/or
2. Develop a short drama about worry. Have someone pace up and down the chancel as he/she expresses a multitude of worries. After a few moments, have a second person express the words of Jesus, slowly and distinctly.

Proclamation of the Good News
1. Either explore the Scripture directly; or
2. Ask, in advance, five or six persons to give three-minute messages about what happened to them in regard to the message on their stars. Then, invite three or four, not asked in advance, if they would like to share their experiences.

Stewardship Challenge

Hand out the Epiphany stars only to those who have not yet received them. Once again, Epiphany represents Jesus' coming to the whole world. Jesus the Christ now is in the whole world through us. How will we show his presence and power to a world dying to hear the Good News?

Response

Instead of the usual doxology, sing "I'm Sending You" (words and music by Billie Hanks, Jr., in *Folk Songs for Choirs*, Hope Publishing Company. See Appendix I for address).

Charge to the Congregation

What are your plans, what is your goal for reaching out to God's world this week, next week, this year, next year?

Meditation

"Worry does not empty tomorrow of its sorrow; it empties today of its strength" (Corrie ten Boom). "The great sin of the church is to be so interested in serving those within it that it cannot serve the needs of those without" (Albert T. Rasmussen).

Music Possibilities In Addition To Those Already Suggested

Music for Preparation: Medley of Epiphany hymns, or "Chaconne" by Buxtehude.

Hymn of Praise: "All Creatures of Our God and King," Francis of Assisi, 1225; para. by William H. Draper, 1855-1933.

Response to the Children's Message: "Seek and Ye (You) Shall Find," Kentucky-Tennessee Gospel Song. Found in *New Wine*. (See Appendix I for address.)

Response to the Newer Covenant: (Choir) "The Prayers I Make," Jane Marshall.

Hymn of Dedication: "All Hail the Power of Jesus' Name," stanzas 1, 2, Edward Perronet, 1779, 1780; alt. stanzas 3, 4 John Rippon, 1787.

Keep the people informed about composers and places and times of the music. We have a rich heritage, way beyond the ten hymns that many wish we would sing every week.

Response to the Benediction: "Jubilate Chorus" only to "Now On Land and Sea Descending."

Music for Dismissal: Medley of Epiphany hymns. Invite the congregation to remain, to listen to, and to sing the hymns used this Epiphany season, to end the season and to prepare for Lent.

The Season Of The Evangel

The Transfiguration Of The Lord

Liturgical Color: White

Gospel: Matthew 17:1-9

Theme: *The Transfiguration of Our Lord.* Getting off of the mountain into the valley and pits of life.

Adoration And Praise

Invitation to the Celebration

"Joy is the most infallible sign of the presence of God" (Teilhard de Chardin). In addition to joy, what signs do we bring today? Some of these signs may be painful, as the disciples found when they wanted to stay on the mountaintop, and Jesus insisted that they come down to earth. If no one responds, enjoy the silence.

Response to the Invitation

"Heleluyan/Alleluia" (Native American, Muscogee, The United Methodist Publishing House). Have the choir sing it first, then the congregation, then as a round.

Prayer of Praise

Fashion the prayer around the theme of getting off of the mountain into the center of life.

Hymn of Praise

"God, You Spin the Whirling Planets" (Austrian hymn, words by Jane Parker Huber, from *A Singing Faith* and *A Joy in Singing*, The Joint Office of Worship, 1044 Alta Vista Road, Louisville, KY 40205).

The Community Examines Itself

The Act of Recognizing Our Humanity

On top of the mountain, Jesus forced the disciples to take a careful look at themselves. I can't *force* you to do so; I do *invite* all of us to examine ourselves carefully during these moments.

P: O God, whose handiwork we see in the grand scale of the universe, as well as in your mastery of the smallest detail, forgive our insensitivity and carelessness.

M: "O Lord, you have searched me and known me! You know me when I sit down and when I rise up! You discern my thoughts from a long way away. Even before I speak a word, you know it!" What an amazing thought to me.

P: Forgive our carelessness with words; for blundering into your presence in prayer with a shower of syllables, usually wanting something, banking on a sick sentimentality, thoughtless and insensitive.

Men: Is this true? Does God know when we deceive deliberately to impress others? Does God hear our unspoken, bitter thoughts under our smooth words?

M: "You harass me wherever I go, and lay your hand on me. Such knowledge is too great for me; it is too high, I can't reach it."

Women: I feel uncomfortable to be known that well by anyone. I fear exposure to that kind of intimacy.

P: "Where shall we escape your Spirit? Where shall I hide from your eyes?"

M: We think that we can hide from God behind our bushes of security. We are afraid to be seen by God and each other, even as Christians in the same congregation.

P: "If I take the morning's wings, and dwell in the depths of the sea, even there your hand shall lead me, and your right hand shall hold me."

M: Forgive my carelessness with the world; for using the earth, as if it were my private playground to do with as I please, with resources to be plundered, and beauty to be ravished. Teach me, God, to respect the balance of nature, that can feed and clothe and shelter me, and nourish my spirit as well, but only when I have the patience to think your thoughts after you.

Men: Can we not escape God, no matter where we go, no matter how we treat God's world? Why does God, who gave us dominion over the earth, pursue us — to judge us, to condemn us?

Women: Can it be that God pursues us to love us, to forgive us, to use us as salt and light, for mission, for ministry in God's world of nature, animals, people?

M: Because God pursues us to convince us of our unconditional acceptance, then, forgive my carelessness with God's creation: allowing myself to be obsessed with the success of numbers, measuring everything in the mass, and standing in awe of statistics. Teach me, God, the importance of one: one sparrow, one sunset, one rose, one person, one Lord, one baptism, one God and Father/Mother of us all.

P: "Search me, O God, and know my heart! Try me, test me, and know my thoughts! And see if you can find any wicked way in me; lead me in your eternal way."

M: Teach me, teach us, God, the discipline of saying what I mean, so I will mean what I say (source unknown, revised).

(Two minutes of silence.)

The Act of Receiving New Life

Look around the sanctuary, slowly. Do you see each other in a new light? God accepts our humanity.

M: We embrace our humanity because Christ embraces us.

P: God in Christ has set us free from the burden of our favorite sin, security, the one which the disciples wanted to keep enjoying on the mountain.

M: We are free to get back down the mountain, not because *we* say so, but because *Christ* says so.

P: God in Christ calls us to experience newness in everything, person, song, day.

M: We celebrate life in the presence and power of the living, reigning Christ.

P: So be it!

M: Yes, indeed!

All: So be it! Yes, indeed!

Listening And Proclaiming

Message with the Children of All Ages

In advance, ask several people to act out the scripture, as a contemporary event. We like vacations, and we want to stay forever. And, we need to get back home to do what we need to do to be the people that God has called us to be.

Proclamation of the Good News

Because this is "Criminal and Justice System" Sunday, invite someone who works in that system to speak. God calls the church to seek justice on behalf of the poor and powerless; and often, the church prefers to ignore that part of its calling to maintain its security blanket.

Stewardship Challenge

Somewhere in the world, 40,000,000 children die every day from lack of food and pure water. 40,000 children in the U.S. live in poverty. Obviously, we cannot minister to the whole world. What will we do in our immediate world?

Charge to the Congregation

Our response as people of faith, hope, love to Christ's mission is not, "Will you join us, Lord?" but rather, "We choose to join you, down in the valley and pits where people live and hurt and die. Thanks for inviting us."

Meditation

"When we do offer our thankful response, we discover a new dimension to our lives" (WHK). And we discover that a "Christian is an 'alleluia' from head to foot" (Saint Augustine).

Music Possibilities In Addition To Those Already Suggested

Consider these hymns to be integrated throughout the worship:

"O God of Light, Your Word, a Lamp Unfailing," Sarah E. Taylor, 1952, 1972.

"O Morning Star, How Fair and Bright," Philip Nicolai, 1599; trans. by Catherine Winkworth, 1863; alt.

"Be Thou My Vision," Ancient Irish Hymn; trans. by Mary Byrne, 1927.

"We Thank Thee, Lord," Bortiansky, for the Adult Choir.

"Swiftly Pass the Clouds of Glory," Thomas H. Troger, 1985; George Henry Day, 1940.

"Jesus on the Mountain Peak," Cyril Vincent Taylor, 1907; Brian Wren, 1962, 1988.

"O Wondrous Sight, O Vision Fair," "The Agincourt Song," England, c. 1415; trans. John Mason Neale, 1851; alt. 1861.

Lent
The Season Of Renewal

Liturgical Color: Purple
(Ash Wednesday to Easter)

The Lenten season extends over a 46-day period. The six Sundays in Lent are not included as a part of Lent; so the season consists of forty days. Sundays, weekly commemorations of the First Easter (though every Sunday is Easter), have always been excluded from this traditional fast season. Holy Week begins with Palm Sunday and serves as a review of the events of Jesus' Passion. Passion refers to the sufferings of Jesus after the Last Supper and on the Cross.

The beginning of Lent appears to have been associated with a period of discipline, reflection, and abstinence in order to imitate Jesus' self-denial and to prepare for the celebration of Easter.

Lent developed for two reasons:

1. As a period of fasting which preceded Easter. At first, this fasting period was held on Saturday, the day before Easter, lasting until 3:00 a.m., Easter morning when the Lord's Supper was celebrated, recalling Christ's resurrection in the early morning. Later, this fast was extended to six days and eventually became separated into the events of Holy Week. Holy Week, then, is an older season than the entire Lenten season.

2. For the baptism of persons into the faith on Easter eve. Because the early church existed "underground," candidates were carefully screened after a long period of preparation. The strictest part of this probationary period came just before baptism. A fasting of forty days was required, suggested by Jesus' fasting forty days in the wilderness, Moses' fasting at Mount Sinai, and Elijah's fasting on the way to the Mount of God. Eventually, this period of preparation for baptism evolved into a general period of preparation for Easter to be observed by all Christians.

The days of Holy Week have the following significance:

Palm Sunday — Jesus' triumphal entry into Jerusalem.

Monday — Jesus' cleansing of the temple.

Tuesday — Jesus' verbal conflicts and confrontations with his enemies.

Wednesday — Jesus' silence and retreat in Bethany.

Thursday — Jesus' initiation of the Lord's Supper. Maundy takes its name from the "New Commandment" which Jesus gave to the disciples to love.

Friday — Jesus' crucifixion. The term "good" probably comes from "God's Friday."

The Season Of Renewal

Ash Wednesday

Liturgical Color: Purple

Gospel: Matthew 6:16-21

Theme: Ash Wednesday provides an opportunity for us to let God's Spirit examine us anew. How often do we listen to, and expect, the benefits of our faith, and ignore its sterner demands? In this hour, God invites us to see, not only that God is love and mercy, but also holiness and justice. How will we see and respond to life differently if we know that God brings justice and calls us, the church, to seek justice on behalf of the risen one?

Prior to worship, ask the congregation to bring some writings about the beginning of Lent which they would be willing to share with the congregation. Give them the opportunity to do so, as the Spirit leads them.

Somewhere in the worship, have people read the Scripture slowly and deliberately from different versions of the Bible. Invite them the previous Sunday to bring their Bibles with them for this purpose.

Read silently, or sing quietly, the hymn, "Forty Days and Forty Nights" (George Hunt Smyttan, 1856; alt. attr. Martin Herbst, 1676).

Give plenty of time for silence. Where appropriate, ask for sentence prayers along the way as people are led by the Spirit.

Dismiss the people with a silent benediction, by raising your hand, and by their raising their hands over one another as they leave the sanctuary.

Meditation

The road to hell is paved not so much with the harmfully obvious for Christians, but with the subtly "unharmful." Our danger is to give first-rate importance and power to second-rate causes.

The Season Of Renewal

Lent 1

Liturgical Color: Purple

Gospel: Matthew 4:1-11

Theme: *The Temptations of Jesus.* He was tempted *in every way* as we are tempted.

The Community Gathers

Invitation to the Celebration
In the name of the Christ who was tempted in every way as we are. Yes, that's what the Scripture says. Today, we examine those temptations of popularity, power, prestige. So, now that Epiphany has ended, are you ready to begin the season of Lent? We begin our Lenten journey.
P: The call of God in Christ is the call to life.
M: It is the call to live with love and hope, and with a deep sense of our own worth.
P: I invite us to respond in the name of the Christ, who was tempted in every way as we are tempted, and live as his forgiven, empowered people.
M: We celebrate the life that he has given us, and rejoice in its unlimited possibilities.

Hymn of Praise
Many of the Lenten hymns are subjective; select an objective hymn, one in which God is the focal point, not in which the worshiper is the focal point.

The Community Takes Responsibility For Itself

The Act of Recognizing Our Humanity
We will examine Jesus' temptations in the light of our own.
1. How do we try to become popular? By being a bookworm? A beach show-off? An athletic star? List some other possibilities; and ask the congregation to do the same. Follow this with one minute of silence.
2. Power. How do we try to gain power? Through money? Clothes? Bragging? List some other ways; and ask the congregation to do the same. Follow this with one minute of silence.
3. Possessions. Is more better? List others; ask the congregation to do the same. Follow this with one minute of silence. Take your time in this confession.

Response
"Have Mercy, Lord, on Me" (Marcello Montoya; trans. George P. Simmons, 1968). Read it a second time silently. Then, have a guitarist play it while the congregation sings.

The Act of Receiving New Life
Someone has said that the only things some people give up for Lent are their New Year's resolutions. Someone else responding to the same question suggests that we give up our independence, putting our lives completely into God's hands. Most of us probably have never done this, and point to Mother Teresa as one who has. What would our life resemble if we chose to make Christ the center of our thoughts, feelings, words, and behavior? We might only feel guilty for failing. Despite our failure to be

perfect, would we live in, by, and through the grace of God, who knows that we fail, and is constantly available to us? Do we believe the truth that God seeks us out and wants to have a relationship with us, even when we fail?
P: I invite us to remember the Good News of our liberation.
M: In Christ, our self-worth has been declared.
P: We have been forgiven, accepted, received.
M: God has given the present new meaning. God has filled the future with possibilities.
P: I invite us to live fully and responsibly. Be free! Be responsible! For true freedom exists only in responsible living!
M: Indeed we shall! So be it! Amen.

Response
"That's For Me" (words and music by Kurt Kaiser, from *Sacred Songs*, a division of Word, Inc. Song found in *Folk Encounter*, Hope Publishing Company. See Appendix I for address).

The Community Responds To God's Truth

Message with the Children of All Ages
Review the temptations in their language and experience. Let them do most of the talking; and for goodness' sake, as well as God's sake, avoid making a moralism of the lesson. Someone once referred to children's messages as "little liquor lectures."

Reading of the Newer Covenant
Have your drama group, informal or formal, act out the temptations in a modern setting. It takes only two people. Portray the struggle Jesus experienced; it was a horrendous struggle!

Proclamation of the Good News
Whereas some liberals have difficulty with the divinity of Jesus, some conservatives have difficulty, extreme difficulty, with his humanity. For the brave, refer to Nikos Kazantzakis' *The Last Temptation of Christ*. Recall how some religious groups in America responded to the book and movie; many of them had never seen it. After referring to it in worship one Sunday, my friend was picketed by one of the church's members in the sanctuary the next Sunday. She handed out material condemning him. Either Jesus was tempted in every way as we are, or he is not our Savior!

Stewardship Challenge
Jesus kept himself in the world, confronting every evil that needed confronting; he calls us to do the same. How will we live out our stewardship this week doing what Jesus did?

Response (to replace the Doxology)
"Today, We All Are Called to Be Disciples" (English Country Songs, 1893; H. Kenn Carmichael, 1985; arr. and harm. Ralph Vaughan Williams, 1906).

Charge to the Congregation
Brazilian educator Augusto Boal calls us from being spectators to "spec-actors," that is, those who see and act.

Meditation
"I believe in hot water. I think it keeps you clean" (G. K. Chesterton).

Music Possibilities In Addition To Those Already Suggested

Music for Preparation: Medley of Lenten hymns.

Hymn of Praise: "We Praise Thee, O God, Our Redeemer," Julia C. Cory.

Response to the Confession: "Lord, Who Throughout These Forty Days," Claudia F. Hernaman, 1873.

Response to the Assurance of Pardon: (a round) "For Your Gracious Blessing," harmonized by David Smart, copyright 1972, in *Music For Young Voices*, Hope Publishing Company. See Appendix I for address.

Offertory: "O Sacred Head," J. S. Bach.

Music for Dismissal: Medley of Lenten hymns.

Note: To introduce a new hymn, use it several weeks in a row. For example, use a new Lenten hymn for the first half of Lent; then introduce another the second half. A surefire way to introduce new music is during the time of the children's message. We can do many things there that we can do nowhere else.

The Season Of Renewal

Lent 2

Liturgical Color: Purple

Gospel: John 3:1-17

Theme: *Nicodemus and Jesus.* Conversion is a matter of "internal combustion," and for most of us is "a long day's journey into light" (idea suggested in a sermon by James T. Cleland).

The Community Gathers

Invitation to the Celebration
  In the name of the Christ who confronts us, as he did Nicodemus, with our "new birth status." Today, we consider the first step of what it means to call ourselves Christians. Are you ready to do that, even though you may have called yourself a Christian for fifty years? Please raise your hand if you are.
P: Fellow adventurers in the new life in Christ, a new life which needs renewing each day, we belong to each other. Christ has made us a new breed of humanity, filled us with his own Spirit, and released us to be persons for others. We praise him for this fellowship, in which we are learning to love him, ourselves, one another, our enemies, and the world.
M: And we are new, not perfect, men, women, boys, girls through him. Even so, as transformed, renewed, released people, we celebrate with adoration and praise.
P: The living Christ is here, even as the living Jesus was with Nicodemus. Our communion is with him, and through his love, with each other. I invite us to open ourselves to him, as did Nicodemus, and to each other, as the did the disciples, at least sometimes. In Christ's name, I invite you to greet those around you. Use your favorite greeting.

Hymn of Praise
  "To God Be the Glory" (Fanny Jane Crosby, 1875; William Howard Doane, 1875).

Prayer of Praise
  Ask, in advance, one of the young people, perhaps a new Christian, to offer the prayer. Offer the idea that this is a prayer of praise, not a subjective prayer.

The Community Takes Responsibility For Itself

The Act of Recognizing Our Humanity
  Think about this statement as we come to this time of confession: "We don't want to be saved, liberated, made whole in our humanity; we want to be fished out of it" (author unknown). Think about this for two minutes; and write down your thoughts; you will have an opportunity to respond. *(Wait two minutes. Ask for response.)* Some may have some great ideas; some may remain confused, no differently from Nicodemus. For me, one idea is that we only want the furniture of our life rearranged, rather than our buying new furniture.

Response
  "Eternal Light, Shine in My Heart" (Alcuin, c. 735-804; paraphrase Christopher Idle, b. 1938; Jane Manton Marshall, b. 1924).

The Act of Receiving New Life

Often, we rush through this act of worship to get to the "important stuff," whatever that's supposed to mean. In silence, consider your personal battle about being born again and receiving the Good News. Did your conversion come easily; or did you do battle with God? After a few minutes of silence, invite the people to offer sentence prayers of thanksgiving.

Response

"Eightfold Alleluia."

The Community Responds To God's Truth

Message with the Children of All Ages

Do you ever argue with your parents? Or do you always do what you are told, immediately? Did you know that many of the people in the Bible argued with God? Sometimes, they were confused; sometimes they were angry. Did you know that it's okay to be confused and angry with God and it's okay to tell God? Give two or three examples: Abraham, Moses, Nicodemus. Tell them the essence of the Nicodemus story and what it means for them.

Reading of the Newer Covenant

Act out the story. You will need a reader, a Nicodemus, and a Jesus. Update the language.

Proclamation of the Good News

Years ago, Elton Trueblood referred to our generation as the "cut-flower" generation. It has no roots. The contemporary church has plenty of activity but little depth. So, take the people back to the basics of the faith through the example of Nicodemus. At the end of the message, ask the people if they have any questions or confusions.

Stewardship Challenge

In which of these two choices, as the stewards of God, are you most involved: Church work, or the work of the church? Do we know the difference? After the offering, ask a layperson to pray about the difference, without the person preaching to the "unsaved."

Charge to the Congregation

On a scale of 1 (mild religion) to 10 (vital faith), where do you put yourself? If you give yourself a one, what are you willing to do to move toward a ten? We are here to help each other.

Meditation

"Many a church member would be terribly frightened if he/she could only feel his/her spiritual pulse and find out how nearly dead he/she is" (from *Uplift,* Stonewall Jackson Industrial School). Does that description fit us or do we have a vital faith which sustains us on the mountaintops and valleys and pits?

Music Possibilities In Addition To Those Already Suggested

Music for Preparation: Medley of Lenten hymns, or "Prelude and Variation," Franck.

Choral Introit: "O Lamb of God," Weiss.

Prayer of Praise: "Christ of All My Hopes, the Ground," Ralph Wardlaw, 1817. (Hymn for first half of Lent; use the hymn, and other hymns, in different places in the worship. Be certain that they fit the proper section of the worship.)

Response to the Confession: "God is Love," C. J. Rivers.

Response to the Newer Covenant: (Choir) "O Savior of the World," text and music by John Goss.

Offertory: "Crucifix," Jean-Baptist Favre.

Hymns of Commitment: 1) "Of the Father's Love Begotten," Aurelius Clemens Prodentius, 348-410 A.D.; John Mason Neale, trans. 1851 and Henry W. Baker, 1859; alt. 1972. 2) "Love Divine, All Loves Excelling," Charles Wesley, 1747; alt.

Music for Dismissal: Medley of Lenten hymns, or "In My Deepest Grief," Bach.

The Season Of Renewal

Lent 3

Liturgical Color: Purple

Gospel: John 4:5-42

Theme: *Jesus and the Woman of Samaria.* "The function of worship is to focus, sharpen, and deepen new response to the world and to other people beyond the point of proximate concern, that is, of liking, self-interest, limited commitment, to that of ultimate concerns; to purify and correct our love in the light of Christ's love; and in him to find the grace and power to be the reconciled and reconciling community. Anything that achieves this, or assists toward it, is Christian worship. Anything that fails to do this is not Christian worship, be it ever so 'religious' " (John Robinson, *Honest to God*).[1]

The Community Gathers

Invitation to the Celebration

Why have you come to worship today? Out of habit? To see your friends? To enjoy the singing? To hear the sermon? To learn something? To get help for the coming week? To restore your sense of values? For 100 other reasons? *(Pause.)* And, now that we're here, let us worship, in the Name of God the Parent, God the Child, God the Spirit. And all the people said, "Right on!"

Response

"Holy, Holy, Holy! Lord God Almighty!" If you have an instrumental group, always use it; if you have none, form one. The congregation probably has many musicians who need only a little encouragement to use their talents in this way.

The Community Takes Responsibility For Itself

The Act of Recognizing Our Humanity

"The first step toward the spirit's recovery in our lives is the awareness and knowledge of the sin committed" (Seneca, 4 B.C. to 65 A.D., slightly revised). Now, I invite us to respond silently to the petitions in this bidding prayer. Let us confess:

1. Our superficial understanding of sin, because we prefer to focus on sins. *(Silence)*
2. Because of our superficial view of sin, let us confess our lack of personal joy. *(Silence)*
3. Let us confess our lack of enthusiasm for the ministry of wholeness. *(Silence)*
4. Let us confess our lack of belief to the point of practice in the truth of the Good News of Christ. *(Silence)*

Follow this with a brief prayer by the pastor or one of the church officers.

Response

"Let the Spirit In" (words and music by Richard Blank, from *The Genesis Songbook* by Agapé, Hope Publishing Company. See Appendix I for address).

The Act of Receiving New Life

Read, or have someone sing, these words of the popular song: "There will be a new tomorrow; there will be a brighter day. There will be a new tomorrow; love will find a way."

P: "No condemnation now hangs over the heads of those who are 'in' Christ Jesus. For the new spiritual principle of life 'in' Christ lifts me, lifts us, out of the old vicious circle of sin and death."

M: So, Lord, help us to believe and act upon this truth with our new intellect and new emotions. Yes, indeed!

Response

"The Lord Is My Shepherd" (the Junior Choir).

The Community Responds To God's Truth

Message with the Children of All Ages

Plan well ahead to use two people to act out the dialogue between Jesus and the Samaritan in the Gospel reading. They need not speak the text exactly; encourage them to have a conversation in a contemporary setting. Show the people how it would sound today. After the drama, ask the people if they have ever had a similar conversation with Jesus.

Proclamation of the Good News

It is not our job to coerce, argue, persuade others into the Kingdom; it is our privilege to invite them, with our words and our lives.

Stewardship Challenge

No one really trusts God until he/she trusts God with his/her money.

Charge to the Congregation

The ministry of worship never ends with the benediction. When Christ is Lord, all of life becomes a ministry of worship — how we relate to each other ... how we spend our money ... how we use our time ... how we care about others ... how we use our resources ... how we allow the Spirit of Christ to sensitize us to the world of hurting people. All of life for the Christian becomes a letter of concern, a poem-praise, a song of joy, in the Name of God, the Creator, Liberator, Sustainer, Energizer, and all the people said, *(your favorite amen)*.

Meditation

"Priorities for the person of faith are difficult to maintain when one fails to read the Bible, pray, study, or worship faithfully, daily" (WHK).

Music Possibilities In Addition To Those Already Suggested

Music for Preparation: Medley of Lenten hymns, or musical version of Psalm 95.

Choral Introit: "O Lamb of God," Weiss.

Hymns of Praise: "Christ of All My Hopes, the Ground," Ralph Wardlaw (for the first half of Lent). And "O, Come and Sing Unto the Lord," the Psalter, 1912; alt., 1955 (based on Psalm 95:1-6).

Response to the Confession: "Open My Eyes, That I May See," stanza 1.

Response to the Proclamation: "What's That I Hear," words and music by Phil Ochs, copyright 1963, by Appleseed Music, Inc. (Use only stanza 2, which begins, "What's that I see ...").

Offertory with soloist: Popular song, "I Only Have Eyes For You," admittedly poor English. Introduce it by applying it to the relationship between God and us.

Hymn of Commitment: "Open My Eyes, That I May See," Clara H. Scott, 1895. Use the entire hymn to conclude worship.

Music for Dismissal: Medley of Lenten hymns, or a musical version of Psalm 143.

---

1. Used by permission of Westminster/John Knox Press. Also published by SCM Press Ltd., 9-17 St. Albans Place, London N1 0NX. Permission not necessary in the U.S.A.

The Season Of Renewal

Lent 4

Liturgical Color: Purple

Gospel: John 9:1-41

Theme: *Physical and Spiritual Blindness.* Do we have any blind spots? What do we do when someone points them out? What if that someone is, in reality, God speaking to us?

The Community Gathers

Invitation to the Celebration
Last week, I asked *why* we came to worship. This week, I ask *how* did we come today:
1. As spectators, waiting for someone to do something for, to, with us; or as participants making something happen?
2. As people ready to say "yes" to God; or as people who say "no, maybe, later"?
3. As humble ones who have more questions than answers; or as self-righteous ones who pretend to have all of the answers?
4. Do we come breezing in, or dragging in?
5. With openness or with calculations?
6. Joyfully or morosely?
7. Do we come broken or whole or a mixture?

Choral Response
"O Come, Let us Celebrate" (Richard Gerig, 1975).

Affirmation of Joyful Expectations   Pastor and Ministers
P: Come on! Let's celebrate the presence and power of God, no matter what our condition — the God who is Creator, Sustainer, Liberator, Energizer of all, the God who came in Jesus the Christ to transform the world and begin the new creation.
M: We come to celebrate the presence and power of God, despite our blind spots. We are the people of God, despite our blind spots — new persons in the new creation made possible by the death and resurrection of Jesus the Christ. We come to affirm that the old has passed away and behold the new has come, is coming, and will come!
P: No matter how blind we are, Jesus the Christ is Lord!
M: And we are new, not perfect, persons through him! As transformed, renewed, released people, we celebrate with adoration and praise!

Hymn of Praise (with drums, or drum substitute; use your imagination)
"O God the Creator" (music by Joy Patterson, 1989; text: c. 1977, Elizabeth Haile and Cecil Corbett).

The Community Takes Responsibility For Itself

The Act of Recognizing Our Humanity
Jim Crane, in his book *On Edge*, has a contemporary man, cigarette in mouth, briefcase in hand, speaking to the prophet Amos. "I enjoyed your talk, Mr. Amos, but I would like to hear more of what's

right with Israel." True of us? If so, then we will do our best to silence the messenger, because we want no one, not even God's messenger, to reveal our blind spots; we will silence the messenger, if not by outright killing him/her, then by gossip to destroy a person's character; or by ignoring the person, even during the social hour following worship; or by ridiculing a person behind his/her back; or by *(what's your favorite way?)*. Blind spots are dangerous to a person's spiritual health. *(Three minutes of silence to consider and write down the content of our blind spots.)*

Response
Offer the opportunity to confess their blind spots, and to ask forgiveness both from God and the congregation. Offer one of your own.

The Act of Receiving New Life
Only the Spirit of God transforms us from our blind spots to an openness to acknowledge them. Only the Spirit of God transforms us from excuse-making, "I just couldn't help myself ... I didn't know!" to obedient decision-making: "I am responsible for myself!" So, if it's true that God is, that God refuses to lie, then, believe me, we are forgiven of the past, reconciled in the present, equipped for the future — with our blind spots revealed in the name of the Christ of the Cross.

Response
"Open My Eyes That I May See" (Clara H. Scott, 1895).

The Community Responds To God's Truth

Message with the Children of All Ages and the Reading of the Newer Covenant
Again, this Scripture provides an excellent opportunity for a powerful drama, preferably memorized, but also as a reading. It requires the following characters: Jesus, the blind man, the Pharisees, the blind man's parents. At the points of the parents' participation, the whole thing is a comedy. Be sure to stress the comedic side of the drama.

Proclamation of the Good News
You may want to use this illustration: A woman went to a play and sat there the whole evening. It was bitter cold outside. While the woman sat inside, she was moved to shed tears at the drama. While she wept over the play, her coachman was freezing outside.

Stewardship Challenge
Do we have any blind spots with our money? Before presenting the offering, consider, and write down, your blind spots. After the offering, ask members of the congregation to offer sentence prayers.

Charge to the Congregation
Ask the congregation in general, though you may want to have asked three or four well before worship, what charge they would like to give each other in regard to blindness; and what, in God's name, they plan to do about it.

Meditation
A farmer who lived on the same farm all of his life wanted a change. He subjected everything on the farm to his blind and merciless criticism; he appreciated nothing about it. So he finally listed the farm with a realtor. He was ready to sell. The realtor prepared an advertisement for the newspaper. He read to the farmer a very flattering description of the property. He talked of the farm's advantages, its ideal location, its up-to-date equipment, its fertile acres, its well-bred stock. "Wait a minute; read that to me again," insisted the farmer, "and read it slowly." The realtor did as asked. "Changed my mind," said the

farmer, "I'm not gonna sell. All my life I've been looking for a place like that!"[1] (J. Wallace Hamilton, in *Ride the Wild Horses!* Revell, revised.)

Music Possibilities In Addition To Those Already Suggested

Music for Preparation: Medley of Lenten hymns.

Hymn of Praise: "Father Eternal, Ruler of Creation," Laurence Housman, 1919; alt.

Response to the Prayer of Praise: "Let Us Sing to the Lord" (Psalm 95), Moyer. Adult Choir.

Response to the Confession: "When We Are Tempted to Deny Your Son," David W. Romig, 1965.

Offertory: "A Prayer for the Innocent," McKay.

Hymn of Commitment: "Where Cross the Crowded Ways of Life," Frank Mason North, 1903; alt., 1972 (hymn for the second half of Lent).

Response to the Benediction: "Fourfold Amen," your choice.

Music for Dismissal: Medley of Lenten hymns, or "Benedictions," McKay.

---

1. Permission to use given by "the heirs of J. W. Hamilton," signed by Joan Hamilton Morris.

The Season Of Renewal

Lent 5

Liturgical Color: Purple

Gospel: John 11:1-45

Theme: *Lazarus' Death and Resurrection; Jesus' Teaching about Resurrection; Jesus Weeps.* "Christianity is the heart of a world without a heart" (author unknown).

The Community Gathers

Invitation to the Celebration

In the name of the Christ who approaches the Cross, welcome to the fifth Sunday in Lent, the season of renewal. What new or renewed insights have you received this Lenten season? How have those insights influenced your behavior? Would anyone care to respond? You may want to ask two or three persons before worship if they would be willing to share during the worship.

P: The Call of Christ is no easy one, even though we want to make it easy.
M: It is an invitation to self-giving and sacrificial giving.
P: It requires hard work in the face of disappointments and disillusion.
M: It means going on when, seemingly, everyone else has given up.
P: We will need to support each other if we are to follow Christ.
M: We offer our support to each other as we celebrate life together.

Response

"Help Us to Accept Each Other" (words by Fred Kaan, music by Jim Strathdee, from *Singing the Lord's Song*, distributed by Discipleship Resources, P. O. Box 189, 1908 Grand Avenue, Nashville, TN 37202).

Prayer of Praise

Merciful and Holy God, to whom all generations have turned for help, look upon us with your Maternal and Paternal compassion. Grant that your presence may come upon us, and your love surround us, this Lenten season. Keep on making yourself known to us, in whatever way necessary for us to pay attention to your presence. Grant that we will spend our time in the light of your presence, even when it seems that we prefer the darkness; so that we may see anew that the Good News is *good news*, for our health and not our destruction. Indeed!

Hymn of Praise

"Blessed Jesus, at Your Word" (Tobias Clausnitzer, 1663; Johann Rudolph Ahle, 1664; trans. Catherine Winkworth, 1858; alt. 1972; harm. Johann Sebastian Bach, 1658-1750, alt.).

The Community Takes Responsibility For Itself

The Act of Recognizing Our Humanity   Pastor and Ministers

"What counts is change, so I struggle so hard to stay the same" (from *On Dusting the Wind*, David P. Young). We say that we want Christ to change us; yet we prefer to run our own lives. As we enter into the confession, review that remark in regard to our own decisions.

P: Almighty God, you alone are good and holy. Purify our lives and make us brave disciples. We ask, not for you to keep us safe, but keep us loyal; so we may serve the Christ, who, though tempted in every way as we are, remained faithful to you.

M: Make it so, Lord.

P: From cowardice that dares not face truth; from laziness content with half-truth; from arrogance that thinks it knows it all;

M: O God, deliver us.

P: From artificial life and worship, from all that is hollow or insincere;

M: O God, deliver us.

P: From cynicism about others; from intolerance and cruel indifference;

M: O God, deliver us.

P: From being satisfied with things as they are, as the church or in the world; from failing to share your indignation;

M: O God, deliver us.

P: For everything in us that may hide your light;

M: O God, light of life, forgive us, and show us how to forgive each other.

The Act of Receiving New Life

The choir will sing the antiphon; the congregation will speak the responses as follows:

Choir: The living Christ works in our hearts. Through us, with us, he saves. *(The choir will write its own tune to those words.)*

Congregation:

1:     Knowledge opens our hearts to you; show us the secret to your love.
2:     Absorbed in you, we find ourselves; we now accept your plans for us.
3:     The seeds have been planted by you; make them grow, working in us.
4:     May our community sprout with your love; let it open that love to the world.
5:     Guide our hands as we reach to help; be with us as we are with others.
6:     Make us, Christ, extensions of you, as we think your thoughts, say your words.

The Community Responds To God's Truth

Message with the Children of All Ages and the Reading of the Newer Covenant

Again, this Scripture provides an excellent opportunity for a drama. By now, perhaps, you have several people interested in forming a drama group. At the end of the drama, you may want to point out the humanity of Jesus, his weeping. Someone has said that "tears represent the purest form of prayer."

Proclamation of the Good News

You may want to emphasize the following: Show why Abraham, Esau, Joseph, King Hezekiah, Peter, Paul all wept. Paul said, "Out of such affliction and anguish of heart, and with many tears, I wrote to you...." Yes, boys and men do cry, and for good reason. In tears, we find our true humanity.

Stewardship Challenge

How would you describe the stewardship of your tears? Over what do we weep? The death of 40,000 children each day? Poverty in Third World countries? Alcohol and drug-related deaths? Pentagon overkill? Greedy politicians? Millionaire CEOs? Before receiving the offering, ask the congregation what they cry about.

Charge to the Congregation

Tears represent love, and love is not weak but strong. In tears, we discover our humanity. Ecclesiastes tells us, "There is a time to weep and a time to laugh." Unless we know how to weep, we will never know how to laugh in healthy ways. Jesus knew how to do both. He accepted his humanity, with all of its emotions. He invites us to live our humanity to its fullest.

Meditation

"Tears are the substance that heals wounds that are too deep for hands and words to touch" (author unknown).

Music Possibilities In Addition To Those Already Suggested

Music for Preparation: Medley of Lenten hymns, or "Therefore, So Great a Sacrament," Bedell.

Choral Introit: "The Lord Is King," Conder.

Hymn of Praise: "Whate'er Our God Ordains Is Right," Samuel Rodigast, 1674; Catherine Winkworth, trans. 1858, 1863; alt., 1972.

Response to the Reading of the Newer Covenant: "When Jesus Wept," William Billings, 1770; as in *New England Psalm Singer*, 1770.

Response to the Prayer after the Proclamation: "Hear Our Prayer, O, Lord," George Whelpton, 1897.

Offertory: "But the Lord Is Mindful of His Own," Mendelssohn.

Hymn of Commitment: "Where Cross the Crowded Ways of Life," Frank Mason North (hymn for the second half of Lent).

Music for Dismissal: Medley of Lenten hymns, or "Postlude," J. Cramer; or, "Lord, from the Depths to You I Cry," para. in the Scottish Psalter, 1650; alt.

The Season Of Renewal

Passion/Palm Sunday

Liturgical Color: Purple

Gospel: Matthew 26:14—27:66

Theme: *Palm Sunday and Jesus' Passion.* When Jesus entered Jerusalem, the crowd cheered, for all the wrong reasons.

The Community Gathers

Invitation to the Celebration

In the name of the Christ who creates, liberates, sustains, energizes us, welcome to this Palm Sunday/Passion Sunday celebration. Here comes Jesus! Let's make him welcome! Enter into the Mardi Gras spirit! Laugh and dance and sing and rejoice! Our King is coming! Our King is here! (In advance, invite any in the congregation to bring their musical instruments; have palm leaves for the children to carry as they process to the chancel.)

Response

"Here He Comes" (Richard Avery and Don Marsh, from *The Avery and Marsh Songbook*, Hope Publishing Company. See Appendix I for address).

Prayer of Praise

Thanks for coming, Lord. We can hardly wait for you to fulfill the promises of the prophets. What a week this is going to be! We're ready. So be it!

Hymn of Praise

"Hosanna, Loud Hosanna" (Jenette Threfall, 1873).

The Community Takes Responsibility For Itself

The Act of Recognizing Our Humanity and Act of Receiving New Life Bidding Prayer

Often, in our prayers, which sound more like demands, we ask God to change others or situations (as the people hoped to do with Jesus); we begin by placing ourselves before the judgment and mercy of God. So, in the power, presence, and purpose of God,

1. Let us pray for one change to take place in our life which blocks us from others, perhaps the elimination of false pride, prejudice, laziness, indifference, hatred, jealousy. *(Silence)*
2. Let us ask God to remove one barrier from us which keeps us from a growing, maturing relationship with a specific neighbor; with a particular classmate or co-laborer; with a member of our immediate family, biological, or church family. *(Silence)*
3. Let us ask God's Spirit to invade the indifferent person, the casual participant, who seems not to care, or who seems untouched by the Word, knowing that we are sometimes that person; the hostile, angry person who has been "turned off" or hurt by fellow Christians, or who has misunderstood (sometimes deliberately, sometimes inadvertently) the church's intention, knowing that we are sometimes that person; and the cool, those who resist God's Spirit with a facade of sophistication and self-sufficiency, knowing that we, too, are that person on occasion.

For a few moments, think about this prayer in the light of how Jesus was treated the last week of his life. We can say that we would have acted differently if we had been there, but would we really? Would we have taken his side; or would we have given in to the pressure of the crowd? *(One minute of silence.)* Then, if it's true that prayer changes people, so that they can and will change events, situations, relationships, then I invite us to become answers to God's promise that "if anyone is in Christ Jesus, that person is new. Old things have passed away; behold, everything is new." And all the people said, "Yes! Yes!"

Response

"Jesus Christ, Whose Passion Claims Us" (Jane Parker Huber, 1982; Early American, found in *Joy In Singing*. See Appendix I for address).

The Community Responds To God's Truth

Message with the Children of All Ages and the Reading of the Newer Covenant

Select one of the many events to dramatize. We need to see how the people treated this Jesus who identified with us in all ways, and refused to behave as we would have. These conversations that Jesus had with those around him make for powerful drama.

Proclamation of the Good News

Consider this for the sermon thesis: "I Like You, Him, Her, Them so long as I agree. I don't like You, Him, Her, Them when I don't." "When I agree with you, I support you; when I disagree, I don't." We can apply that theme politically and religiously, as we see in the last week of Jesus' life, and as we see it in our own lives.

Stewardship Challenge

If Jesus were to ask you what kind of giving you give, what would you say? Does our giving represent Cross-bearing giving; that is, "Lord, what will you have me do?" Or, my kind of giving; that is, leftover giving, after we take care of everything else first?

Prayer after the Offering

Forgive us, Lord, for confusing our burdens with your Cross. Lead us, Lord, to learn from Your Spirit the difference between bearing the normal burdens of humanity and picking up your Cross in obedient love, not because we have to, but because we choose to, for your sake and the world's.

Charge to the Congregation

God calls, and has always called, the church, that is, you and me, personally and corporately, to give ourselves away. If we are willing to respond to God's invitation to give ourselves away, we will discover the abundant, eternal life. That's God's promise, not mine!

Response

I invite you to read today's Gospel lesson each day of Holy Week. Write down what insights you receive, in preparation for the Easter event.

Meditation

"Many of us hate the cross because it means a salvation, not of our own choosing or making, but rather of God's grace and mercy. We hate the cross because it means a salvation which is unearned, undeserved, unmerited. We would much prefer God to punish us than to forgive us, because that would mean that God is dependent on us, and needed our obedience to be our God" (from *Free in Obedience*, William Stringfellow, Seabury Press).

Music Possibilities In Addition To Those Already Suggested

Passion Sunday

Music for Preparation: "Whither Am I To Flee," Zachau.

Choral Introit: "The Lord is in His Holy Temple," Edmundson.

Hymn of Praise: "All Praise Be Yours; for You, O, King Divine," F. Bland Tucker, 1938, 1972.

Response to the Reading of the Newer Covenant: Adult Choir to sing, "Bless the Lord, O My Soul," Ippolitov-Ivanov.

Offertory: "Andante," Tomlinson.

Hymn of Commitment: "Where Cross the Crowded Ways of Life," Frank Mason North (hymn for second half of Lent) or, "To God My Earnest Voice I Raise," *The Psalter*, 1912.

Music for Dismissal: Medley of Passion hymns, or "Be Glad, My Soul," Walther.

Palm Sunday

Music for Preparation: Medley of Palm Sunday hymns, or "Cortege and Litany," Dupré.

Choral Introit: One which captures the excitement of that Palm Sunday crowd.

Hymn of Praise: "All Glory, Laud, and Honor," Theodulph of Orleans, c.a. 820; John Mason Neale, trans. 1851; alt., 1859.

Response to the Act of Praise: (Children's or Youth Choir) "Hosanna, Hallelujah," Richard Avery and Don Marsh, from *Let the People Sing*, Hope Publishing Company. (See Appendix I for address.)

Response to the Prayer after the Proclamation: "Were You There?" (Consider leaving off the final stanza.)

Offertory: "O Sacred Head," Bach.

Hymn of Commitment: "In the Cross of Christ I Glory," John Bowring, 1825. Ask the people to read the words silently before singing it.

Response to the Benediction: "Lonesome Valley," Spiritual. As the people sing, invite them to walk slowly toward the cross. When they arrive, ask them to remain in silence for as long as they want, and then, to leave the sanctuary in silence.

Music for Dismissal: Medley of Passion hymns.

The Season Of Renewal

Holy Thursday/Maundy Thursday

Liturgical Color: Purple

Gospel: John 13:1-17, 31b-35

Theme: *Jesus Washes the Disciples' Feet, and the New Commandment.* "They (the Christians) know one another by secret marks and signs, and they love one another almost before they know one another" (in "The Octavius of Minucius Felix," 210 A.D.).

For this worship, use a small room for closeness that can be expanded easily to accommodate those who participate.

As people enter the room, offer to wash their feet; or if that is too radical, simulate footwashing by shining their shoes. Expect that some will refuse either act of grace.

Use plenty of silence.

Read the Gospel lesson, slowly and deliberately, with guitar or piano background music, played softly.

Following the reading, give the people five minutes of silence. Ask them to write down their thoughts during the silence.

Invite them to come to the communion table when they choose. Use dark brown bread; and say to each one as he/she receives the bread, "For you, *(name)*, the dark brown body of Jesus." Use wine, or grape juice, laced with vinegar. Jesus' death was no easy one. As each person receives the cup, say, "For you *(name)*, the rich, red blood of Christ." After receiving the elements, invite each person to return to his/her seat and remain in silence.

Invite people to use their silence creatively, by rereading the Scripture or some of the Holy Week hymns found in the hymnbook. Especially make them aware of the hymn, "An Upper Room Did Our Lord Prepare" (Fred Pratt Green, 1973; English folk melody).

Invite the people to leave in silence when they choose.

Meditations

1. "Love must be learned, and learned again and again; there is no end to it. Hate needs no instruction, but waits only to be provoked" (Katherine Anne Porter).

2. "To be out of love is to be in hell" (author unknown).

3. "You should love your crooked neighbor with all your crooked heart" (W. H. Auden).

4. Through love, one creates his/her own personality, and helps others create theirs" (from a college dorm bulletin board).

The Season Of Renewal

Good Friday

Liturgical Color: Purple

Gospel: John 18:1—19:42

Theme: *The Last Hours of Jesus' Life and his Burial.* "The whole world has never been the same since God died" (author unknown).

Print these statements at the beginning of the order of worship: We are here to discover the meaning of death so that we, on Easter, will experience the joy of life. We will experience resurrection only after we experience crucifixion. We cannot have one without the other.

After ten minutes of silence, read, slowly and deliberately, Jesus' last words from the Cross. After the reading of each, give two minutes of silence; during the silence, ask the congregation to write down their thoughts and feelings. Following the silence, ask those who choose to share their insights and awarenesses. Prior to worship, you may want to ask three or four people to be prepared to share. Include children and young people in the experience. Give permission to everyone not to respond verbally. Also, ask someone from the back of the sanctuary to pound nails into a piece of wood, only during the reading of Jesus' words.

If you offer a meditation, consider these ideas: a) "One of the most solemn facts in all of history is the fact that Jesus was murdered, not merely by hooligans on a country road, but also he was condemned by everything that was most respectable in that day, everything that pretended to be most religious — the religious leaders of that time, the authority of the Roman government, even the democracy itself, which shouted to save Barabbas the killer in preference to a manifestly good and innocent man" (Henry Butterfield). b) Jesus plainly says that "you will recognize me in the gaunt faces of the hungry, the parched throats of the thirsty, the shivering bodies of the naked, the feverish brows of the sick, the concealed masses of the imprisoned; and when you respond to such people, you are resurrected in my name" (author unknown).

Print these words in the bulletin: a) What, for me, is holy about Holy Week? b) How do I contribute to today's crucifixions with my time, resources, money, energy? c) Do I have anyone from whom I am alienated? What am I willing to do about that so I can pray, truthfully, the Lord's Prayer, "Forgive me my debts as I forgive my debtors"?

Conclude worship by singing, quietly, several of the Good Friday hymns; conclude the singing with "He Never Said a Mumblin' Word" (African-American spiritual).

Leave the sanctuary in silence.

Meditations

1. "A candle loses nothing by lighting another candle" (author unknown).

2. "Common to all Christians and Jews and any creature created by God is the great commandment of love. True charity admits of no substitute. If we prostitute our love by admitting some and excluding others from our affections because they differ from us in race, religion, color, political beliefs, then we are counterfeit religionists and traitorous Americans" (Bishop Mark K. Carroll).

Easter
The Season Of The Resurrection

Liturgical Color: White
(Easter to Pentecost)

Christianity focuses on, and revolves around, Easter Day. (No such term as Easter Sunday exists.) Christianity either stands or falls on the Resurrection of Jesus the Christ. If we can get rid of the resurrection, however we understand it, we can get rid of the church.

The Easter season begins on the eve of Easter and ends on the eve of Pentecost, fifty days later. The movable days and festivals of the church year depend on the date of Easter. Easter is always the first Sunday after the full moon falling on or after March 21st, the first day of Spring. If the full moon occurs on Sunday, Easter occurs on the following Sunday. Easter can occur between March 22 and April 25. This method of dating makes it coincide with the Feast of the Passover, because the first Easter coincided with that feast.

Easter is the oldest festival of the church year. The period of fifty days after Easter is older than either Lent or Advent. This entire season from Easter to Pentecost was once observed as one continuous festival. Later, in the fourth century, the season was separated into the Resurrection, the Ascension, and Pentecost.

Ascension Day comes on the fortieth day after Easter and is always a weekday, Thursday. It is seen as the final act in God's drama of redemption. It marks the completion of Christ's ministry on earth. The season continues for ten days and corresponds to the length of time the disciples waited in Jerusalem for the gift of Holy Spirit who came at Pentecost.

The color for the Easter season, including Ascension Day, is white (though not in all cultures), signifying God's victory over the powers of evil, the perfection of God's work, and our personal and corporate joy.

The symbols for Easter are the Cross and the Crown. The Crown signifies the fact that Christ has been raised in power to the Lord of lords and King of kings. To this King, every person shall bow!

The Season Of The Resurrection

Easter Day

Liturgical Color: White

Gospel: John 20:1-18 or Matthew 28:1-10

Theme: *Resurrection of the Christ.* "Easter is preceded by Good Friday; we will not experience life in Christ until we first experience death to our old ways." "Easter is the one day in the year when anyone may attend worship without incurring the suspicion that he/she is deeply committed to the Christian faith " (author unknown).

A Return To Good Friday For Those Who Want Life Without Death

Prepare, in advance, someone to simulate "Jesus" on an old rugged cross. This person is to take his position on the Cross about seven minutes before the beginning of worship. Two people can hold and steady the Cross, which is on eye-level with the people, and at the front or in the middle of the sanctuary. A soloist will sing the first stanza only of "Jesus Walked That Lonesome Valley." The pastor will read a brief meditation on the death of Jesus, which then leads into the pastor's repeating Jesus' "Seven Last Words from the Cross." As the pastor reads, someone offstage pounds nails into wood. "Jesus" dies and then leaves the sanctuary. Give one minute of silence. The congregation then sings stanzas 2, 3, 2 of "Lonesome Valley," as the people come forward and stand before the Cross. After the singing, one minute of silence. The people who come forward wait until after the pastor's invitation to the celebration, and then scatter throughout the sanctuary to welcome each other to worship.

A Celebration Of Resurrection

Pastoral Invitation to the Easter Celebration
   I trust by now that you've heard the Good News — Christ lives! That ought to make a difference in our lives; and it does, even if we choose not to accept its reality personally. It could make more of a difference, though, if we refused to put limits on the Risen Lord in our lives. Because when Jesus' body died, he got a new body, the church, the living, breathing body of the Risen Christ. Easter goes on, in and through us! So, with that message, I invite us to greet one another.

Choral Response
   "Eightfold Alleluia." Second stanza, "He is Risen." Third stanza, "We do praise him."

Meditation
   "The stone was moved, not to let Jesus out, but to let the disciples in" (G. Ashton).

Declaration of Joyful Expectations *(with enthusiasm)*   Pastors and Ministers
P: God loves the world!
   Right Side: Alleluia!   Left side: Hurray!
P: God calls us to celebrate the Good News of Christ!
   Right Side: Alleluia!   Left Side: Hurray!
P: Glorious things God has done, is doing, will do for us, to us, with us, through us.
   Right Side: Alleluia!   Left Side: Hurray!
P: Joy is ours, because we are Christ's!
   All: (three times) Alleluia! (three times) Hurray!

Hymn of Resurrection
"Jesus Christ Is Risen Today." Stanza 1: Solo and handbells and whatever musical instruments the congregation brings. Stanza 2: Quartet and musical instruments. Stanzas 3 and 4: Let all that breathes and moves praise the Lord!

Prayer of Praise   Congregational Amen
P: The Lord be with you, friends.
M: The Lord be with you, too, pastor.
P: Praise the Lord.
M: The Lord's Name be praised.
P: Prayer of Gratitude for the Risen Christ.

Recognizing Who We Are And Whose We Are

The Act of Recognizing Our Humanity
Peruse the previous day's newspaper. Select several items to read which cover the gamut of human behavior. Someone has suggested that we are to read the newspaper and the Bible together; the former merely updates the latter. Select Scriptures which illustrate the daily news. Perhaps some of the people would be willing to add their own, yes, even the children.

The Act of Receiving New Life
Develop the prayer around the events you have read. Ask, what kind of newspaper headlines are you writing each day that never make it into the daily newspaper? Jesus died and rose for the rest of the world and for you, too. What a relief!
P: Jesus declares a new humanity.
M: He accepts our lives, forgiving the past and opening the future.
P: He calls us to face life and to see it through with our eyes open, our ears alert, our minds active.
M: He calls us to celebrate, in and through and with and by his power. Let it be!

Response
Chorus only, popular song, "Let It Be."

The Teaching

Message with the Children of All Ages
As a symbol of new life and growth, use the various stages in the development of an avocado bush, beginning with its large pit. A biblical comparison is the mustard seed. Do more than tell the story; involve the children, even using their own birth and growth and its great mystery.

Response
"Allelu" (words and music by Ray Repp, F.E.L. Church Publishing, Ltd.; found in *Folk Encounter*, Hope Publishing Company. See Appendix I for address).

Reading from the Newer Covenant
Traditionally, people stood for the reading of the Gospel; so ask them to stand, not only this but every Sunday. Ask the organist or pianist to play some Easter music as background while you read.

Response
"Thanks to God Whose Word Was Written" (R. T. Brooks, 1954; alt. Peter Cutts, 1966).

Proclamation of the Good News

Incorporate these ideas: If we read and hear this passage from the outside looking in, the whole thing sounds similar to a *Wizard of Oz* fairy tale. We struggle with our believing the witness of the disciples and the early church. Are they reliable? Can we trust them? That's a strange question, considering the outright lies and half-truths we believe without batting an eyelid, as for example, "Jews deserve to die; blacks are inferior; Indians are savages; anyone who votes for that political candidate can't possibly be a Christian; if I can't have you I'll go crazy; blonds have more fun." If we repeat, or hear repeated, those lies and half-truths often enough, we believe them, even though they make no sense, even though they are pure baloney and banality, even though they fail the test of reality.

Response

Adult choir and youth or children's echo choir singing an anthem of gratitude, or a resurrection anthem.

Stewardship Challenge

"To withhold help is to participate in the authorship of misery that Jesus came to change. Violence slays thousands; but supine (passive) negligence slays millions" (Bishop Fulton Sheen). One life, your life, matters, to many more than you will ever know.

Charge to the Congregation

A church school teacher one day asked her students, "What do you think Jesus said when he first came out of the tomb?" "I know, I know," shouted a second grader. "He said, 'Tah-dah!'" (This, of course, makes a great sermon title.) (Story taken from *The Joyful Noiseletter*, published by The Fellowship of Merry Christians, Cal and Rose Samra, P.O. Box 895, Portage, MI 49081-0895.)

Hymn of Commitment

"The Strife is O'er, the Battle Done." The choirs sing the fanfare before and after this hymn.

Benediction

With power. Ask the people to look at each other, for whom Jesus rose. His act puts us all in the same boat, which Martin Luther called the church.

Response

"Every Morning Is Easter Morning" (Avery and Marsh, Hope Publishing Company. See Appendix I for address).

Meditation

"The world is not done with the Cross — but it is done without it" (author unknown).

Music Possibilities In Addition To Those Already Suggested

Music for Preparation: Medley of Good Friday hymns.

Choral Introit: An enthusiastic "Hosanna" piece.

Hymn of Praise: "The Day of Resurrection," John of Damascus (675?-749? A.D.), John Mason Neale, trans., 1862; alt.

Response to the Proclamation: (Choir) "It Is a Great Day of Joy" (Alleluia Fugue), from "Jesus — the Life of Jesus in Twelve Contemporary Songs," music by Claude Henri Vic; texts by Jacques Hourdeaux, produced by Avant Garde Records, Inc., 250 West 57th Street, New York, N.Y. 10010.

Offertory: "Rejoice Ye Christians," Bach.

Hymn of Dedication: "Good News Is Ours To Tell," Jane Parker Huber, 1978, from *Joy In Singing*. (See Appendix I for address.)

Choral Response to the Benediction: "Amen Chorus," from "Lilies of the Field." Ask the people to sing as they leave.

Music for Dismissal: Medley of Easter hymns, or "Carillon for a Joyful Day," McKay.

The Season Of The Resurrection

The Week Following Easter

Bright Monday

Bright Monday, also called Easter Monday, acknowledges the fact that God has the last laugh over sin and death and the grave! Easter/Bright Monday parties resurrect an old and unfortunately an often forgotten tradition that goes back to the early centuries of Christianity. According to an article in *The Joyful Noiseletter*, publication of The Fellowship of Merry Christians (F.M.C.), "The early fathers and mothers of the church encouraged God's people to celebrate continually. Many of the great religious figures of all denominations have passed down through the centuries the same message." So, for your Bright Monday celebration, invite members, nonmembers, guests, people off the streets, to a party, in which they will provide the laughter and fun. Invite them to use their varied talents: poetry, jokes, stories, music, painting, you name it. They are urged to use the talents and interests that God has given them. Conrad Hyers, a Presbyterian pastor, captures the essence of this celebration. "If the Gospel really is Good News, when do we get to shout, 'Whoopee!'?" I ask a similar question, "When do we get to shout, 'Tah-dah!'?"

F.M.C. also encourages congregations to continue the Easter celebration on the Sunday after Easter as "Bright Sunday" and to observe April as "Holy Humor Month."

For more information, write to Cal and Rose Samra, F.M.C., P.O. Box 895, Portage, MI 49081-0895; or, call toll-free, 1-800-877-2757 (orders only), 8 a.m. to 8 p.m., E.S.T., Monday-Friday. For all other inquiries, call 616-324-0990.

As a member of F.M.C, and an occasional writer for *The Joyful Noiseletter*, I know that you will be glad you did! And all the people said, "Tah-dah!"

A Bright Sunday Celebration
On April 6, 1997, I led worship at the South Beach Presbyterian Church in Westport, Washington. I began this way: "In the name of the risen Christ, welcome. As we continue, remember that all worship is interactive. You are invited to interrupt at any time, even though the authority persons insist that you never interrupt, even when they make no sense. It is okay to participate other than standing, sitting, singing on cue.

"Last week I asked John, your pastor, to encourage you to wear bright clothes today. Thank you for doing so. Now, how many of you know that this past Monday, the Monday after Easter Day, is known as Bright Monday? *(No hands.)* How many of you know that today is Bright Sunday? *(No hands.)* (Someone said, after worship, 'Now we know why you wanted us to dress this way.')

"Who of you knows the meaning of Easter (and every Sunday is Easter) other than the reality that Christ arose? *(No response.)* I'm going to tell you. Easter signifies that, in Christ, God has the Last Laugh over sin, death, the grave! So, have you ever laughed with God and each other over that great event? *(No response.)* Today, we have this unique opportunity. I invite all of us to laugh with God and each other. Yes, I know that you'll feel embarrassed. To help us with our dis-ease, I brought with me a Spike Jones laughing record. If you prefer not to laugh outright (maybe no one has ever given you permission to guffaw), you can lip-sync with the record."

We laughed, then, and throughout the Bright Sunday Celebration.

For the offering, I directed them to Jesus' remark, "God loves a cheerful giver." The biblical word for "cheerful" is "hilarious." God loves hilarious givers. And I will know that the Kingdom will have arrived in its wholeness when we roll in the aisles with laughter during the offering.

Following the benediction, I, telling no one in advance, including the musicians, invited the people to sing the "Ho Ho" song, three times, and faster each time. And then I concluded with this: "And all the people said, 'Tah-dah!' "

The Season Of The Resurrection

Easter 2

Liturgical Color: White

Gospel: John 20:19-31

Theme: *Jesus' Appearance to the Disciples, including Thomas, and the Purpose of the Book.* "Christ has turned all our sunsets into sunrises" (Clement of Alexandria).

A Celebration Of Resurrection

Invitation to the Easter Celebration
Welcome to the second Sunday of Easter. If Easter ended for you last Sunday, then it never began. For Easter is not so much a day on the calendar, but an ongoing event in our lives. So rejoice, and keep on rejoicing. And all the people said, "Tah-dah!"

P: So, again I ask, have you heard the news, with heart, mind, body, spirit?
M: Yes, we have! And tell us again. We need reminding.
P: God has sent a rescue party to search out those cut off from the truth.
M: Tell us more! We need to hear more.
P: The leader is Jesus. He has broadcast, "I have come to seek and to save the lost."
M: Is he doing this alone?
P: He began alone. In fact, he was killed in the effort. But God raised him from the dead. Now, he has millions assisting him in the search. If you have received him into your life, you are counted among those millions.
M: We celebrate the presence and power of this God who cared enough to send the very best.

Response
"Christ is Risen! Shout Hosanna!" (Ludwig von Beethoven, 1824; adapt. Edward Hodges, 1796-1867; alt. Brian Wren, b. 1936).

Prayer of Praise
"O God, the One who has given us permission to be in history, we stand judged by the great mystery of the Easter event, admitting that we have not understood it or lived by it. The event spoke to us of authentic life, but we are preoccupied with making a living. This event speaks to us of life today, but we see the present chaos as too large to deal with. This event speaks to us of life in the future, but we would rather restore the familiar patterns of the past. This event speaks to us of faith, but we are more at home with what can be measured and programmed. This event speaks to us of hope, but we limp along on wishful thinking. This event speaks to us of love, but we prefer our stance of indifference." Invite the congregation to complete this prayer, written by Robert E. Deckert, Charbonier United Methodist Church, Florissant, Missouri.

Response
"Easter for the World" (Avery and Marsh, from *The Second Avery and Marsh Songbook*, Hope Publishing Company. See Appendix I for address).

Recognizing Who We Are And Whose We Are

The Act of Recognizing Our Humanity

Have any of you even had any doubts about the point of all this church business? Have you ever asked yourself, "Why bother? What does all of this church activity mean? Is it worth it?" Or, perhaps your doubting goes even deeper. "Did Christ really rise from the dead?" With Thomas, "I won't believe until I can get some tangible proof." Well, Thomas did doubt; and Jesus refused to reject him. So, doubting not only is okay, it is essential to a growing faith. Suggest that people read Leslie Weatherhead's *The Christian Agnostic*. Doubting is a part of faith, not apart from faith. So I invite all of you doubters to pray this prayer (source lost): "Lord God (in case you exist), on the basis of your word (in case you said it), I ask you (in case you can hear me) to forgive my sins; be with me in my anxiety, comfort me in my loneliness, show me my neighbor, and kindle love in my heart. Let me discover that, in good times and bad, in all the high points and frustrating times of my life, it is your hand that reaches out to me, shepherds me along, bears my burdens, strokes my brow in times of trouble, and makes death easier by cradling my head. I will get up tomorrow, making the most of my opportunities for you, and serving my neighbors 'as though' you exist. Then you will break out of the great silence surrounding you, and you suddenly will be with me."

Response

Two minutes of silence, followed by "Lord, I Want to Be a Christian" (African-American Spiritual).

The Act of Receiving New Life

Doubting is not the "Unpardonable Sin." Healthy doubting leads to healthy growth. So, all you agnostics out there, stop being so hard on yourself! Give yourself a break today! Wrestle with God until you know the truth!

Response

(Ask the people to stand.) Choir: "As Long As Men On Earth Are Living," (Portuguese Tune, arranged by Paul Abels. *Change "men" to "all."* From *Workers Quarterly: Hymns for Now*, published by the Walther League. See Appendix I for address).

The Teaching

Message with the Children of All Ages

Deal with doubting on their level. For example, a friend has lied to them, and they doubt that they can ever trust that person again. Let them know that Jesus never turned Thomas away because he doubted.

Response

"O Sons and Daughters, Let Us Sing" (French tune, fifteenth century, attr. Jean Tisserand, d. 1494; trans. John Mason Neale, 1852).

Proclamation of the Good News

In advance, ask several people what form their doubts took before they became Christians, and what doubts they continue to raise, even if they've been Christians for fifty years. If they prefer not to speak in worship, ask them to write a paragraph which you will read to begin the proclamation.

Response

Use a second time, "O Sons and Daughters, Let Us Sing."

Stewardship Challenge

(Even though you may have used this before) Before the offering: "If we gave our tithes and offerings in a face-to-face encounter with Christ, would we give him the same amount that we will put in the offering plate in a few minutes?" After the offering, "Thank you, Lord, for helping us to see you as you are, so that we will serve you as you will."

Charge to the Congregation

Again I say, if Easter is now over for us, it never began. For Easter is not a day on the calendar, sandwiched between the first day of spring and the opening of the fishing season. Easter is an experience of the heart, will, mind, body. Easter goes on, in the lives of the Easter people who have said "yes" to the Giver of Life, with renewed, enriched, abundant life. We are the Easter people, now! And, all the people said, "Tah-dah!"

Meditation

"I rate a man (person) or a church, not by the reasons they give for things, but by the things for which they give reasons" (written by George Bernard Shaw in a letter to the Archbishop of Canterbury). Simeon Stylites, in *The Christian Century,* years ago commented on that letter with these words: "Our faith is not in the reasons we give for things but in the experiences for which we are impelled to give reasons. The experience of Easter comes first. The finding of reasons for it comes afterwards. The experience is our response to the tremendous affirmation that Christ is and is present with us."

Music Possibilities In Addition To Those Already Suggested

Music for Preparation: Medley of Easter hymns.

Hymn of Praise: "Come, You People, Rise and Sing," Cyril A. Alington (1872-1955); alt., 1972.

Response to the Act of Pardon: "Come, You Faithful, Raise the Strain," attr. to John of Damascus (675? - 749?); trans. John Mason Neale, 1859; alt., 1972.

Response to the Newer Covenant: "When We Are Tempted to Deny Your Son," David W. Romig, 1965.

Response to the Proclamation: "The Tree Springs to Life," Fred Kahn.

Offertory: "Rejoice, Ye Christians," Bach.

Music for Dismissal: Medley of Easter hymns.

The Season Of The Resurrection

Easter 3

Liturgical Color: White

Gospel: Luke 24:13-35

Theme: *Jesus' Walk to Emmaus.* Detour, there's a muddy road ahead. Whom will you invite to walk it with you?

A Celebration Of Resurrection

Invitation to the Easter Celebration
In the name of the risen Christ, welcome to the third Sunday in Easter. Whom have you met on your Emmaus road this past week? We will explore that theme today.

P: Good morning! Shalom! Peace! And God be with you on your highway!

M: We're glad we're here! But what does it mean? Who knows or cares that we're here?

P: Someone knows all about you, even as that someone knew those fellows who met and finally recognized him on that Emmaus road long ago.

M: Yes, yes! We know that we're counted among the living; we know that we're on record, because we have been counted.

P: And there's more to it than your being counted. The really up-to-date news is that you are known by someone more than a computer.

M: And how do we know this?

P: Because of the Good News experienced by those men on the Emmaus road; and because that same Jesus comes to us on our own Emmaus road. Thank God!

M: Alleluia! Amen! and Tah-dah!

Response
"He's Alive" (Avery and Marsh, from *The Avery and Marsh Songbook*, Hope Publishing Company. See Appendix I for address). Have the choir director teach this to the congregation; have the children lead the congregation in the action. Respond as the hymn writers suggest.

Prayer of Praise
This prayer always focuses on the person of God. Ask a young person to offer it. Give that person only the help that he/she asks for.

Hymn of Praise
"Sing Praise Unto the Name of God"   (attro Matthaus Greiter, 1525; Genevan Psalter, Fred Anderson, 1983, 1989).

Recognizing Who We Are And Whose We Are

The Act of Recognizing Our Humanity
Take a few moments to examine the road you traveled this past week. Smooth driving? Any ruts? Any barriers? Write down your experiences. *(Two minutes.)* Have a soloist sing, "Detour, There's a Muddy Road Ahead." Before the person sings, ask the people to think about how the message of that song fits their journey in life and in their life this past week. After the song, ask if any would be willing

to share one insight. Share one of yours, though not necessarily one that you might discuss with your therapist.

The Act of Receiving New Life
Does the act of confession make any real difference in your life; or do you get stuck on the confession and never hear the pardon? If you have never heard the pardon part before, I invite you to hear it now.
P: Jesus the Christ meets us on the road and declares a new beginning, now!
M: He walks with us, recognizes us, accepts us, forgiving our past, and opening up the future.
P: He gives us a "faith-lift" in order for us to face life and see it through.
M: Therefore, we celebrate, in and through and by and with his power. Yes!

Response
"Let It Be," popular song, chorus only. Sing it several times; ask different groups to sing it, for example, children, the boomers, senior citizens, and so forth.

The Teaching

Message with the Children of All Ages and the Reading from the Newer Covenant
Ask three people to dramatize the passage. Ask a group of children to accompany the two men. Give them the freedom to speak to Jesus also, whatever is on their minds.

Proclamation of the Good News
Contrast this statement by Roy Eckardt with the experience of the disciples on the Emmaus road: "Our Easter finery has about as much power to save us as the Easter bunny."

Response, if you serve Communion
"Come, Risen Lord" (George Wallace Briggs, 1931; Alfred Morton Smith, 1941).

Stewardship Challenge
If you have met Christ on your personal Emmaus road, does that make a difference about what you put in the offering plate?

Charge to the Congregation
Recognizing Christ on our Emmaus road makes a difference in response to God's action. Christ openly declared his authority by reconciling black and white and red and yellow, rich and poor and everyone in between, ambitious and lazy, intelligent and stupid, hopeful and hopeless, to the living God. The authority of God came to live in a manger, hung on a cross, broke loose from death, meets us all on our Emmaus road, and empowers all who choose to be empowered. That marked the beginning of a new way of life in which we are invited to share (paraphrase and revision of a statement by Arthur Fay Sueltz).

Meditation
The pessimist says, "All roads lead nowhere." The optimist insists, "All roads lead. Know where." Which idea guides you?

Music Possibilities In Addition To Those Already Suggested

Music for Preparation: Medley of Easter hymns.

Hymn of Praise: "That Easter Day with Joy Was Bright," Latin hymn before the eighth century; trans. John Mason Neale, 1851; alt.

Response to the Newer Covenant: (Choir) "Song of the Lord Among Us," Huub Oosterhuis, English version by C. M. DeVries.

Response to the Proclamation: (Choir) "Song of God's Presence," Huub Oosterhuis, English version by Walter Van Der Haas, Peter-Paul Van Lelyveld, et al.

(These two responses are found in *Workers Quarterly,* July 1967, Volume 39, Number 1, published by the Walther League. See Appendix I for address.)

Hymn of Dedication: "O, For a Closer Walk with God," Scottish Psalter, 1635; William Cowper, 1772 (two tunes).

Music for Dismissal: Medley of Easter hymns or Communion hymns.

The Season Of The Resurrection

Easter 4

Liturgical Color: White

Gospel: John 10:1-10

Theme: *Jesus the Good Shepherd who Brings Abundant Life.* Does the culture or does the Christ define what the abundant life looks like?

A Celebration Of Resurrection

Invitation to the Easter Celebration
In the name of God, the Creator, Liberator, Sustainer, Energizer, welcome to the fourth Sunday of Easter. How have you come? Glad, sad, mad, or a mixture of all three? No matter how you came, what do you hope to get out of this worship? And, by the way, how you came probably will give you different expectations. So, what do you want to get? A little uplift? Something to think about? A jog to your conscience? Marching orders for the week? What? Mark Twain once said, "Blessed are those who expect nothing, for they will not be disappointed." And I add, "Blessed are those who come, not as spectators, not as observers, but as participants, responsible to God, to each other, to oneself; for they shall be filled." (Sidelight: A response I once received to this invitation was this from a parishioner: "I never bothered to formulate my expectations; that's the pastor's job." Really, now!)

Response
(During the response, have the organist, pianist, or orchestra play some energetic music.)
P: God, our God, we praise you for our hearts,
M: which respond in love to your mercies.
P: We praise you for our minds,
M: which open up broad avenues of understanding.
P: We praise you for our wills,
M: which can be tuned into the Good Shepherd for obedient action.
P: We thank you for salvation by grace and for wisdom by revelation,
M: that all persons may come to know your shepherding qualities, and thus, to trust you as the One who possesses the nurturing of Mother and Father.

Hymn of Praise
"Praise Ye (You) the Lord, the Almighty" (Joachim Neander, 1680; trans. Catherine Winkworth, 1863; alt.).

Recognizing Who We Are And Whose We Are

The Act of Recognizing Our Humanity
To confess our sins means to "cut them out." Write down those sins that you *need* to cut out. *(Give three, yes, three, minutes of silence.)* Now, cross out the ones that you *will* cut out. *(Two minutes of silent prayer, followed by a pastoral confession, if you think that it's really necessary.)*

Response

Soloist, preferably a teenager, to sing "Amazing Grace" while the congregation hums it. *(I substitute the word "someone" for the word "wretch." Perhaps the people can find one that fits them.)*

The Act of Receiving New Life

I invite us to remember that forgiveness has nothing to do with our feelings; it has everything to do with God's promise, and our acting on that promise. It is an act of God's will and our will.

Ministers: God, because we can hide nothing, no part of ourselves, from you, we have confessed our alienations and brokenness. We rejoice that you forgive us, even when we "feel" unforgiven and guilty. Remove from us the guilt and shame which get in the way of you and others, despite the promise of the Good Shepherd, who promises us the abundant life. Remove all of those barriers, especially fear and anxiety, which betray our trust in you and others, beginning with the members of our own biological family, and extending to our church family. In the name of Christ, the sin-bearer, reconciler, and Good Shepherd.

Response

Now, have the soloist sing "Amazing Grace" once again. Ask the congregation if they heard and responded to it any differently now than previously.

The Teaching

Message with the Children of All Ages

Several weeks in advance, ask the children, and any members of the church who are in touch with their inner child, to write their version of Psalm 23. One person who works with inner-city children began his version, "The Lord is my probation officer ..." Use this time to encourage the children to share their versions. You may want to begin by sharing your version. While reading, ask the organist to play "The Lord Is My Shepherd."

Reading of the Newer Covenant

In advance, ask a member to memorize the passage and present it, as if he/she were simulating Jesus.

Proclamation of the Good News

Expose the vocation of the shepherd during Jesus' time; and apply those qualities to our lives this week.

Stewardship Challenge

Here is someone who knew the Good Shepherd personally: A woman of ill health had to give up many activities. Wishing to express sympathy (though most of us prefer empathy), a friend said to her, "Illness does color life, doesn't it?" "Yes," she replied, "it does; but I intend to choose the colors." What does our giving have to do with "choosing colors" in the presence and power of the Good Shepherd?

Charge to the Congregation

If we celebrate the presence and power of the Good Shepherd in all of our relationships and experiences to let everything that breathes praise God; to say "yes" to life's mysteries, as a Chicago teenager has said, "Even in the midst of absurdity"; a "yes" as Martin Luther has said that "we make merry even when there's nothing to be merry about," what a difference life would be. We would move from a fear of life to a cheer for life. Everything would speak to us of the realities of life, instead of allowing us to wallow in our illusions. The whole world, in the shadow of the Good Shepherd, would shout to us of the Creator's goodness. All of our experiences, even the painful ones, would elicit praise, thanksgiving, gratitude for everything under the sun.

Meditation

"Do not fear that your life shall come to an end, but rather, fear that it shall never have a beginning" (Cardinal Newman, updated language). No wonder that a person responding to a remark of someone who believed in the immediate return of the Christ said, "Thousands of people now living are already dead." In the presence and power of the Good Shepherd, we make our life count for something, lest it fall for everything.

Music Possibilities In Addition To Those Already Suggested

Music for Preparation: Medley of Easter hymns, or "Andante Religioso," Thomé.

Choral Introit: (Choir) "Hosanna, In the Highest."

Hymn of Praise: "Come, Christians, Join to Sing," Christian Henry Bateman, 1843; alt.

Response to the Newer Covenant: "Shepherd of Eager Youth," ascribed to Clement of Alexandria, c. 200 A.D.; trans. by Henry M. Dexter, 1846; alt.

Hymn of Commitment: "In Christ There Is No East or West" (two tunes), John Oxenham, 1908; alt. Alexander Robert Reinagle, 1836.

Offertory: "Priere," Lemmens.

Music for Dismissal: Medley of Easter hymns, or "Fanfare," by Handel.

The Season Of The Resurrection

Easter 5

Liturgical Color: White

Gospel: John 14:1-14

Theme: *Jesus, the Way, the Truth, and the Life.* "The New Testament does not claim that Christianity is absolute, or that it is the best religion, or that the Christian or the church is superior. The New Testament does claim that there is a unique revelation which God has made, that God has made once and for all time, that Christ has revealed the nature of God, of humanity, of life, of the universe. It insists that there is universal validity, not in any religion, including Christianity, but in that unique revelation which has been made in Jesus the Christ, and that the measure of value in any religion is Jesus the Christ. He is the criterion of truth and value" (T. Watson Street, slightly revised).

A Celebration Of Resurrection

Invitation to the Easter Celebration

When God got ready to turn a world free from its bondage, it took everything that God had. There was no other way, truth, life. No pain, no birth. No suffering, no salvation. No crucifixion, no resurrection. No death, no life. No cross, no crown. For, once again, now on this fifth Sunday of Easter, Easter is not some date that appears on a calendar, but rather, an event that happens to the heart, mind, strength, will of us humans, thanks to the gift of the one who is the way, the truth, and the life. We celebrate the presence and power of that one who offers us that gift.

P: So, let's celebrate the Author of that gift.
M: But we don't see God on television, or hear God on radio.
P: Nevertheless, let us celebrate the way, God's way!
M: But God has no broadcast time and no family tree.
P: Even so, let us celebrate the truth, God's truth!
M: But the world is scary, and so are we.
P: All the more reason to celebrate the life, God's life!
M: But under what label? How can we know God?
P: The only true God has no label, no heritage.
M: Then, how can we know who God is?
P: We can't know God unless God chooses to reveal the God-Self to us; and God has done precisely that in Jesus the Christ, the Way and the Truth and the Life. Thank God! Are you glad? If so, respond in your favorite praise word!

Response

"Allelu!" (words and music by Ray Repp, F.E.L. Church Publications, Ltd., found in *Folk Encounter*, published by Hope Publishing Company. See Appendix I for address). Use all musical instruments, all choirs; have the ones who can, walk around the church sanctuary as they sing.

Prayer of Praise

Ask people to call out praise words, repeat them, and then have the congregation repeat your repeating. Make this an enthusiastic response.

Hymn of Praise
"Here, O Lord, Your Servants Gather" (Tokuo Yamaguchi, 1958; Japanese gagaku mode; trans. Everett M. Stowe, 1958; alt. 1952, Isao Koizumi).

Recognizing Who We Are And Whose We Are

The Act of Recognizing Our Humanity
As we enter into this act of worship, think about how Jesus, the way, the truth, and the life, reveals to you your brokenness, and how you respond to him in your daily walk. What of your life do you plan to bring before God today, and which will you continue to hide from God? Someone has said that we cannot and will not put our sins behind us until we face them. Which ones will you face today, knowing that Jesus is the way, the truth, and the life?

Response
(Unison prayer. However, before praying verbally, read the prayer silently. Consider praying only those parts which pertain to you. Ask the organist or pianist to play "Beneath the Cross of Jesus" as the congregation prays.) "Forgive us, Lord, for our cowardices which hold us back from courageous action when we know what is right; for our prejudices which keep us from looking facts in the face; for our silences which keep us from speaking out for justice and truth; for our selfishness which hinders us from responding to our neighbor's need; for our pride which will not permit us to admit that we are wrong, or acknowledge the part we play in the wrongs of others. Pardon us through the merits of Jesus the Christ, our Lord, the way, the truth, and the life. Fill us with his strong, courageous love" (resource lost).

The Act of Receiving New Life
After several moments of silence, introduce the act with these, or similar words: No matter what your past has been, your future is spotless, in the name of God, the Creator, Liberator, Sustainer, Energizer.

P and M: God's love never changes. Against all who oppose or ignore God, God expresses love and wrath. In the same love and wrath, God took on self-judgment and death in Jesus the Christ, to bring us liberation and new life.

P: I declare to you who mean business with God, in the name of the Christ, the way, the truth, the life, you are forgiven. Do you hear that central biblical message? You are forgiven. Rejoice!

M: We do hear. Thank you, Lord. We receive your gift. Yes, we do!

Response
"For Your Gracious Blessings" (source unknown; harm. by David Smart; found in *Folk Encounter*, Hope Publishing Company. See Appendix I for address).

The Teaching

Message with the Children of All Ages
Explore the healthy and unhealthy ways in which children and young people are living. Perhaps you will find some examples in yesterday's newspaper. Without becoming legalistic, reveal to them Jesus' way, even though sometimes, it hurts.

Reading of the Newer Covenant
Dramatize the passage, using someone to be Jesus, Thomas, and Philip.

Stewardship Challenge

"The world is not a supermarket in which we can buy anything we want" (author unknown). Do we need to reorder our priorities around the One who is the way, the truth, and the life? If so, how will we go about doing that?

Charge to the Congregation

In Malaya, during World War II, a sympathetic native was helping an escaping prisoner of war to make his way to the coast. Stumbling through the well-nigh impenetrable jungle, with no evidence of human life and no sign of a trail, the soldier turned to his guide and asked, "Are you sure this is the way?" To which came the reply in faltering English, "There is no way. I am the way" (source lost).

Meditation

"It's the set of the sail, and not the gale, that determines the way you go" (author unknown).

Music Possibilities In Addition To Those Already Suggested

Music for Preparation: Medley of Easter hymns, or "Fantasie in C-Minor," Bach.

Hymn of Praise: "Earth and All Stars," Herbert Frederick Brokering, 1964; David N. Johnson, 1968.

Response to the Newer Covenant: "He Is the Way," W. H. Auden, 1944.

Response to the Message with the Children: "Truth Shall Make You Free," John F. Wilson, found in *Folk Encounter*, Hope Publishing Company. See Appendix I for address.

Offertory: "A Morning Song," by Charles Wesley.

Hymn of Commitment: "I Greet Thee, Who My Sure Redeemer Art," attr. John Calvin; *French Psalter*, Strassurg, 1545; adapt. from Genevan 124; trans. Elizabeth Lee Smith, 1868.

Music for Dismissal: Medley of Easter hymns.

The Season Of The Resurrection

Easter 6

Liturgical Color: White

Gospel: John 14:15-21

Theme: *Promise of Holy Spirit.* "Some people like surprises, at least the enjoyable ones; others do not, even the enjoyable ones" (WHK). Ready or not, God promises a coming one.

A Celebration Of Resurrection

Invitation to the Easter Celebration

In the name of the risen, living Christ, welcome to this sixth Sunday of Easter. What's been going on with you these past weeks since Easter Day? Anyone care to share? *(Wait for a few moments. Silence is okay. You may want to share one of your own insights.)* Today's worship, centered around John 14:15-21, marks a new phase of the liturgical year, a promise that God fulfills in a few weeks. I prefer not to give away the surprise just yet. Today's Good News centers around and focuses on God's love and God's commandments; and remember, these were commandments, not suggestions or recommendations. God shows the love of Christ to us by giving us the commandments. And as Saint Augustine has said, "We can know only that which we love." *(Repeat Augustine's remark, and give a few moments of silence for it to sink in.)*

P: God loved, and loves, the world so much that God gave, gives ...
M: God loves the world!
P: You mean, of course, the good people, the nice people, God's own people?
M: No!
P: Are you saying that God loves the proud, cruel, greedy, lustful, lost and lonely, rebellious people of the world? All of them? People such as we? All of us?
M: Yes, God gave the unique, one-of-a-kind Son for the whole world; and God lives in our midst, wooing us, pursuing us, seeking us.
P: If that's true, and I have no reason to doubt you, then I invite all to praise this living God, who has placed us in such a world. I invite us to celebrate God's Presence and Power in our lives for the sake of the world that needs to know it is loved.

Hymn of Praise

"Love Divine, All Loves Excelling" (Charles Wesley, 1747; Rowland Hugh Prichard, 1838).

Prayer of Praise

Include a hint of what's to come, namely, the Holy Spirit.

Response

"Easter for the World" (Avery and Marsh, from *The Second Avery and Marsh Songbook*, Hope Publishing Company. See Appendix I for address).

Recognizing Who We Are And Whose We Are

The Act of Recognizing Our Humanity

Have you ever noticed how much we want God's love for ourselves in comparison with how much we give God's love to others? *(Silence, for one minute)*. On a scale of 1 to 10, where do you put your emphasis? Five would be 50-50. Jot down your number. *(Offer a few more moments of silence.)* Now, I invite us to pray the following prayer. After each "I" insert your name: God, I *(name)* recognize the many needs that I *(name)* have: the need to be loved, to have others take an interest in me, to have them listen and care about what is happening to me and within me. I *(name)* also know of my need to love, and to share myself with someone, to do things that give satisfaction, and contribute to life. Sometimes, I *(name)* find these needs being met, and life becomes rich and full. At other times, they go unfulfilled, and I feel frustrated and hurt. I *(name)* pray that I may grow in this ability to receive and give. Help me, through the Holy Spirit, to be real, and in being real, to discover my purpose in your will. I *(name)* take this prayer to heart.

Response

Ask a soloist to sing the popular song, "Both Sides Now" (words and music by Joni Mitchell, Siquomb Publishing Corporation).

The Act of Receiving New Life

Former Sister Corita said, "To believe in God is to have somebody who knows you through and through and likes you (loves you) still and all."

Thanks, Lord, for giving me *(name)* another chance, this year, this day, this hour, this moment, both to receive your forgiveness and to share your forgiveness. I *(name)* haven't the slightest idea why I *(name)* have been spared to live another moment, and others haven't. But because I *(name)* have, help me *(name)* to put quality into my life. Help me *(name)*, God, more than anything else, to care for others as persons, even though I *(name)* may differ. If there is anything that we need, it is to know that people care about us, love us, not in some superficial, obnoxious way, but from the depths of our being. We thank you for loving us, even while we were still your enemies; help us to love each other so that we will be friends, in the name of the living, loving, caring, compassionate Christ.

Response

"Love Them Now" (words and music by Richard Avery and Don Marsh, Hope Publishing Company. See Appendix I for address). Invite the children to teach this to the congregation.

The Teaching

Message with the Children of All Ages

Teach the congregation the song, "Love Them Now." Ask the children to whom they would like to dedicate the song, the longer the list the better.

Reading of the Newer Covenant

Invite someone to memorize the text and present it to the people.

Proclamation of the Good News

Many people, inside and outside of the church, want God's love without obedience to God's commandments.

Stewardship Challenge

If you were to give yourself a stewardship challenge before putting your money in the offering (again, *not* collection) plate, what would you give? Instead of the doxology, use the hymn, "God So Loved the World ..."

Charge to the Congregation

"The greatest gift to the totalitarians is religious and political indifference and apathy. At the last judgment, the balcony-sitter may plead, 'I never harmed a fly.' But the Judge will say, 'The fly you never harmed carried the plague to millions' " (Franklin Littell, *Wild Tongues*).

Meditation

"It's much easier to talk about, and to expect, God's love for us than to talk about, and to give, our love to God, which is given to the hungry, thirsty, stranger, naked, sick, imprisoned" (WHK).

Music Possibilities In Addition To Those Already Suggested

Music for Preparation: Medley of Easter hymns.

Hymn of Praise: "O Sons and Daughters, Let Us Sing!" Jean Tisserand (d. 1494) et. al.; John Mason Neale, trans., 1851; alt.

Response to the Good News: "Gloria Patri," any version.

Offertory: "Antiphon," Dupré.

Hymn of Dedication: "Gracious Spirit, Dwell With Me," Thomas Toke Lynch, 1855; or, "We Are One in the Spirit," Peter Scholtes, 1966.

Response to the Benediction: "Sevenfold Amen."

Music for Dismissal: Medley of Easter hymns, or "Love Divine, All Loves Excelling," Charles Wesley, 1747; alt.

The Season Of The Resurrection

Ascension Day

Liturgical Color: White

Gospel: Luke 24:44-53

Theme: *The Ascension of Christ.* "When it comes to this strange Scripture, we have no business idolizing the event, while ignoring its content" (WHK).

A Celebration Of Resurrection

Invitation to the Easter Celebration

Good morning, church! Welcome to Christ's world; and I emphasize the reality that the world belongs to Christ, even when we act as though we own it. Today we consider an event that may seem strange, if not weird, to you. So, as we begin, I invite all of you to write down what you know and believe about Jesus' ascension. *(Two minutes of silence; and if no one uses the silence for the assignment, that's okay. We need much more silence in worship, anyway.)* Following the silence, ask the congregation, at least a few, to take the risk of sharing verbally what they wrote. If no one says anything, what a great opportunity to educate the people. Express your own wonderings about this event. Many have been more interested in how and what happened than wanting to know the significance of the event.

P: We have come because the living God has invited us to come.
M: We have come to affirm who we are, whose we are, what we do, where we go, in the power of the ascended Christ.
P: We affirm our life, all of it, in the presence and power of the Holy Spirit, for the sake of the world, which God loved so much that God gave.
M: Be it so! So be it!
Choir: *(sing)* "Allelu! Allelu! Allelu!"
One-half of the Congregation: *(sing)* Praise the Lord!
One-half of the Congregation: *(sing)* Christ is Sovereign!
Sing it together three times; then, have all sing their parts, and applaud!

Prayer of Praise

Develop the prayer around the Ascension, focusing on the Lordship of Christ.

Hymn of Praise

"A Hymn of Glory Let Us Sing" (the Venerable Bede, 673-735; "The Agincourt Song," England, c. 1415; based on E. Power Biggs, 1947; arr. Richard Proulx, b. 1937).

Recognizing Who We Are And Whose We Are

The Act of Recognizing Our Humanity

John Alexander, writing in *The Other Side*, says, "If the church (you/I/we) is not genuinely different from the world — if it is not a contrast society — then the Messiah hasn't come," and I add, "at least for us." And, of course, if the Messiah hasn't come, then the Messiah has never ascended to become our Lord. In silence, think about and write down how we block the Lordship of Christ, not only in our own life, but in the life of the world around us. Give time for people to consider this.

Response

Remember that his ascension declared his Lordship over the whole earth. Have a soloist sing "Song of the Lord Among Us" (Huub Oosterhuis and Bernard Huyers, English Version by C. M. DeVries; arranged by Paul Abels. From *Hymns for Now*. See Appendix I for address).

The Act of Receiving New Life

Kenneth Clarke in a *Pulpit* Magazine sermon asks these probing questions to the disciples, then and now: "Why do you stand looking into heaven? Why do you continually attempt to confine my Lordship to the church? Why are you afraid to practice goodness in business and in politics? Why do you think that the people who go around asking others if I am their personal savior are my best witnesses when you know that I came on behalf of the world, every acre of it? In short, do you really believe in my kind of lordship or not?" *(Read slowly and give several moments of silence.)*

P: "While we deliberate,
M: Christ reigns.
P: When we decide wisely,
M: Christ reigns.
P: When we decide foolishly,
M: Christ reigns.
P: When we serve God humbly, loyally,
M: Christ reigns.
P: When we serve God self-assertively,
M: Christ reigns.
P: When we rebel and seek to withhold our service,
M: Christ reigns" (William Temple).

Response

Chorus only to "Lord of the Dance" (American Shaker melody; Sydney Carter, 1963). Invite the children to come forward and lead the congregation. Sing the chorus several times, until the people sing it enthusiastically. Let them know that, in the Pentecost Season, they will learn and sing the entire hymn.

The Teaching

Message with the Children of All Ages

After they teach the hymn, tell them about the meaning of the chorus, and offer a summary of the hymn.

Reading of the Newer Covenant

Have someone who has memorized the passage be "Jesus" and have several disciples standing around waiting for him to do something, anything. After Jesus has ascended, have the disciples dashing throughout the sanctuary and telling the joyous news.

Proclamation of the Good News

Integrate these ideas: The Ascension marks, with absolute certainty, the beginning of Christ's rule, not of rules, but of grace and justice. The Ascension points to Pentecost, when the Holy Spirit empowered the disciples.

Stewardship Challenge

Who is lord of your pocketbook and charge card and A.T.M.? Give several moments of silence before receiving the offering.

Charge to the Congregation

The Ascension means "taking Christ's lordship seriously. It means being unafraid of the world, because it is his world. It means being willing to seek him in it, and being able to identify him for others in the midst of it. It means being open and flexible to the guidance of his Holy Spirit in the creation of new forms of ministry and the burial of old ones. As Bishop Pike has said, 'It means distinguishing the package from the packaging.' "[1]

Response

The power and lordship of Christ be yours as you enter the world each day! (Male soloist to sing "I'm Sending You"; words and music by Billie Hanks, Jr. in *Folk Songs for Choirs*, Hope Publishing Company. See Appendix I for address.)

Meditation

Jesus said to Mary after the Resurrection, "Go, tell! Don't stand clinging to me, but go to my brothers and sisters. I have been installed in authority and power."

Music Possibilities In Addition To Those Already Suggested

Music for Preparation: Medley of Ascension hymns, or "Pastorale" by Milhaud.

Hymn of Praise: "Lord Jesus Christ, Our Lord Most Dear," Heinrich von Laufenberg, 1429(?); Catherine Winkworth, trans., 1869; alt.

Response to the Confession: "We Bear the Strain of Earthly Care," Ozora S. Davis, 1909.

Response to the Newer Covenant: "Earth's Scattered Isles and Contoured Hills," Walter Pelz, 1977; para. Jeffery Rowthorn, 1974; adapt. W. Thomas Jones, 1980.

Offertory: "Grave and Allegro," A. Scarlatti.

Hymn of Dedication: "Crown Him with Many Crowns," Matthew Bridges, 1851; George Job Elvey, 1868.

Music for Dismissal: Medley of Ascension hymns (see the Scriptural references in your hymnbook), or "O Gracious God," Dupré.

---

1. From the sermon, "Why Do You Stand Looking Into Heaven?" by Kenneth E. Clarke, in *Pulpit* Magazine, copyright 1966, Christian Century Foundation. Reprinted from the May 1966 issue of *The Christian Pulpit* by permission.

The Season Of The Resurrection

Easter 7

Liturgical Color: White

Gospel: John 17:1-11

Theme: *Jesus Prays for his Disciples.* "Prayer is the wire surrendering to the dynamo, the flower surrendering to the sun, the child surrendering to education, the patient surrendering to the surgeon, the part surrendering to the whole, life surrendering to Life" (E. Stanley Jones).

A Celebration Of Resurrection

Invitation to the Easter Celebration

If you want to set your people free, or make them thoroughly uptight, consider this idea, either on Easter Day or on the last Sunday that you celebrate the Season of the Resurrection: As Worship leader, enter from the back of the sanctuary laughing, yes, guffaw laughing; if you prefer to do this with others, invite as many as it takes to enter the sanctuary from every entrance, so you will have stereophonic laughter filling the sanctuary. When all of the "laugh-ers" have arrived in the chancel, say: "Come one, come all, laugh with us. It's the season of Easter when God had the last laugh over sin and death! If that Good News fails to bring joy and laughter, what will? Greet each other with God's Holy Laughter." *(After a few minutes, begin this response:)*

P: "Look! Christ is here to stay and that's enough!" (WHK)
"Look! Love is here to stay and that's enough!" (former Sister Corita)
Right Side: Hallelujah! Left Side: Gladness is ours!
P: Hallelujah! Gladness is ours!
Right Side: Hallelujah! Left Side: Sing to the Lord with thanksgiving!

Response

Sing chorus only to "Allelu!" Sing it until the congregation sings it enthusiastically and with energy. (Words and music by Ray Repp, F.E.L. Publishing, Ltd., found in *Folk Encounter*, Hope Publishing Company. See Appendix I for address.)

Prayer of Praise

O God, Parent, Child, Spirit, we rejoice that you have invited us to come laughing and rejoicing today and every Sunday, and that today, we have said, "Yes!" Prepare our hearts, minds, wills, to receive the truth of Jesus, the reason for our laughter, as we think and act upon your word, and celebrate your Presence and Power in Scripture and song, in the prayers and the proclamation, in the offering and the sacraments, and in willing, and sometimes not so willing, obedience. For Christ's sake, the world's sake, our sake. And all the people laughed and said, "Tah-dah!"

Recognizing Who We Are And Whose We Are

The Act of Recognizing Our Humanity

Authority! Authority! Authority! How we hate that word! Some of us can hardly wait to sing "Take This Job and Shove It" by Johnny Paycheck. *(Have someone sing it.)* We would rather **have** servants than **be** servants. Notice the Lotto ads, which basically say, "Win the Lotto, you can quit your job and have servants, and anything else your heart desires." Consider, silently, how we view authority, negatively, and positively. Write down your responses. *(Two minutes.)* Ask, what are your responses toward human authority, toward God's authority over our lives? Do we really want anyone telling us what to do, where to go, including our own family members? *(One minute of silence.)*

In silence, I invite each of us to read the Gospel for today. What do you think that Jesus says about authority, and how does he deal with it; and how does he ask us to deal with it? *(Ask for responses; expect none — too scary — so ask the people to jot down and put in the offering plate, unsigned, one idea from their reading.)*

Response

"Lord, Have Mercy Upon Us" (arr. David N. Johnson, 1972; or John Merbecke, 1550, arr. Healey Willan, 1930).

The Act of Receiving New Life

Have you ever wondered why Jesus, of all people, prayed, and needed prayer? My guess is that he recognized the source of his power and authority. So many of us pray the way rabbits nibble, a little here, a little there, dashing here, dashing there. Now, if we believe that God in Christ has conquered life and death, I invite several of you to offer laughing prayers of joy and thanks.

Response

"What Surging Well of Joy This Is" (from *Psalmody in Miniature,* 1783; adapted by Edward Miller, 1790. Jane Parker Huber, 1983).

The Teaching

Message with the Children of All Ages

Tie it in with the Scripture. Begin by asking, "Do you know that when Jesus prayed for his disciples, he also prayed, and keeps on praying, for you. And not only that, he enjoys hearing your laughter. Show them pictures of Jesus laughing. (The Fellowship of Merry Christians has several. Order from F.M.C., P.O. Box 895, Portage, MI 49081-0895.) Too often adults have used Jesus to discipline their children harshly.

Reading the Newer Covenant

Have someone memorize the words of Jesus, and present them as Jesus might.

Proclamation of the Good News

Someone has offered the following outlets of power: 1) through our life, who we are; 2) through our lips, what we say; 3) through our service, what we do; 4) through our money, what we do not keep; 5) through our prayers, what we claim in Jesus' name.

Stewardship Challenge

Before the Offering: We give cheerfully (the biblical word is "hilariously"), not for services rendered, not for what we can get, not even on the basis of what we receive for ourselves. We give as joyful "thankers."

After the Offering: Gracious and Holy God, the Source of our laughter, it's easy to talk; it's difficult to act. It's difficult to act because we're both afraid and confused — afraid of what people might think of us, and confused about where to start, or even if we **want** to start. By your pursuing Spirit, work in the lives of each of us this week, and always, that we will receive both your insight about where to begin, and courage to begin, even though we're not always sure where, or even if, we want to begin. Fulfill within us your purposes for us as a community of faith at this time, beginning now. We offer this prayer, and ourselves, in the name of the living Christ.

Hymn of Dedication
"God of Love and Joy and Laughter" (Jane Parker Huber, 1985. "Hymn to Joy," Ludwig von Beethoven, 1824; arr. by Edward Hodges, 1796-1867).

Charge to the Congregation
From this day forward, as the joyful, laughing people of Christ, live in his power, with his promise, for his purpose — for the sake of his world! And all the people said ...

Response
"O Let's Get On" (words and music by Avery and Marsh, *The Avery and Marsh Songbook*, Hope Publishing Company. See Appendix I for address).

Response to the Benediction
Personal: "*(name)*, the joy and laughter of Christ are yours!"
Corporate: "Amen Chorus," from "Lilies of the Field." Repeat, as often as you want, as the people leave the sanctuary.

Meditation
"Prayer is the Divine in us appealing to the Divine above us" (C. H. Dodds). Substitute the word "laughter" for "prayer."

Music Possibilities In Addition To Those Already Suggested

Music for Preparation: Medley of Easter hymns or laughter songs.

Choral Introit: "Hallelujah," Warner.

Hymn of Praise: "All Glory Be To God On High," based on "Gloria Excelsis," attr. to Nikolaus Decius, 1525; trans., Catherine Winkworth, 1863; alt.

Response to the Prayer of Praise: "Almighty Father, Hear our Prayer," Felix Mendelssohn, arr. 1846.

Response to the Newer Covenant: "Wondrous Love," Christiansen.

Hymn of Commitment: ""Upon Your Great Church Universal," J. M. de Carbon-Ferriere, 1823; trans. Margaret House, 1949; alt., 1972. Or "God is Our Strong Salvation," from Psalm 27; para. by James Montgomery, 1822; alt., 1972. Or "Come Down, O Love Divine," Bianco da Siena, c. 1367; trans., Richard F. Littledale, 1867; alt. 1972. (Change the sexist language as you sing.)

Music for Dismissal: "Psalm 119," Marcello.

Pentecost
The Season Of The Holy Spirit

Liturgical Color: Red/White/Green

Pentecost (formerly Kingdomtide [Trinity] — Season of the Kingdom of God on Earth), meaning "fiftieth day," has its roots in the ancient Jewish Feast of Weeks, a celebration of the first harvest, seven weeks after the spring sowing of the grain. Later, the Jews associated Pentecost with the giving of the Law to Moses on Mount Sinai. For Christians, Pentecost has a twofold significance independent of Jewish tradition. It commemorates the event in Acts 2 when two things occurred: 1) Holy Spirit came in the fulfillment of Christ's promise to his disciples; 2) The Church of Christ launched upon its world mission.

Pentecost, sometimes called "Whitsunday," may refer either to the wearing of white robes by candidates for baptism, or to the old Anglo-Saxon word "wit," meaning "wisdom" — an allusion to the outpouring of the Spirit of wisdom (Ephesians 1:17).

The color for the Pentecost season, which lasts seven days, is red. Red signifies divine fire, in addition to the fervor of the church's faith. The dove serves as the most common symbol of the Holy Spirit, and is found in the story of Jesus' baptism. The wind provides a third symbol.

The Season of the Holy Spirit, longest of the church year, begins on the Sunday following Pentecost, and continues until the season of Advent. Depending on the date of Easter, this season can contain 22 to 27 Sundays. This season serves as the instructional half of the church year and an attempt to keep God's commandments. Spiritual nourishment received from the observance of the first half of the church year now brings forth Christ-like living.

Four cycles divide the Pentecost Season:

I. Apostolic Age: Pentecost to the end of June (June 29, the Feast of Peter and Paul). Christians are taught how they are called to their new life in Christ.

II. Age of Persecution: (June 29 to August 10, the Feast of Saint Lawrence). Christians are instructed about how to live their life in Christ.

III. Church at Work Today: (August 10 to the end of September, the Feast of Saint Michael, September 29).

IV. Church Triumphant: (September 29 to Advent).

Generally, Pentecost has included two patterns or traditions:

I. Pentecost Sunday followed by 27 Sundays, designated "After Pentecost."

II. Pentecost Sunday, followed by Trinity Sunday, followed by 26 Sundays as "After Trinity." Some others labelled the whole season after Trinity Sunday as "Kingdomtide." Those who omitted any observance of Trinity Sunday claimed that "Trinity" was a doctrine, whereas "Pentecost" was an event. The emphases, originally during the Season of Pentecost, were designated, generally, as the Church, the Word, the Sacrament, and the Christian Hope.

Thanks to Donald Macleod, Francis Landey Patton Professor of Preaching and Worship, Emeritus, Princeton Theological Seminary, Princeton, New Jersey.

The Season Of The Holy Spirit

Pentecost

Liturgical Color: Red

Gospel: John 7:37-39

Theme: *Rivers of Living Water; Anticipation of the Coming of the Holy Spirit.* "Have you received the Holy Spirit?" "Received it? We've never heard of it!"

Pre-preparations for Pentecost

1. Invite, several weeks in advance, the people to wear red, the color for Pentecost. Ask them also to bring their favorite symbol for Pentecost. Let them know that two of the symbols are wind and fire.
2. Order from the American Bible Society, "The Best Gift: Acts of the Apostles, Chapter 2:1-47"; and ask them to read it before Pentecost Sunday.
3. Order a Pentecost button to hand out as people come to worship; and encourage them to wear it wherever they go. People in the community will ask them what it means, and it will provide a simple and effective way to witness.

The advantage of Pentecost over the other Holy Days is that the mass media haven't yet discovered how to make a few billion dollars with it.

The Community Gathers To Celebrate The Coming Of The Holy Spirit

Invitation to the Celebration

In a few moments, I will ask those of you who brought Pentecost symbols to share them if you choose. First, I invite us to listen to two Pentecost hymns. One symbol is fire; listen and follow in your hymnbook as the organist plays "Holy Spirit, Truth Divine." Write down the message that you think God is giving you. Another symbol is wind. The pianist will play "There Is a New Wind Blowing." Write down the message that you think God is giving you.

Response

Would any of you be willing to share your Pentecost symbol? Share your own favorite, and why.

Declaration of Joyful Expectations   Pastor and Ministers

P: The Holy Spirit is here! The Holy Spirit is the power and presence of Christ! The Holy Spirit is the healing force in and of the world.

M: Thank God, we have heard of the Holy Spirit! So, we come to celebrate the Spirit's presence and power, the wind and the fire.

P: I invite us to open ourselves, our needs and the needs of others; our relationship to God and to each other; the world of joys and sadnesses and angers — to Christ's Spirit.

M: We come with expectations, some of which we're aware, some of which we're not. We come to experience what the Holy Spirit of God will do with our lives, open and receptive. We are ready!

Hymn of Praise

"Come, O Spirit" (Union Harmony, 1837; John Dalles, 1983; harm. Hilton Rufty, 1934).

Prayer of Praise
Ask those who brought Pentecost symbols to offer a sentence prayer focusing on their particular symbol.

Response
And all the people shouted *(reverently, of course)*, "Happy birthday to the church." Now that we've said it, I invite us to sing it.

The Community Takes Responsibility For Itself

The Act of Recognizing Our Humanity
A member of the church one day asked his pastor, "Why can't I receive power, as the early disciples did, and do the same things as did Paul and Stephen?" The pastor said, "You shall receive power when the Holy Spirit has come upon you. How did they prepare to receive the Holy Spirit? How do you prepare?" He had no answer. So, how do we? Because, as someone has said, "Only the disciplined change the world."

All: God, we confess that, while we have been aware of Your Spirit, we want it through some kind of David Copperfield illusion.
P: The Spirit of Christ has said, "SWIM!"
M: Some of us have responded, "The water is too cold!"
P: The Spirit of Christ has said, "SWIM!"
M: And some of us have responded, "I don't know how!"
P: The Spirit of Christ has said, "SWIM!"
M: And some of us have responded, "This is not the time or the place!"
All: Lord, throw us into the water and teach us there, or else we may never get in!

Response
Ask the people to symbolize the splashing of water over themselves. Some will act confused, so show them how.

The Act of Receiving New Life
"The Gospel is dynamite, but we treat it like dried leaves" (Nicholas Berdyaev, Russian philosopher).
P: God's Word is clear: Forgiveness comes whenever we make honest confession. God cannot forgive those who think that they need not confess. The Good News demands a response. What will you do?
M: We will sing with our voices; we will speak with our lips. We will pledge our lives to be Pentecost people.

Response
Have a liturgical dancer, with the children, teach the congregation simple body response to "Spirit of the Living God, Fall Afresh on Me." Tell them, "It's okay not to be embarrassed."

The Community Responds To God's Truth

Message with the Children of All Ages
Have the children lead the congregation in response to the act of receiving new life. Thank them; children need to hear thanks often, especially in the sanctuary, not for their performance, or their cuteness. They need to be recognized and accepted as the church of today, not the church of tomorrow.

Reading from the Newer Covenant
Have your liturgical dancers interpret Acts 2:1-4, 43-47.

Proclamation of the Good News

Consider incorporating these ideas: 1) "Just as atomic energy represents the release of hidden forces in the physical world, so Pentecost represents the release of hidden invisible forces in the realm of personality" (Lloyd Ellis Foster). 2) Has the church missed the point that it now needs a set of new pews, a new organ, a new carpet, a new pastor, to give it a shot in the arm, rather than a steady flow of power from the Holy Spirit?

Response

(Choir) "Come, O Spirit, Dwell Among Us" (Janie Alford, 1979; Thomas John Williams, 1890).

Stewardship Challenge

In groups of three or four, where you sit, share signs and gifts of the Holy Spirit that you see in each other. After a few moments receive the offering.

Charge to the Congregation

There is no need to starve to death with so much nourishment available. Christ has given us his resources, his love, his Spirit — Power and Presence — and he has given us each other to live full, wholesome, abundant lives — so let's do just that, in the name of Christ's Spirit. Alleluia and Hurray; and all the people said, "Tah-dah!"

Meditation

"A common criticism of a play is that 'it lacks the courage of the first act.' One of the great needs of the church today is to regain the courage of the first act — at Pentecost" (Halford E. Luccock).

Invite the people to a "Happy Birthday" party for the church. Plan, as much as possible, everything in red.

Music Possibilities In Addition To Those Already Suggested

Music for Preparation: Medley of Pentecost hymns; list the pages in the hymnbook where they are located. Encourage the people to read the words, as they wait for formal worship to begin. Or, "Adagio for Strings," Samuel Barber.

Hymn of Praise: "On Pentecost They Gathered," Jane Parker Huber, from *A Singing Faith*, Westminster Press, 1987.

Singing the Older Covenant Reading: Select one of the Psalms and find it put to music.

Response to the Proclamation: (All the choirs) "It Is a Great Day of Joy" (Alleluia Fugue), from *Jesus: The Life of Jesus in Twelve Contemporary Songs,* Avant Garde Records, Inc., 250 West 57th Street, New York, N.Y. 10019.

Hymn of Dedication: Either, "Come, Holy Spirit, Heavenly Dove," Isaac Watts, 1707 (if you want to end worship on a quiet note); or "The Lord of the Dance," Sydney Carter (if you want to end worship on a more dramatic note).

Response to the Benediction: "Allelu," words and music by Ray Repp, Hope Publishing Company. It is okay to use a hymn more than once. Remember that only about one-third of the congregation is present on any given Sunday, unless you have a most unusual congregation.

Music for Dismissal: Medley of Pentecost hymns.

The Season Of The Holy Spirit

Trinity Sunday

Liturgical Color: White

Gospel: Matthew 28:16-20

Theme: *The Great Commission in Response to the Trinity.* When the church speaks about God in three persons, it doesn't mean three separate individuals, but three ways by which God expresses the God-Self.

The Community Gathers To Celebrate The Trinity And Great Commission

Invitation to the Celebration

Begin this way: In the Name of God, Father, Son, and Holy Spirit, and/or, In the Name of God the Parent, the Child, the Holy Spirit, and/or, In the Name of God the Father/Mother, God the Human, God the Present One, welcome to our celebration of the Eternal One who comes to us in many ways to show us the Way.

P: Rejoice in our God who is revealed as having the qualities of Mother/Father.
M: We do rejoice! We do respond!
P: Rejoice in our God who has come to us as one of us.
M: We do rejoice! We do respond!
P: Rejoice in our God who has come to us as daily Presence and Power.
M: We do rejoice! We do respond!

Response

"Come, Thou Almighty King" (Felice de Giardini, 1769; *Collection of Hymns for Social Worship*, 1757; alt.).

Prayer of Praise

Include a reference to each member of the Godhead.

Hymn of Praise

"Holy, Holy, Holy, Lord God Almighty!" (Reginald Heber, 1783-1826; John Bacchus Dykes, 1861; as in *Hymns Written and Adapted*, 1827).

The Community Takes Responsibility For Itself

The Act of Recognizing Our Humanity

At this point, even though we may have difficulty understanding the Trinity, we can know this: "We will never be good enough to merit Christ's love; we will never be bad enough not to merit Christ's love." Despite our understanding, or misunderstanding, of the Trinity, we acknowledge both our brokenness, I-centeredness, alienation, and, at the same time, that You invite us to acknowledge Your desire for fellowship with us. Cleanse us as we pray this prayer of confession: Holy God, Parent, Child, Spirit, we confess that we are timid, slow to speak, and reticent in action. We know that You have given us the answer to the riddle of life in the person of Jesus the Christ. In him, and through his spirit, You have shown us Yourself, and revealed what life is meant to be. The solution to life You have given us, if written large, could solve the problem of our war-weary, frustrated, and lusty world. Why do You wait for us to make it known? Why do You trust people such as us? You have given us spiritual power, placed us in spheres of influence, and imbued us with authority to speak truth about You in love. Do you have no other plan for a time such as this? We wonder ... *(one minute pause)*. Lord, forgive us, and awaken us to our heritage as Your children, communicators of Your grace, vessels of Your Spirit. Give us courage to claim our authority to speak and act as fearless prophets of power. You are our only security; whom shall we fear? To glorify You and enjoy You is our chief purpose; how can we be afraid? Overcome our introverted self-concern with the wonder of Your Grace, so that we will speak what we have seen and heard! Yes! Yes! Yes!

Response
"Gloria Patri (et al)" (Carlton Young, *The Genesis Songbook*, Hope Publishing Company).

The Act of Receiving New Life
To respond to God, the Father/Mother, Child, Spirit, is to practice love and loving. It means that we never give up on anyone, including ourselves. To give up is to deny God. Love, however, looks for ways of being constructive. As we read and digest the Great Commission, how will we look for ways of being constructive, today, this week, this month?

Response
"Catch Fire!" (words and music by Ferdinand Rodriguez, in *Folk Encounter*, Hope Publishing Company).

The Community Responds To God's Truth

Message with the Children of All Ages
(Reminder: Wait until all of the children arrive before beginning.) Today we have a hard lesson. Tell me what you know about the Trinity. *(If no response, ask those who didn't come forward to respond.)* One church school teacher, not, of course, in this congregation, summed up the Trinity by saying, "It is a kind of heavenly panel." That definition sends us clergy into deep despair! Think of the Trinity as a human trinity. You are a son/daughter, brother/sister, cousin. You are not three people; you are one person who relates to different people in different ways. God is similar to that.

Proclamation of the Good News
Incorporate these ideas:

1. Dorothy Sayers analyzed what many Protestants think about the Trinity, "the Father incomprehensible, the Son incomprehensible, and the whole thing incomprehensible."

2. Presently, the word "person" refers to a single individual, separate and distinct. Initially, it had a theatrical meaning. Actors, then, took more than one part in a play. For each character they portrayed, they wore a different mask, or "persona," which means, "the part that one plays." So then, when people talked about "God in Three Persons," they meant not three individuals, but three ways in which God expressed Self. One writer suggests, "God has more than one way of being God; Father, Son, and Holy Spirit is our Christian way of saying so."

3. If we take God seriously, then we also take God's Commission seriously. We authenticate God's reality through our witness.

Response
(Choir) "O Praise the Lord with One Consent" (Handel).

Stewardship Challenge
Laypeople are "the frozen assets, the credits of the church, but they must become 'liquid cash' to spend and be spent" (Heindrich Kraemer).

Charge to the Congregation

No one needs to tell us to go into all the world. We often confine that kind of thinking to "foreign missions." God already has placed us in all the world, the world of science, the classroom, economics, politics, community, vocation, vacation, home, neighborhood, supermarket, mall, you name it! God penetrates the world through us, into every area, every structure, every organization, with the recognition that Jesus the Christ is the Lord of all life!

Benediction for Action

We now go into the world in peace, having courage, holding on to what is good, returning no one evil for evil. We go out to strengthen the fainthearted, to support the weak, to help the suffering, to honor all people, to serve the Lord, rejoicing in the power of the Holy Spirit.

Response

"It Is Christ's World, After All" (tune: Disney's "It's A Small World, After All"). Sing while walking around the sanctuary, and leaving for ministry.

Meditation

"You shall be my witnesses in *(name your city)*, throughout your *(name your county)*, to the state *(in which you live)*, and the other 49 states, to the North American continent, and to every last place in the world."

Music Possibilities In Addition To Those Already Suggested

Music for Preparation: Medley of Trinity hymns (see the Trinity section of the hymnbook) or "Panis Angelicus," Thiman.

Hymn of Praise: "Come to Us, Mighty King," *Anonymous tract*, 1757; alt., 1972.

Response to the Newer Covenant Reading: "Nicene Creed," Herbert G. Draesel, Jr., from *Hymns for Now*, Workers Quarterly; Walther League. See Appendix I for address.

Response to the Message with the Children: "Magic Penny," copyright 1955, 1959 by MCA Music, a division of MCA, Inc.; found in *New Wine: Songs for Celebration*, by the United Methodist Church. See Appendix I for address.

Offertory: "Pavane," Warlock.

Hymn of Dedication: 1) "I Am the Light of the World," Howard Thurman and Jim Strathdee, copyright 1969 by Jim Strathdee. 2) "Called by Christ to Love Each Other," Jane Parker Huber, 1980, from *Joy in Singing*, Jane Parker Huber, Presbyterian Church U.S.A. See Appendix I for address.

Response to the Benediction: "Glory be to God on High. Alleluia. Father, Son, and Holy Ghost. Alleluia."

Music for Dismissal: Medley of Trinity hymns. (Ask the congregation to read the words as the musician plays them.)

The Season Of The Holy Spirit

Propers One, Two, Three

Liturgical Color: Green

Gospels: Matthew 5:21-24, 27-30, 33-37; 5:38-48; 6:24-34

Proper One
Episcopal: Matthew 5:21-24, 27-30, 33-37

Proper Two
Episcopal: Matthew 5:38-48

Proper Three
Episcopal: Matthew 6:24-34

These three Gospel lessons are duplicated on the sixth, seventh, and eighth Sundays after Epiphany.

The Season Of The Holy Spirit

Proper 4, Pentecost 2, Ordinary Time 9

(Sunday between May 29 - June 4, inclusive)

Liturgical Color: White/Green

Gospel: Matthew 7:21-29

Theme: *Self-deception; Hearers and Doers.* "We say that we want to spend eternity with God; but how much time do we spend with God each day?" (WHK).

The Community Gathers To Celebrate The Season Of The Holy Spirit

Invitation to the Celebration
Select which Trinitarian greeting you prefer in your welcome. The Spirit of Christ makes us come alive. We use that phrase often. What does it mean? Ask for response from the people. Here is another idea of what it means: "Coming alive is when the grass no longer seems greener somewhere else, but in the relationships and responsibilities which are knocking at our door today" (from *Celebrations on Coming Alive*, author unknown). (R.S. - Right Side; L.S. - Left Side)

P: Clap your hands, stomp your feet! Let your bodies and voices explode with joy!
R.S.: God is not some human concoction. God is for real and is here!
L.S.: Despite all attempts to rationalize God out of existence, God is in the world and reigns over the universe.

(If the congregation is dragging through the call, begin again, and again, until the people show some enthusiasm about being in God's presence.)

P: The rulers of the nations often ignore God, and so do you and I.
R.S.: People of learning often pass God by, and so do we.
L.S.: The masses of God's creation substitute their own little gods, and worship the things they can see and feel, and so do we.
All: Others build fortresses around themselves, and display no need for God, and so do we.
P: Our God will not be ignored. No, indeed!
All: God will remain in this world, no matter how we react. Therefore, we recognize God's Presence and we fill the air with God's praises! Yes! Yes!

Response
"Eightfold Alleluia" (source unknown).

Prayer and Hymn of Praise
These center upon, and focus on, the God whose presence and power we celebrate. This is no time for subjectiveness!

The Community Takes Responsibility For Itself

The Act of Recognizing Our Humanity
How do you respond to Jesus' words in the Gospel for today? "Not everyone who says to me, 'Lord, Lord,' will enter the Kingdom of Heaven." Often, I come to that statement and have a list of folks who I know won't make it. How about you? Do you have that list in your head? If so, would you be willing

to write down the names of those people who you think will not make it; and then, after each name, tell God why you think they won't make it? *(Pregnant pause!)* After a few moments, invite the people to read, silently, Matthew 7:21-23, to let the Spirit of God examine them, and to make their personal confession of sin. *(Three full minutes.)*

Response
Pastor to offer a corporate prayer of confession. Incorporate the idea that such behavior represents lives built on sand.

The Act of Receiving New Life
Now, please read Matthew 7:24-29, silently. As you read, what new insights of awareness do you have about yourself, and about the local congregation of which you are a part? Write down your thoughts. After a two-minute pause, ask if any want to share their discovery. Offer one of your own. What does it take to build our house, our life, on rock rather than sand?

Response
"Let All That You Do" (words and music by Gary Hasson, in *Folk Encounter*, Hope Publishing Company).

The Community Responds To God's Truth

Message with the Children of All Ages
If possible, bring a sandcastle; if not possible, talk about sandcastles at the beach — how long they take to build, and how quickly they are wiped out by the incoming tide. Talk about things that do not last. Perhaps they can list several. And even though houses built on rock last for a time, they, too, disappear. Jesus asks us to build our lives on his love which never disappears. Use illustrations from your life.

Reading from the Newer Covenant
This passage makes for a dramatic presentation. It includes a person, a reader, and Jesus. Begin by having that person knocking loudly on a sanctuary door entrance. "Hey, let me in!" Use the first part of the text; and give permission for the person to be creative, so long as he/she maintains the content of the passage. Then, Jesus will respond appropriately. The reader concludes with verses 28-29.

Proclamation of the Good News
Consider the difference between religion and Christianity. Identify some of the barriers that keep people from the Kingdom, barriers which are nothing more than sandcastles. To name the barrier is to have power over it. Here are some examples: a deceitful liaison; a full pocketbook; a fear of failure; an unwillingness to risk; a demand for false recognition; a hope based on illusions. These may well keep us from entering the Kingdom. Then, invite the people to allow the presence and power of the risen Christ to replace it, that secondary god, with a primary loyalty to him who came to bring life in all of its richness, fullness, wholeness.

Response
"Have Thine Own Way, Lord" (Adelaide A. Pollard; George C. Stebbins).

Stewardship Challenge
Our faith begins and ends, not by our obedience to rules; not by our achievements, measured by ourself or others; not by our finding God through our efforts; not by how much or how little we put in the offering plate; but, rather, by God's unconditional acceptance of us. Our response, during the offering, and throughout our life, is thankful gratitude. I invite us to offer our grateful thanks to God now.

Charge to the Congregation

The Holy Spirit reveals the irresistibility of God's authority let loose among people in Jesus of Nazareth — not in Buddha, not in the Bahgwan, not in Mohammed, but in Christ; not in authoritarianism, religion, or otherwise, but in Christ. In Jesus the Christ, God openly declared God's authority by reconciling black and white, rich and poor, ambitious and lazy, intelligent and stupid, hopeful and hopeless, sinner and saint, to the Godself. The authority of God came to life in a manger, hung on a cross, broke loose from death, and lives for *all* people — the ones we like and the ones we don't like. We are invited to share that life with the world — today and every day.

Response

Use Disney's tune, "It's a Small World, After All," again this week. "It Is Christ's World, After All."

Meditation

"Everyone expects to go to heaven, but no one wants to die" (WHK). "If Christianity were a little more willing to put miracles and Resurrection under wraps, it would be far less offensive and worth almost nothing" (S. Lewis Chamberlain).

Music Possibilities In Addition To Those Already Suggested

Music for Preparation: Medley of Pentecost or Holy Spirit hymns; or "Chaconne," Buxtehude.

Hymn of Praise: "When Morning Gilds the Skies," German hymn, eighteenth century; trans. Edward Caswall, 1854; 1858; alt.

Response to the Prayer of Pardon: (Choir) "My Soul Doth Rejoice," Homilius.

Response to the Message with the Children: "Seek and Ye (You) Shall Find," Kentucky-Tennessee gospel song, from *New Wine: Songs for Celebration* (see Appendix I for address).

Offertory: "Benedictus," Couperin.

Hymn of Dedication: "My Hope Is Built on Nothing Less," Edward Mote, c. 1834; William Batchelder Bradbury, 1863; or "Jesus Shall Reign," Isaac Watts, 1719; based on Psalm 72.

Music for Dismissal: Medley of Dedication hymns.

The Season Of The Holy Spirit

Proper 5, Pentecost 3, Ordinary Time 10

(Sunday between June 5 - 11, inclusive)

Liturgical Color: Green

Gospel: Matthew 9:9-13, 18-26

Theme: *The Call of Matthew and Several Healings.* "If we say, 'Yes!' to God's call, then we also have God's power to bring healing to others, don't we?" (WHK)

The Community Gathers To Celebrate The Season Of The Holy Spirit

Invitation to the Celebration
God calls us to worship and service, both active ingredients in all of our faith celebrations. Because God calls us, corporate worship is an act of the total community of faith, hope, love — not just when we feel like it; but weekly, as was Jesus' custom, not because we agree or disagree with the pastor, for we do both; not because we do or do not feel stimulated, but in spite of how we feel. Basically, we worship, not to get or to give anything, only to celebrate the Good News of Christ's presence and power. The style of our celebration is thanksgiving and thanksliving. Do you agree? If so, how will you let each other know? *(Wait for a response. How will you let the congregation know about your presence today, other than getting paid?)*

Hymn of Praise
"Called by Christ to Love Each Other" (Dimitri S. Bortniansky, 1818; Jane Parker Huber, 1980, in *Joy in Singing*, Hope Publishing Company. See Appendix I for address).

Prayer of Praise
Focus on the One who calls us from death to life.

The Community Takes Responsibility For Itself

The Act of Recognizing Our Humanity
Spend several minutes helping people to get in touch with God's call to them. In how many ways did God seek to reach you, and you kept saying, "No, later, maybe." Review those ways, and write them down. During that time, what kind of a call were you expecting? Thunder and lightning? Still small voice? An angel, heavenly or earthly? What do you suppose God was thinking during this struggle? Did you experience God struggling with you? If so, what form did it take? Go slowly. Let the people digest their awarenesses. After some time, let them know that God is more interested in our salvation, our wholeness, than we are. And God will continue to seek, literally, to pursue us as the "Hound of Heaven," in Francis Thompson's poem. So rejoice!

Response
Stanza 1 only of "When I Had Not Yet Learned of Jesus" (Yongchul Chung, 1967: Yoosun Lee, 1967; para. Jane Parker Huber).

The Act of Receiving New Life

Psalm 23:6 in the Hebrew language is translated this way: "Of a certainty! God's covenant grace and steadfast love shall hotly pursue us all the days of our lives ..." Wow! Did you hear that? God refuses simply to hang back, to follow us casually. God pursues! Rejoice and be glad!

Response

"What Wondrous Love Is This" (American Folk Hymn, c. 1811; Walker's Southern Harmony, 1853).

The Community Responds To God's Truth

Message with the Children of All Ages

Focus on the call as we experience it in everyday life. Mother and father call us to dinner; the teacher calls the class to order; your friends call you to play. We receive many calls. Take the magic out of God's call to us. Ask one or two adults to share with the children how God called them. And emphasize the reality that God uses people most of the time.

Reading from the Newer Covenant

Dramatize Matthew's call. Have the Pharisees sitting around talking about this Jesus for a few minutes before Jesus arrives on the scene. Then, have someone who reads well read the remainder of the text while standing in the middle of the sanctuary. Use a microphone if necessary.

Proclamation of the Good News

Perhaps you will want to begin with this story: A man sitting in the barber chair says to the barber, "It's a good thing for you that it grows, isn't it?" The barber responds, "Not really. Maybe I would have gotten into something worthwhile ... If I had it to do it over again, I wish ... but what's the use, I quit wishing years ago." Secondly, when we accept the call of God, we do bring healing to others, maybe not the dramatic healings viewed on *The Benny Hill Show*, but healings nevertheless. Words and actions do bring healing to those around us; our money does bring healing.

Stewardship Challenge

I make only one New Year's resolution, and I renew it each year, and I break it often; that's why I keep renewing it. It's this: "What is the most loving thing I can say or do at any given moment?"

Charge to the Congregation

Here is one who takes his calling to heal seriously: A pastor sat with Dr. S. P. Raju, an engineer and scientist, in India one hot night. Dr. Raju invented the smokeless oven used by Indian villagers. He has designed a one-room house, approved by his government, that could drastically change the living conditions of the lowly peasant in his land. He is an official in the Indian government. He is also a remarkable Christian. As the two men sat there, Dr. Raju placed in the pastor's hands a rumpled piece of paper on which he had paraphrased Paul's words. Listen. "Raju, a servant of Jesus Christ, called to be an engineer, separated unto the Gospel of God in the evangelism of irrigation research for growing more food and bringing redemption from hunger ... Also separated unto the Gospel of God in the evangelism of housing research for the poor, for bringing 'preventive redemption' to those from congestion, dirt and disease, which are the potential sources of moral evil and sin." I charge each of us to write down the meaning of our call from God, and how that call brings healing. You are urged to share them in worship or the newsletter.

Response

"It Is Christ's World, After All." Encourage people to sing as they leave the sanctuary.

Meditation

"Do not fear that your life shall come to an end, but rather, fear that it shall never have a beginning" (Cardinal Newman, updated language).

Music Possibilities In Addition To Those Already Suggested

Music for Preparation: Medley of Holy Spirit hymns or hymns which center on God's call, or "Chorale," by Franck.

Hymn of Praise: "Praise, My Soul, the King of Heaven," from Psalm 103, Henry Francis Lyte, 1834; alt. Sing stanza 4 in unison; organist will play the alternative harmonization.

Response to the Assurance of Pardon: (Choir) "'Alleluia, Glorious is Thy Name," Olson.

Response to the Message with the Children: "Of My Hands," Ray Repp, text and music copyright 1966 by F.E.L. Church Publications, Ltd., 1925 Pontilus Ave., Los Angeles, CA 90025; phone: 213-478-0053.

Offertory: "Berceuse," McKay.

Hymn of Dedication: "Whate'er Our God Ordains Is Right," Samuel Rodigast, c. 1674; trans. Catherine Winkworth, 1858, 1863; alt., 1972.

Music for Dismissal: Medley of Hymns of Healing or "Carillon for a Joyful Day," McKay.

The Season Of The Holy Spirit

Proper 6, Pentecost 4, Ordinary Time 11

(Sunday between June 12 - 18, inclusive)

Liturgical Color: Green

Gospel: Matthew 9:35—10:8 (9-23)

Theme: *Few Laborers and the Disciples' Mission.* "The mission of Jesus cannot be defined without speaking of us humans as being lost" (Henri Blocher, from the European Congress on Evangelism, Amsterdam, The Netherlands, 1971).

The Community Gathers To Celebrate The Season Of The Holy Spirit

Invitation to the Celebration

In the Name of God, the Creator, Liberator, Sustainer, Energizer, welcome to the celebration of the Good News. How do we come? As spectators? Or as participants in the worship-drama? As we come, what expectations do we bring, not of others' performances, but rather of our own response to God's call? Because we have come, what difference will we make in the world, God's world — from now on? So, in God's Name and Power, the same Name and Power who called the first disciples, welcome, and ON GUARD! — especially if we want nothing to do with God's Spirit challenging and invading us, changing the way we think, feel, respond. God will have some surprises for us, if we hear and respond, or even if we don't. Therefore, ready or not, we continue to worship in the Name and Power of God, Parent, Child, Spirit. So be it!

Hymn of Praise

"God Is Here!" (Fred Pratt Green, 1979; rev. 1988; Cyril Vincent Taylor, 1941).

Prayer of Praise

Thank God for sending the Holy Spirit into the disciples. Name each of them. And acknowledge the fact that if they had not gone out, in God's Presence and Power, we would not be here this morning.

The Community Takes Responsibility For Itself

The Act of Recognizing Our Humanity

Confession has at least two dimensions:
1. We look inside. What sin (or sins) do we bring before God in this moment? I urge us not to get stuck on the world's (and often, the church's) definition of sins, chief of which seem to be murder (homicide, suicide, abortion, with abortion as number one), adultery, theft, homosexuality. Instead, I urge you to look at the Bible's definition of sin as "living off-center"— as not only "missing the mark, but aiming at the wrong target" — as looking for scapegoats by "attempting to justify our thoughts, words, actions." *(You may want to use each of these definitions on separate Sundays, and illustrate them.)* What do we allow to keep us in bondage? To what, to whom, do we give our time, energy, money, which keep the radical-to-the-core teachings of Jesus from getting and maintaining a toehold on our heart, mind, will, pocketbook? *(Two minutes of silence. Ask the people to make notes on their thoughts.)*

2. The second dimension of confession is to look beyond ourself. So, I invite us to look at each other, also the subject and object of God's love and justice. To do this, we will need to give up, at least temporarily, the "don't stare" messages we learned as a child. We have a strange phenomenon in our society. It's okay to look at someone, so long as we are talking, no matter how bland or stupid the conversation. Instantly, when we stop talking, we get embarrassed, and begin to look all around the world. *(Pause.)* Now that we have cleared that hurdle, I invite us to look around at one another, to realize that we're all in the same boat; that no one is superior or inferior to anyone else; that no one is any stronger or weaker than another; that we all play, basically, the same games of living off-center, missing the mark, and justifying our own actions to make ourselves appear better than others. As we look around, I invite us to ask ourselves, silently, "I wonder what those people think about my Christian witness? And, what do I think about their witness as Christians?" Are others saying/am I saying, "What a powerhouse for God!" or "They're/I'm perfectly harmless; they/I would never hurt a fly"? All of us, no exceptions, come to God needing forgiveness and new life. Thank God! *(Two minutes of silence. Ask people to make notes. Invite them to take the initiative to share in future worships, during the act of confession.)*

Response
"Lord, Have Mercy" (John Weaver, 1984).

The Act of Receiving New Life
Because so many of us were, or are, raised on guilt, the gift that keeps on giving forever if we let it, we more easily hear the confession than we do the assurance of pardon. *(To correct that, print the confession less often, and the assurance more often.)* The Scriptures insist that, for the Christian, the past is forgiven, every second of it up to this one! The Christ has come to urge us to give up thoughts, words, behaviors which de-energize and dehumanize us and others; to move us beyond our fear of others, and what they might say about, or do to, us; to empower us to share good news of how the Spirit has changed our lives. So, are we willing to let God renew, reaffirm, reactivate that power now — knowing that God accepts us unconditionally, as we are — this moment? *(Three minutes of silence. Please take notes; and share at a later worship.)*

Response
"A New Creature" (words and music by John F. Wilson, *The Genesis Songbook*, Hope Publishing Company. See Appendix I for address).

The Community Responds To God's Truth

Message with the Children of All Ages
Jesus called/invited the disciples to follow him; at the time, they had no idea where. They never got his message until after the Resurrection. Give a one- or two-line biography of each disciple and the legends about how they died.

Reading from the Newer Covenant
Ask, a week before worship, twelve people to be Jesus' "disciples." Have them seated with the rest of the people. Call them to come forward one by one. Have "Jesus" present to them their mission. Encourage them to respond as modern-day disciples might respond to Jesus' call. Some possibilities: "No, not yet; maybe; see me later; I'll call you; yes."

Proclamation of the Good News
Consider these ideas:
1. "Mission is not a special function of a part of the church. It is the whole church in action. It is the body of Christ expressing Christ's concern for the whole world. It is God's people seeking to make all

persons members of the people of God. Mission is the function for which the church exists" (Donald Miller).

2. "The mission of the church is to reproduce the life of Jesus in the life of the world" (J. E. Lesslie Newbigin).

Stewardship Challenge

"We have become a generation of people who know the price of everything, and the value of nothing" (Oscar Wilde).

Charge to the Congregation

"Don't ever say that we have no opportunity to reach people. It is not that the chances are missing, but that we are missing the chances" (Charles Guillot).

Meditation

The attitude with which we came today will determine what we heard and how we respond. Did we hear that? "Missions, or mission, is not a part of the work of the church; it IS the work of the church" (author unknown).

Music Possibilities In Addition To Those Already Suggested

Music for Preparation: Medley of Holy Spirit hymns, or "Toccata in D-Minor," Froberger.

Hymn of Praise: "Sing Praise to God, Who Reigns Above," Johann J. Schutz, 1675; trans. Frances E. Cox, 1864; alt.

Response to the Assurance of Pardon: "The Lord's Prayer," West Indies Version, by Paul Abels.

Response to the Newer Covenant: "Salvation is Created," Tschesnokoff.

Offertory: "God of the Ages, By Whose Hand," Elizabeth Burrowes, 1956, 1971.

Hymn of Dedication: "O Be Joyful in the Lord," Curtis Beach, 1958; alt., 1972.

Music for Dismissal: Medley of Mission hymns, or "Credo," Haydn.

The Season Of The Holy Spirit

Proper 7, Pentecost 5, Ordinary Time 12

(Sunday between June 19 - 25, inclusive)

Liturgical Color: Green

Gospel: Matthew 10:24-39

Theme: *Whom to Fear; Not Peace, But a Sword.* "Christianity requires us participants (saints, priests, angels) to come out of the grandstand onto the playing field; because, 'the church is the one institution in society that exists primarily for those outside of itself' " (author unknown).

The Community Gathers To Celebrate The Season Of The Holy Spirit

Invitation to the Celebration
How (not why) did we come today?
1. As spectators waiting for someone to do something for, to, with us; or as participants making something happen?
2. As people ready to say "yes" to God and fellow humans; or as people who say, "No, maybe, later"?
3. As humble ones who have more questions than answers; or as self-righteous ones who pretend to have all of the answers? *(Pause.)* Do we come breezing in, or dragging in? With openness, or with calculation? Joyfully or morosely? Do we come broken or whole, or a mixture?

Response
(Choir) "O Come, Let Us Celebrate" (Richard Gerig, 1975).

Affirmation of Joyful Expectations   Pastors and Ministers
P: Come on! Let's celebrate the Presence and Power of God, the God who Creates, Sustains, Liberates, Energizes; the God who came in Jesus the Christ to transform the world and begin the new creation!
M: We come to celebrate God's Presence and Power. We are the people of God, new persons in the new creation made possible by the death and resurrection of the Christ. We come to affirm that the old has passed away; and behold, the new has come!
P: Jesus the Christ is Lord! Yes, he is!
M: And we are new persons through him. As transformed, renewed, released people, we celebrate with adoration and praise!

Hymn of Praise
(with drums and any other available instruments) "O God the Creator" (music by Joy F. Patterson, 1989; text, c. 1977, Elizabeth Haile and Cecil Corbett).

The Community Takes Responsibility For Itself

The Act of Recognizing Our Humanity
Jim Crane, in his book *On Edge*, has a contemporary man, cigarette in mouth, briefcase in hand, speaking to the prophet Amos. "I enjoyed your talk, Mr. Amos, but I would like to hear more of what's

right with Israel." True of us? If so, then we will do our best to silence the messenger, if not by outright killing him/her, then by gossip to destroy character; or by ignoring the person, even during the social hour (even though we're such a friendly church); or by ridiculing behind a person's back; or by ... what's your favorite way? *(Three minutes of silence.)* Then, a summary prayer of confession.

The Act of Receiving New Life

Only the Spirit of God transforms us from excuse-making, "I just couldn't help myself!" to obedient decision-making, "I am responsible for myself!" So, if it's true that God is, that God refuses to lie, then, believe me, we are forgiven of the past, reconciled to the present, equipped for the future — with no excuses, no barriers — in the Name of the One who inspired and energized that first Pentecost, and everyone since!

Response

Liturgical dance to Acts 2:1-4. If you have no children liturgical dancers, take this opportunity to invite the children who come forward, and the adults who remain in their seats, to act out the passage.

The Community Responds To God's Truth

Message with the Children of All Ages
See above.

Reading from the Older Covenant

Whenever possible, have the Scripture signed, even if you have no deaf person in the congregation. Perhaps you will have deaf persons, if you are known as a congregation which reaches out to all conditions.

Reading from the Newer Covenant

Again, have someone memorize the words of Jesus and speak them, as the person walks around the sanctuary.

Stewardship Challenge

The church exists, not for our enjoyment, comfort, security. It exists for the doing of God's work in God's Spirit for the fulfilling of God's purpose. So, notice the meditation at the beginning of the order of worship. The church is the only institution in society that exists primarily for those outside of it. *(Ask people to raise their hands if they believe that.)* Remember that we believe, not what we say, but what we practice. So, this week, how will we put into practice what we say we believe?

Charge to the Congregation and Receiving the Invitation

God invites, calls, urges us to grapple courageously, to cooperate creatively, to venture cooperatively, for the sake of the way, the truth, and the life.

Hymn of Dedication
"Be Thou My Vision" (Irish Ballad).

Meditation

The purpose of life is not, "Don't worry; be happy!" but rather to make a difference, even when we seem alone, forsaken by family and friends and fellow church members. Christ's spirit transforms the *merely* or *drearily* routine into the *dearly* routine. The routine of life, penetrated by God's vision, though perhaps frustrating us, will never destroy us, not if we allow the Christ to take it, and us, in order to make both the routine and us responsible citizens of the Kingdom (WHK).

Music Possibilities In Addition To Those Already Suggested

Music for Preparation: Medley of Holy Spirit hymns or "Before Thy Throne" by Bach.

Hymn of Praise: "God of Our Fathers, Whose Almighty Hand," Daniel C. Roberts, 1876.

Response to the Act of Recognizing Our Humanity: "Eleanor Rigby," Lennon/McCartney, copyright 1966, Northern Songs, Ltd., 71-75 New Oxford Street, London, W. C. 1, England.

Response to the Newer Covenant: "Blessed Are You," Emma Lou Diemer.

Offertory: "Pastorale," McKay.

Response to the Offering: Change the tune occasionally as, for example, traditional words to the tune of "Lasst Uns Erfreuen L.M. with Alleluias."

Hymn of Commitment: "Call Jehovah Thy Salvation," James Montgomery, 1822; Rowland Hugh Prichard, 1855. (Update sexist language as you sing.)

Music for Dismissal: "Put Your Hand in the Hand," words and music by Gene MacLellan. (Ask the congregation to sing as they leave and to grasp each other's hands.)

The Season Of The Holy Spirit

Proper 8, Pentecost 6, Ordinary Time 13

(Sunday between June 26 - July 2, inclusive)

Liturgical Color: Green

Gospel: Matthew 10:40-42

Theme: *Rewards.* "One of these days, you're gonna get yours! So, 'make my day!' " How do we usually interpret that statement? In what ways, if any, does it fit with Jesus' remark about "the reward of the righteous"?

Celebrating The Presence Of God

Invitation to the Celebration

In the name of the Living Christ, welcome, welcome, welcome! Hear the promise of Jesus: "Whoever welcomes you welcomes me, and whoever welcomes me welcomes the one who sent me." So, let's spend a few moments welcoming each other in the name of the Christ. (R.S. - Right Side; L.S. - Left Side)

All: Allelu! Allelu! Allelu!
R.S.: Praise the Lord!
L.S.: Christ is Sovereign!
All: Praise the Lord! Christ is Sovereign! *(three times)*
All: *(Speak your part and applaud!)*

If this is awkward the first time, practice it several times. And, it's okay not to do it perfectly. The goal is to free the people to respond with enthusiasm and energy. In a sense, you, the pastor, are the cheerleader to help make this happen.

Response

"Allelu!" (words and music by Ray Repp, *Folk Encounter*, Hope Publishing Company. See Appendix I for address).

Prayer of Praise

Focus on the theme of welcoming, how God has welcomed us and how God calls us to welcome each other and a world that's dying to hear Good News.

Hymn of Praise

"O God the Creator"   (Elizabeth Haile and Cecil Corbett, 1977; Joy.Patterson, 1989). It's okay to use the same hymn within the same month. One way to teach a congregation a new hymn is to use it as a hymn of the month.

Celebrating The Act Of Forgiveness

The Act of Confession

"We have become so 'sensitive' to the needs of individuals that we give all of our emphasis to acceptance and none to accountability" (from *Pastoral Administration*). Jesus kept saying, "Go and sin no more." Luther said, "Cut it out." I say, "Give it up — anything which separates you from God, others, yourself." *(Silence.)*

Prayer of Confession

(Unison) As our humanity bumps up against a tense and broken world, it is so easy for us to draw back into ourselves, Lord. We begin to play the role of victim, feeling fearful, angry, powerless, allowing our lives to be determined by outside forces. Soon we become separated from ourselves, performing the acts required by society but out of touch with our real needs, feelings, hopes. We pray that you will reawaken life within us, that we will find the courage to rediscover who we are, and that we will take control of our lives and begin to shape our futures, and the future of your world, as we welcome the world each day that we arise, in the power and presence of Jesus the Christ. So be it!

The Assurance of Pardon

God in Christ invites us to give up those choices that get us into trouble. At the same time, God in Christ welcomes us to God's world, the world to which God sent the unique one-of-a-kind son to bring newness and wholeness.

Response

"There's a Sweet, Sweet Spirit" (Doris Akers, 1962). Have the musicians play through the hymn while the people read it silently; then sing it.

Celebrating The Word

Message with the Children of All Ages

Invite them to think about rewards. When do they get them; when are they withheld? So often, at least with adults, rewards are based on this idea: "I'll do this for you if you'll do that for me," a tit for tat. You may have trouble with Jesus' words. So, explore, on the children's level, how Jesus' reward system differs from ours.

Response

Even though we may have difficulty understanding how God rewards us, we are called to respond out of thanksgiving for what we have received. So, let's sing the chorus only to "O Let's Get On" (words and music by Richard Avery and Don Marsh, *Folk Encounter*, Hope Publishing Company. See Appendix I for address).

Reading from the Newer Covenant

Again, have your scripture reader memorize the passage, and walk around the sanctuary speaking the words of Jesus.

Proclamation of the Good News

Consider this idea: As we respond to the ministry of the Christ, whatever form it takes, do we think about the reward we will receive? Or is the very act of ministry reward enough? It is so easy to become self-righteous, "My works are better than yours." Or, as a well-known church educator said years ago, "If you vote for that particular presidential candidate, you can't possibly be a Christian."

Celebrating Our Gifts

Stewardship Challenge

If we believed that we received no eternal rewards for our faith, that the act alone was our reward, what shape and content would our giving take? *(Silence before receiving the offering.)*

Dedication Prayer
Lord, we give out of gratitude. Do what you will with this money, and with us.

Celebrating Our Departure

Charge to the Congregation
"Just to Live is Holy" (Abraham Heschel).

Hymn of Dedication
"Give to Me, Lord, a Thankful Heart" (Caryl Micklem, 1973).

Meditation
"If I were an angel, I'd say to all the flowers in the world, 'Grow, grow, grow'" (source unknown).
"To take up the cross of Christ is no great action done once and for all (nor is it done to get a reward); it consists in the continual practice of small duties [responses] [some of] which are distasteful to us [while others bring extreme joy, no matter what the reward]" (John Henry Newman; brackets mine, WHK).

Music Possibilities In Addition To Those Already Suggested

Music for Preparation: "The Sound of Silence," words and music by Paul Simon, from Warner Brothers' Publications, Inc., 75 Rockefeller Plaza, New York, NY 10019.

Hymn of Praise: "The God of Abraham Praise," Daniel ben Judah Dayyan, c. 1400; trans. by Newton Mann, 1885; and William Channing Gannett, 1910; alt. (You may want to substitute "God" for "His.")

Response to the Confession: "Gloria Patri." Vary the tune.

Response to the Assurance: "Come, My Soul, You Must Be Waking," Friedrich R. L. von Canitz, (1654-1699). Trans. attr. to Thomas Arnold and Henry J. Bucknoll, 1838, 1841; alt. (Clarify the word "soul" to mean "spirit," in order to clarify the fact that Christians do not believe in the "immortality of the soul.")

Hymn of Praise: "O Lord, You Are Our God and King," *The Psalter*, 1912; alt., 1972. Or "Take My Life, and Let It Be Consecrated," Francis Ridley Havergal, 1874. (You may want to point out that some church members read the hymn, "take my life and let it be.")

Response to the Benediction: "Day by Day," Richard of Chichester (alt.), copyright 1971 by Valando Music, Inc., and New Cadenza Music Corp.

The Season Of The Holy Spirit

Proper 9, Pentecost 7, Ordinary Time 14

(Sunday between July 3 - 9, inclusive)

Liturgical Color: Green

Gospel: Matthew 11:16-19, 25-30

Theme: *Comparison between Jesus and John the Baptist; Jesus' Thanks to the Father; Jesus' Invitation to Us. "To create is to relate" (former Sister Corita).*

Celebrating The Presence Of God

Invitation to the Celebration

In a football game, if a team huddles for more than 25 seconds, it is penalized. The huddle is as important for a football team as the huddle of corporate worships is for the community of faith. All that God ever intended the worship to be is the huddle. We come together for the purpose of going out and hitting the line. For the next hour, or in my case, the next 75 minutes, we huddle in order to get back into the thick of the action — because worship is not primarily something that happens between God and the church, but rather, something that happens between God and the world.

Declaration of Joy   Reverently shouting
(Moffett's Translation of Psalm 150)
(R.S. - Right Side; L.S. - Left Side)
All: Praise the Lord! Praise the Lord! Praise the Lord!
R.S.: Praise God in the sanctuary!
L.S.: Praise God in the heaven of power!
R.S.: Praise God for mighty deeds!
L.S.: Praise God for sovereign strength!
R.S.: Praise God with a bugle blast!
L.S.: Praise God with lute and lyre!
R.S.: Praise God with the drum and dance!
L.S.: Praise God with strings and flute!
R.S.: Praise God with resounding cymbals!
L.S.: Praise God with the clash of cymbals!
All: Let everything that breathes, praise the Lord! Praise the Lord! Praise the Lord! Hallelujah. Amen!
(Sexist language eliminated. During the reading, use the instruments mentioned, or facsimiles, to reinforce the reading.)

Hymn of Praise

"All Creatures of Our God and King" (Francis of Assisi, 1225; trans. and para. William Henry Draper, c. 1910; alt.; harm. Ralph Vaughan Williams, 1906). Augment the organ with all the musical instruments.

Prayer of Praise

Be certain to focus on who God is, the One who invites us to worship, no matter what our situation or condition.

Response

Use a musical version of Psalm 150.

Celebrating The Act Of Forgiveness

The Act of Confession

The story is told of a Scottish preacher (though the response is not limited to Scottish people). One day he stood at the fringe of a Salvation Army meeting on a street in Edinburgh. A young uniformed girl with a tambourine asked him, "Are you a Christian?" He replied sternly, "I am a professor in a theological school." When the girl returned to her companions after his rebuff, she sighed, "What a face for a Christian." Which model do we want for our life, the response to John or Jesus? Or neither? What keeps us from living the joy-life? *(Two minutes of silence.)*

The Assurance of Pardon

(Have someone prepared to give the assurance from where he/she is sitting; make certain that everyone can hear.) From *To Believe in God* (former Sister Corita): "To believe in God is to get so attached to everything that it can't give you up; is to have the great faith that someone, somewhere is not stupid; is to have somebody who knows you through and through, and likes you still and all; is to be able to die and not be embarrassed." And to believe in God is ... *(you finish the sentence; and write it on your friendship card. Print it in the church newsletter).*

Response

"O Rejoice in the Lord Always" (by John F. Wilson; tune: "Michael, Row the Boat Ashore," in *Folk Encounter*, Hope Publishing Company. See Appendix I for address).

Celebrating The Word

Message with the Children of All Ages

Contrast the people's responses between Jesus and John. Bring in a cartoon of Snoopy dancing. To Snoopy, "dancing is the only pure art form." Jesus, too, knew how to dance to life. If some of your congregation are "anti-dancers," offer this definition of Simeon Stylites, writing in the *Christian Century*, April 27, 1967: "By dancing, I mean the feeling of spiritual joy which tells us that here is something too big and lively to permit us to be content with a sedate walk, a joy which needs some rhythm to make it."

Response

"The Lord of the Dance" (American Shaker melody, Sydney Carter, 1963). Ask the teenagers to lead the congregation; and use a variety of musical instruments.

Reading from the Newer Covenant

Have Jesus and John and a group of people. The people, with sarcasm, speak verse 17. Jesus responds to their griping. Jesus then prays to the Father. Have Jesus then walk out in the midst of the people to offer the invitation found in verses 28-30. Ask if anyone has any response to the invitation.

Proclamation of the Good News

Consider the theme: "Learning to Dance." One translation of Psalm 25 reads, "Worship the Eternal in festive attire." Someone said to a friend, "Take your mind out and dance on it. It is getting all caked up."

Response

(Choir) "Ye Followers of the Lamb" (arr. Ferguson; Shaker Tune).

Celebrating Our Gifts

Stewardship Challenge

For the super-brave, ask your people to dance down the aisles to place their money in the offering plates on the communion table. For the less risky, use this remark by a Chicago teenager to the question, "What does it mean to be Christ-like?" "We should dance in the midst of absurdity." The world, in many ways, does seem absurd; but so what, it always has, as for example, when people stoned the prophets, crucified the finest man who ever lived, burned the martyrs, and still do.

Charge to the Congregation

Where do we look for people dancing to life today? Look around this week for the "dancers" and write down what you discover. Are you one of the dancers? If not, what's keeping you from dancing to life?

Celebrating Our Departure

Benediction

You are dismissed to dance with Jesus; for, as Jerome Murphy has said, "If we leave it to the Spirit, there will be nothing left in the church but Jesus and dancing."

Response

Chorus only, "Lord of the Dance." Sing as you leave the sanctuary.

Meditation

Once again, from the lips, so to speak, of Snoopy, "To those of us with real understanding, dancing is the only pure art form." And, "feeling groovy!"

Music Possibilities In Addition To Those Already Suggested

Music for Preparation: Medley of Holy Spirit hymns or "Solemn Prelude," T. Tertius Noble.

Hymn of Praise: "Sing Praise to God, Who Reigns Above," *Bohemian Brethren Hymnal*, 1566; trans. by Frances E. Cox, 1864; alt.

Response to the Proclamation: (Choir) "Awake My Heart," Jane Marshall.

Offertory: "O God, Thou Great God," Karg-Elert.

Hymn of Commitment: "Rejoice, O Pure in Heart," Edward H. Plumptre, 1865; alt. Refrain added in 1883.

Music for Dismissal: Medley of dance tunes or "Postlude," Green.

The Season Of The Holy Spirit

Proper 10, Pentecost 8, Ordinary Time 15

(Sunday between July 10 - 16, inclusive)

Liturgical Color: Green

Gospel: Matthew 13:1-9, 18-23

Theme: *Parable of the Soils.* "Praise is similar to a plow set to go deeply into the soil of believers' hearts. It lets the glory of God into the details of daily living" (C. M. Hanson, slightly revised).

Celebrating The Presence Of God

(Plan ahead to hand out a package of seeds to every person or every family that comes to worship today. Give no explanation for the seeds at this time.)

Invitation to the Celebration

Welcome to God's world. On behalf of all of those who decided not to worship today, we celebrate the Good News, as a body, family, community of persons, called by God, sustained by God, perfected by God, in order to allow the Spirit of God to energize us, to allow the lives of each other to strengthen us, to let the rest of the world know who we are, whose we are, what we do, where we go, in the name of the risen Christ. What a joy!

P: Our help is in the Name of the Lord, the good gardener,
M: Who provided the proper soil in which to grow healthy lives.
P: Praise the Lord for the right nutrients.
M: The Lord's Name be praised, as the gardener who grows healthy lives.

Hymn of Praise

"As Trees from Tiny Seeds Can Grow" (Jane Parker Huber, 1981; Henry K. Oliver, 1832).

Prayer of Praise

Ask, in advance, one of the laypeople who works in the garden to offer the prayer. Remind him/her that this prayer is to focus on the Master Gardener.

Response

"Alleluia, Alleluia! Give Thanks" (Donald Fishel, 1973; arr. Betty Pulkingham and Donald Fishel, 1979). Sing the chorus and the first stanza only. Sing it several times if unknown; ask the young people to lead it.

Celebrating The Act Of Forgiveness

The Act of Confession

Scott Peck has said that sin is anything that stands in the way of our own or another person's growth. How do we see ourself doing that in our home, community, school, job, and so forth? *(Give two minutes of silence; ask the people to write down their responses.)* What are we willing to do about our whacking away at another's seed? *(Follow this with another two minutes of silence.)*

Response
Sing once again, "As Trees from Tiny Seeds Can Grow." Ask if any see themselves differently in light of their confession. Perhaps several would be willing to share their insights. If there is no response, perhaps you, the pastor, would be willing to share one of yours.

The Assurance of Pardon
How do you suppose our lives, and the lives of those around us, would be different if we nurtured the soil of each other's lives? Do you see some specific ways this week that we can make that happen? Write down your specific decisions about how you will be nurturers, rather than complainers. Anyone willing to share?

Response
"Let There Be Peace On Earth" (words and music by Sy Miller and Jill Jackson, copyright by Jan-lee Music, found in *Singing the Lord's Song*, published by Discipleship Resources, United Methodist Church. See Appendix I for address). Change the word "peace" to "growth," and the word "brother" to "neighbor"

Celebrating The Word

Message with the Children of All Ages
Have a master gardener present the message around the text. Perhaps he/she could bring a piece of garden which shows growth in good soil, and death in nonproductive soil. Have them suggest ways to nurture the seeds so they produce well. Ask the same question to those who chose to remain in their seats.

Response
"Help Us Accept Each Other" (John Ness Beck, copyright by Agape, Hope Publishing Company. See Appendix I for address).

Reading from the Newer Covenant
While the children remain, let them serve as the crowd that gathered around Jesus. Have "Jesus" recite, dramatically, only Matthew 13:1-9. After a few moments' pause, have several of the children, warned in advance, ask "why in the world he needed to speak to them in parables." "Jesus" can tell them, and present the last part of the text.

Proclamation of the Good News
If you have a background working with chickens, you may want to compare the four soils with the four kinds of chickens found in every chicken house: the pullets, who are getting ready to lay; the molters who have laid and are now resting and may lay again someday; the cluckers, who go around pretending they have laid, and who may sit on eggs laid by another chicken; and the layers, who must produce for all the others if the farmer is to make a profit. You can readily see how members of the congregation fit into each category.

Response
"God, Give Us Eyes and Hearts to See" (Jane Parker Huber, from *Joy in Singing*. See Appendix I for address).

Celebrating Our Gifts

Stewardship Challenge
How will we take care of the earth, and each of us on it, this week? What will you do with your seeds, both literally and figuratively speaking? One idea to consider: Each time you go for a walk, take a

plastic sack and collect recyclables; you may be surprised to discover how many spread garbage on our living room.

Charge to the Congregation

Meditation: Rod McKuen has said, "I like people with flowers, because they're trying; they haven't given up. People with flowers are always going someplace, to worship, to weddings, to graveyards, home, to attempt to make their empty lives [and I add, their full lives] as full as blossoms."

Meditation

God opens up every day as a flower for us. Yes, God does!

Music Possibilities In Addition To Those Already Suggested

Music for Preparation: Medley of growing or gardening hymns or "O Day of Rest and Gladness," Christopher Wordsworth, 1862.

Hymn of Praise: "O Day of Rest and Gladness," Christopher Wordsworth, 1862.

Reading of the Psalm: Instead of reading the Psalm, find a musical version for the choir and/or the congregation to sing.

Offertory: "Take My Life, and Let It Be Consecrated," Frances Ridley Havergal, 1874. Note again, the hymn does not say, "Take My Life and Let It Be."

Hymn of Praise: "What Signs Has God Revealed to Us?" Jane Parker Huber, from *Joy in Singing*.

Music for Dismissal: "Johnny Appleseed."

The Season Of The Holy Spirit

Proper 11, Pentecost 9, Ordinary Time 16

(Sunday between July 17 - 23, inclusive)

Liturgical Color: Green

Gospel: Matthew 13:24-30, 36-43

Theme: *Parable of the Wheat and the Weeds.* Do we think of ourselves as wheat or weeds, or some of each? How do we plan to get the weeds out of our lives; or do we like living in the weeds?

Celebrating The Presence Of God

Invitation to the Celebration

In the Name of the Eternal Gardener, welcome to the world of wheat and weeds. Following the creation, God pronounced the world "very good," which means, "fit for the purpose for which it was intended." We rejoice in our creation. Thank you, Lord, for putting us here, where you work with us, on us, within us, and through us, to eliminate the weeds in our own lives, and in the life of your church. Yes, thank you, even though we do not always appreciate your gardening methods.

P: God, our Creator and Liberator, has called us, invited us, to worship.

M: We have come — some of us joyfully and expectantly; some of us, dragging our heels; some of us, because we had nothing else to do; some of us, to see our friends; some of us, to hear the Good News; and for a myriad of other reasons.

P: I look and listen for God, and invite you to do the same, in what we do here and now.

M: We seek an invasion of God's Spirit to bring a new dimension to our understanding of wheat and weeds; and to shake us out of our judgmental apathy.

Response

"Lord, We Praise You" (words and music by Otis Skillings, Lillenas Publishing Company, found in *Let the People Sing*, Hope Publishing Company. See Appendix I for address).

Prayer of Praise

Almighty God, make this act of worship an event in our lives. Grant that it shall be an experience that cleanses us at the very center of our being, freshening the springs of life, probing the hidden depths of our hearts, searching out our secret sins, and purifying our aims and ambitions. As we stay here, singing, praying, listening, let your hand shape our lives, let Christ your Son claim us anew for himself, and let the Holy Spirit revive and empower us.

Hymn of Praise

"Immortal, Invisible, God Only Wise" (Welsh Folk Melody; Walter Chalmers Smith, 1867; alt. 1987).

Celebrating The Act Of Forgiveness

The Act of Confession

(Invite the people to take out paper and pencil. Give them time.) Now, I invite you to write down the names of all the people who you wish would confess their sins. You can begin the list in worship, and

complete it sometime this year. *(Two minutes of silence.)* Now, after each name, write down the sins that you wish they would confess. *(Two minutes of silence.)* Compare yourself with the people whose names you've listed. Have you decided which *ones* are the weeds, and which *one* is the wheat? *(Silent prayer of confession.)*

Response
Churches and church members that are closed systems are so insecure and frightened that they believe their survival depends on judging and destroying everyone that differs from them, or does not support them. So, I invite us to respond with "Have Mercy on Us, Living Lord" (Fred R. Anderson, 1986; Hal H. Hopson, 1983).

The Assurance of Pardon
Jesus said to let the weeds and wheat grow together; because no one can tell who's in and who's out of the Kingdom. To attempt to decide is to play God. None of us is wise enough to do that.

Response
This week, also, use "Let There Be Peace On Earth." This time, change "peace" to "truth." Change the word "brother" to "neighbor."

Celebrating The Word

Message with the Children of All Ages
Again, put your master gardener to work. Point out the difference between a garden, in which we get rid of the weeds on a regular basis, and the parable. Draw out of them how they treat those who are different from them.

Response
"Help Us Accept Each Other" (John Ness Beck).

Reading from the Newer Covenant
Ask the children to remain, and have your actor tell the parable in his/her own language. Dismiss the children, and have your actor interpret the text, as did Jesus.

Proclamation of the Good News
We often focus on the results, described in the last few verses of the text. Instead, put the emphasis on the tremendous opportunities that we, Christians, have to salt the earth, and to light the world.

Response
"We Are a New Creation" (Henry Smart, c. 1835; Jane Parker Huber, 1981, from *Joy in Singing*. See Appendix I for address).

Celebrating Our Gifts

Stewardship Challenge
Do we give with no strings attached? If we give with strings attached, we are still in the weeds, attempting to bribe someone.

Dedication Prayer
Take our pocketbooks, Lord, and put them to death for our sake, and bring them to life for your sake.

Charge to the Congregation

Are we willing to accept people where and as they are without our making condemnatory decisions about their faith? Are we willing to recognize that, in our own personal lives, the wheat and weeds grow together? We need to let God make the final decision, without our help. We need to make the decision to share the Good News with the millions of opportunities we have in a lifetime, in our lifetime.

Meditation

"Of what use is eternity to a person who doesn't know how to spend the next half-hour, except in making value-judgments about others?" (WHK).

Music Possibilities In Addition To Those Already Suggested

Music for Preparation: Medley of growing or gardening hymns or "Preludium," Nicholas Lemmens.

Hymn of Praise: "Crown Him (God) with Many Crowns," Stanzas 1, 2, 4, Matthew Bridges, 1851; alt., 1972. Stanza 3, Godfrey Thring, 1874.

Response to the Prayer of Praise: (Choir) "Savior, Blessed Savior," Thomas Morley.

Response to the Assurance of Pardon: (Youth or adult choir) "God is Love," Graham George.

Offertory: Organ Voluntary "Siciliano," J. S. Bach.

Hymn of Commitment: "We Give Thee But Thine Own," William Walsham How, 1858.

Music for Dismissal: In the hymnbook, look for hymns related to today's scripture.

The Season Of The Holy Spirit

Proper 12, Pentecost 10, Ordinary Time 17

(Sunday between July 24 - 30, inclusive)

Liturgical Color: Green

Gospel: Matthew 13:31-33, 44-52

Theme: *Parables of the Mustard Seed, the Yeast, Hidden Treasure, Pearl of Great Price, the Fishing Net.* "If suddenly we lost everything, and had one minute to decide what is most important to us, what would we choose?" (WHK).

Celebrating The Presence Of God

Invitation to the Celebration

In the Name of the Master-teller of parables, welcome to worship. Is anyone joyful? *(Wait for a response; if no one responds to the first asking, ask again, at least until a few respond.)* Is anyone victorious? *(Same procedure.)* Is anyone hilarious? *(Same procedure.)* We live on the A.D., not the B.C., side of the resurrection. We already know that the battle is won. Christ has defeated sin, death, the grave. We will have sad moments; we need not lead sad lives. So, I invite us to celebrate the presence of the risen, living God with our heart, mind, will. And all the people say *(offer your favorite affirmation)*.

Response

"Blessed Be the Name" (Ralph E. Hudson, found in *Folk Encounter*, Hope Publishing Company). Sing as a round: the children one group; the young people a second group; adults a third group; and those over 65 a fourth group.

P: The call of God in Christ is the call to life, abundant, eternal life.
M: It is the call to live with love, hope, and with a deep sense of our own worth.
P: I invite us to respond in the name of Christ, and live as his people.
M: We celebrate the life he has given us, and rejoice in its unlimited possibilities.

Response

Sing "Blessed Be the Name," again as a round. This time, change the designated groups to fit your congregation.

Prayer of Praise

Loving and merciful God, who has created within our restless hearts a longing for you, continue to come to us with your grace that reconciles; enlighten our minds with your truth that disturbs; invade our inmost being with power that makes new; and give to our lives that peace which comes from following you, no matter how far behind we may follow.

Hymn of Praise

"O God, in a Mysterious Way" (*Scottish Psalter*, 1615; William Cowper, 1774; alt.; arr. Thomas Ravenscroft, 1621).

Celebrating The Act Of Forgiveness

The Act of Confession

Do we bring our sin or our sins for confession? If we bring our sins, which ones do we mention; which do we leave out? Today, I invite us to bring our sin which once again Genesis 3 defines as "the attempt to justify our feelings, thoughts, words, actions"; which the New Testament defines as not only "missing the mark, but shooting at the wrong target"; which Sigmund Freud, in his "Pleasure Principle," defines as "I want what I want when I want it, and never mind the consequences." I invite us to confess our sin before we confess our sins. *(Three minutes of silence. Then, invite them to pray the printed prayer of confession, in unison, saying, "Pray only the part of the prayer which you want forgiven; using the following prayer as an introduction, tailor the prayer to fit your situation.")*

Prayer of Confession

We share a common humanity, but it is so hard to get down to it. We have so many facades, so many pretensions, so many social games to play. We have difficulty understanding our own fears, our own needs, our own motivations. No wonder we are so often cut off from our best self and each other. Lord, we pray for the grace to get in touch with ourselves, and at the same time, to reach out to each other. Help us to discover the sense of community necessary to renew your world.

Response

"In This Quiet Moment" (words and music by Larry Mayfield, copyright by Word Music, found in *Let the People Sing*, Hope Publishing Company. See Appendix I for address).

The Assurance of Pardon

The most important fact that we need to know, and we've heard it a million times, is that God already has forgiven our sin and our sins. If not so, then God's grace is a lie. But, it's not a lie; it is, literally, the gospel truth, when we accept it and when we do not.

Response

"Thank You, Thank You" (Richard Avery and Don Marsh, Hope Publishing Company. See Appendix I for address. Follow the directions they suggest for singing).

Celebrating The Word

Message with the Children of All Ages

Remind the children what the word "parable" means. Pick one of the parables and illustrate it; as, for example, a mustard seed, a bowl of flour and yeast. Or, ahead of time, hide something in the chancel; or use your imagination.

Reading from the Newer Covenant

Have the children remain, and focus on parables that you did not include in the children's message.

Proclamation of the Good News

Incorporate this idea: Some pastors handle relationships with the congregation, and some longtime members of the congregation operate, this way: "Here is something to be done; will you do it, and do it the way we want you to do it?" Obviously, the more productive way is this: "What would you find joy, even fun, in doing that would express your inner nature, and at the same time, fill a need in your life, as well as in the life of the whole church?"

Celebrating Our Gifts

Stewardship Challenge

"I like my way of doing things better than your way of not doing them; I like my way of accomplishing something better than your way of criticizing me when I accomplish it" (WHK).

Dedication Prayer

God, we like to think that our pennies and dollars are sufficient, without ourselves. Do not let us get away with that kind of thinking. Take all of us, and all we have, in committed obedience to you.

Celebrating Our Departure

Charge to the Congregation

God has planted in our hearts, minds, wills, spirits, great ideas, insights waiting to be released. God inspires us to respond; God waits for our response. In the Spirit of the living God, what are we willing to discover about ourselves, and share with others, this coming week?

Meditation

"You were born with all that you need to win at life; you were born to win" (author unknown).

Music Possibilities In Addition To Those Already Suggested

Music for Preparation: Medley of music focusing on the Parables listed or "If Thou But Suffer God to Guide Thee," Vetter.

Hymn of Praise: "When Morning Gilds the Skies," German Hymn, eighteenth century; Edward Caswall, trans., 1854, 1858; alt.

Response to the Act of Forgiveness: (Choir and/or congregation) "Where Cross the Crowded Ways of Life," Frank Mason North, 1903; alt., 1972.

Response to the Newer Covenant: "Come, Thou Fount of Every Blessing," Robert Robinson, 1758.

Offertory: "If Thou But Suffer God to Guide Thee," Newmark.

Hymn of Dedication: "Take Thou Our Minds, Dear Lord," William H. Foulkes; stanzas 1-3, 1918; stanza 4, 1920 or "Take My Life, and Let It Be Consecrated," Frances Ridley Havergal, 1874.

Music for Dismissal: Medley of music focusing on the Parables listed or "If Thou But Suffer God to Guide Thee," J. S. Bach.

The Season Of The Holy Spirit

Proper 13, Pentecost 11, Ordinary Time 18

(Sunday between July 31 - August 6, inclusive)

Liturgical Color: Green

Gospel: Matthew 14:13-21

Theme: *Feeding the Five Thousand.* "Bread for myself is a material question; but bread for my neighbor is a spiritual question" (Nicolas Berdyaev).

Celebrating The Presence Of God

Invitation to the Celebration

Welcome in the Name of God, the Gift-giver. God rains gifts, innumerable gifts upon us. *(Invite the people to name a few. You may want to ask several in advance to be ready to respond.)* In light of these gifts, the important ones given freely to us, do you come today with expectation and excitement, or with wait-and-see drudgery? God is ready for us; are we ready for God? Ready or not, God is here!

P: You have heard that God is dead; I say to you, God is living and is here.
M: Praise be to the living God!
P: God is here. Do you *hear* God?
M: We hear God in the word, both spoken and sung: in Bible and hymns, in newspaper and popular songs, in laughter and shouts of joy, in weeping and sobs of anguish.
P: God is here. Do you *see* God?
M: We see God in sacrament and symbol: in Cross and table, in air and water, in bread and cup, in paintings and drawings, in sculpture and architecture, in drama and dance.
P: God is here. Do you *feel* God?
M: We feel God through the Holy Spirit: in fellowship around the table; in support and challenge from Scripture; in common unity of purpose and mission, in persons who love the unlovely, who love their enemies, who love those who persecute them, who love us ...
P: I invite us to celebrate with this God who is living and who is present with us.

Hymn of Praise

"God Created Heaven and Earth" (Taiwanese Hymn, Pi-po melody; trans. Boris and Clare Anderson, 1981; harm. I-to Loh, 1963; rev. 1982).

Prayer of Praise

Almighty God, we rejoice that we can come to One who is more concerned for our welfare, and others' welfare, than we are; more eager to give than we are to receive. We're grateful that we need not bully or cajole you. It is our capacity to take that which needs enlarging, our ambition to live off of you that which needs quickening. So we pray that today's encounter with the Christ may rebuke our piecemeal, hand-to-mouth, shoddy living and set us hungering for the life that is life indeed (source lost; slightly revised).

Response

"The Good News in Five Senses" (Avery and Marsh, from *The Second Avery and Marsh Songbook*, published by Hope Publishing Company. See Appendix I for address).

Celebrating The Act Of Forgiveness

The Act of Confession

Before this confession, read *Peacemaking: On Dusting the Wind* by David P. Young. He suggests, and rightfully so, that many of us sleep through life. We ignore justice issues, unless we want justice for ourselves. We passively accept military spending, corrupt business practices, world hunger. We close our eyes; we sleep our way through life. Develop the following litany to suit your situation. Have someone, or several someones, speak the part, "I was hungry." These persons can remain where they are seated. Then the pastor or layperson will respond with excuses. For example, first person says, "I was hungry" and someone says, "Don't worry; be happy." Or "I'm going out to dinner with my family." Or "God helps those who help themselves." Or "Jesus said that the poor are always with us." Or "You should get a job." You get the idea, I'm sure. After the litany, let the people sit in silence for four minutes, or at least until they feel uncomfortable, the most unfavorite position for many church members.

Response

"Lord, Have Mercy" (harm. Richard Proulx, 1984; found in *The Presbyterian Hymnal*).

The Assurance of Pardon

Invite the people to take out paper and pencil; I have an exam for you. Here it is: 1) I will not _____ my neighbor anymore; instead, I will _____. 2) I will not _____ to my enemy who is _____. Instead, I will _____. 3) I will not limit myself to _____ as I have done in the past; instead, I will _____. 4) I will not prejudge or limit my neighbor in this way _____ as I have done in the past; instead, I will _____.

Response

"Into My Heart" (words and music by Harry D. Clarke, from *Let the People Sing*, Hope Publishing Company).

Celebrating The Word

Message with the Children of All Ages

Ask if any have ever been hungry, even for a while. What was that like? Let them know that, every day, 40,000 children die from lack of food and pure water. Find out if they think that they can do anything about it. Offer one or two ideas.

Reading from the Newer Covenant

Invite the people to stand for the Gospel, a tradition which we need to recapture. The congregation represents the crowd. Ask them to mill around. Appoint, ahead of time, a disciple who will speak the words in the text. Jesus and the disciples get into a discussion about lunch. At the proper time, instead of giving bread to the people, make certain that the disciples reach out to touch each member present. Be careful about the touch; it must be nurturing, and respectful of each individual.

Proclamation of the Good News

Incorporate this idea about identifying with the hungry: For one week, or one day, live on the following: Breakfast, one glass of water; one cup of coffee or cocoa; one slice of toast with margarine. Lunch: One peanut butter and jelly sandwich, one glass of Kool-Aid. Dinner: One helping of collard greens and rice and one cup of tea; or one bowl of chili con carne, one cup of tea or one glass of Kool-Aid; or one helping of macaroni and cheese, one cup of tea. If this fits your thinking, say that you must talk about hunger because it's part of Scripture; "but I come with many tears, and few, if any, answers; with much frustration and little solutions."

Celebrating Our Gifts

Stewardship Challenge
Before receiving the offering, hand around a tea bag and a spoon of rice to represent what two-thirds of the world eats each day.

Dedication Prayer
We offer these gifts, and the gift of our lives, God, to and for a world that's dying to hear the Good News from someone.

Celebrating Our Departure

Charge to the Congregation
The setting is a congregational meeting. You hear reports on your charitable projects and learn, in the end, that your giving has done nothing to reverse the slide into more degradation and poverty. Finally, you hear the chairman saying, "Have we a second to the motion that we sell our building and entire grounds and use the proceeds as a first step in helping the poor?" How would you respond?

Meditation
"The only people who are sick and tired of hearing about hunger are those who are well fed" (WHK).

Music Possibilities In Addition To Those Already Suggested

Music for Preparation: Medley of hunger music or "Study on B. A. C. H.," Walter Piston.

Hymn of Praise: "O Worship the King, All Glorious Above," based on Psalm 104, Robert Grant, 1833; alt.

Response to the Newer Covenant: (Choir) "He Comes to Us," Jane Marshall, text by Albert Schweitzer.

Offertory: "Reverie," by Vierne.

Hymn of Dedication: "Guide Me, O Thou Great Jehovah," William Williams, 1745. Stanza 1, Peter Williams, trans. 1771; stanzas 2 and 3, William or John Williams, trans. c. 1772; or "External God, Whose Power Upholds," Henry Hallam Tweedy, 1929; alt., 1972.

Music for Dismissal: Popular song, "We Are the World," or "O Love That Will Not Let Me Go," George Matheson, 1882.

The Season Of The Holy Spirit

Proper 14, Pentecost 12, Ordinary Time 19

(Sunday between August 7 - 13, inclusive)

Liturgical Color: Green

Gospel: Matthew 14:22-33

Theme: *Jesus Walking on Water; Peter Sinking into Water.* "What's your latest experience of walking on, or sinking into, water?" (WHK).

Celebrating The Presence Of God

Invitation to the Celebration

In the Name of the living Christ, we come to worship, not as passive spectators, but as active participants. We participate through prayer, expectancy, listening, alertness, disagreeing, anticipation, challenging, giving, loving, confronting. This means getting out of the boat into the water. Are you ready for a God-event in your life, in the church's life? Ready or not, we plunge ahead!

P: Please repeat after me:
1. We are here!
2. We are ready!
3. We know that God is here!
4. We know that God is ready for us!

And, all the people said, *(your favorite one-word celebration).*

(If this is awkward the first time, practice it several times. And, it's okay not to do it perfectly. The goal is to free the people to respond with enthusiasm and energy. In a sense, you, the pastor, are the cheerleader to help make this happen.)

Response/Prayer of Praise

(Printed) Holy and Loving God, make this act of worship a life-giving event in our lives. Grant that your Spirit will cleanse us at the center of our being; freshening the springs of life; probing the hidden depths of our hearts; searching our secret brokenness, alienation, self-justifications; teaching us about stepping out of boats into water; and purifying our aims and ambitions. May Christ claim us anew, and the Holy Spirit receive and empower us, in the name of the Christ.

Response to the Prayer

Chorus only, "The Lord of the Dance" (by Sydney Carter).

Celebrating The Act Of Forgiveness

The Act of Confession

Sigmund Freud defined sin, probably without realizing he had done so. He called it the "Pleasure Principle." Here it is: "I want what I want when I want it — and never mind the consequences." It's time to stop debating the "worst" sins, which, of course, are the ones that you commit; and begin to examine our own SIN, namely, of justifying our thoughts, feelings, words, behaviors — and never mind the consequences. *(Give the people four full minutes of silence to consider these remarks; ask them to write down their responses. After the four minutes, ask if anyone would take the risk of getting out of the boat and sharing. Wait; never rush through the confession and forgiveness.)*

The Assurance of Pardon

Forgiveness and reconciliation begin with the confession of our own "I want what I want," not somebody else's, though we do enjoy confessing other people's sinking into the sea. So, because confession begins within us, not outside of us, I invite us to sing a response that we sang during Epiphany: "A New Creature" (words and music by John F. Wilson, Hope Publishing Company. See Appendix I for address).

Celebrating The Word

Message with the Children of All Ages

How many of you have walked on water for one minute? Thirty seconds? Twenty seconds? One second? Doesn't seem possible, does it, unless David Copperfield is around. *(Show the children that taking risks is something they can do, rather than just going along with the crowd.)* Perhaps you can apply this example to your own situation: A high school girl moved to town. Her clothes were delayed in shipment. After wearing her one dress to school the first day, she returned home and insisted that her parents provide her with a new wardrobe. "Your clothes will arrive in a day or so," her mother consoled her. But the girl exclaimed, "I'd rather die than go to school wearing the same dress tomorrow. What would everyone think? How can I possibly face everyone at school?" She preferred the boat to the water. You, too?

Reading from the Newer Covenant

Though you may not simulate a boat and a lake, do simulate the conversation between Jesus and Peter, with plenty of emotion.

Proclamation of the Good News

Security means enjoying, or not enjoying, our slavery in Egypt; faith refers to our willingness to take risks. What's our choice: Boat or water?

Celebrating Our Gifts

Stewardship Challenge

"Make mine the same," may suffice at the cocktail lounge, but never when we are in the business of changing the world. Raymond B. Fosdick has said, "It is always through those who are unafraid to be different that advance comes to humanity."

Dedication Prayer

"Grant, O Lord, that what we have said with our lips, we may believe in our hearts; and that what we believe in our hearts, we may practice in our lives."

Celebrating Our Departure

Charge to the Congregation

It is relatively easy to accept the vows of church membership, and pay one's weekly pledge for its support; it is rather comfortable to sit in one's pew on Sunday morning, and listen to music which inspires and a sermon which reassures; it gives one a sense of social respectability to point to one's church membership as an evidence of good character and good citizenship. And it is an entirely different matter to keep the Lord's Day holy in the midst of a secular society; to take a stand for justice in the face of the respectable people of the church and community; to maintain a family time for study and prayer in these days of disorganization. So, how will we find ways to get out of the boat into the water?

Response

Male soloist to sing "Who Will Answer?" recorded by Ed Ames; Sunbury Music, Inc., 436 Maple Ave., Westbury, Long Island, N.Y. to order the music.

Meditation

"One of the smallest packages we ever saw was a man (could also be a woman) wrapped up wholly in himself (herself)" (author unknown). So, what does a large package resemble? You?

Music Possibilities In Addition To Those Already Suggested

Music for Preparation: "God of Grace and God of Glory," Harry Emerson Fosdick.

Hymn of Praise: "Rejoice, O Pure in Heart," Edward H. Plumptre, 1865; alt. refrain added, 1883.

Response to the Confession: "Guide Me, O Thou Great Jehovah," William Williams, 1745.

Response to the Assurance: "A Mighty Fortress Is Our God," Martin Luther, 1592; trans., Frederick H. Hedge, 1854; alt., 1972.

Response to the Newer Covenant: "Praise to the Lord," Duke Street; or "Bread of Life," Christiansen.

Offertory: "Put on the Whole Armor of God," Humphreys; or "He Shall Feed His Flock," Handel.

Hymn of Commitment: "O God of All the Years of Life," Jane Parker Huber (from *Joy in Singing*. See Appendix I for address).

Response to the Benediction: Lively and energetic Threefold Amen.

Music for Dismissal: "A Mighty Fortress Is Our God," Martin Luther.

The Season Of The Holy Spirit

Proper 15, Pentecost 13, Ordinary Time 20

(Sunday between August 14 - 20, inclusive)

Liturgical Color: Green

Gospel: Matthew 15:(10-20) 21-28

Theme: *That Which Defiles; Faith of the Canaanite Woman.* In light of the Canaanite woman's perseverance, have you ever considered your own "nuisance value"? If not, this is the time to consider it (WHK).

Remembering Whose We Are

Invitation to the Celebration
   I invite us to celebrate the Presence and Power of the Living God, who is revealed as Father/Mother — Creator, as Son/Child — Redeemer, as Fire/Wind — Empowerer. We hear and experience and know of God in many ways. Throughout this worship, you will have many opportunities to hear, experience, know of God in those ways. You are invited to respond at any time.
P: The world which God loves needs a sense of community and family.
M: God has called the church (you and me) into being, has given it (you and me) the Holy Spirit, and continues to offer it (you and me) the Spirit's Presence and Power.
P: God's community and family begin here.
M: God's community and family begin with us. God help us to live our uniqueness in You.

Response
   Chorus only, "We Are the Church" (Avery and Marsh, Hope Publishing Company. See Appendix I for address).

Prayer of Praise
   God, we have carried with us into this house of worship our cares, anxieties, and fears. Help us to lift them into your presence, and to see them against the spacious background of your good purpose. Grant us a sense of proportion that we may see our temporary worries against your permanent love, and our selfish fears against your eternal righteousness. And if we have come today without a care in the world, grant that we shall offer our joy and serenity as a service to you and our fellow worshipers. If we are enjoying vigorous health, joyful family relationships, the precious boon of a good conscience, and a quiet mind, help us to make these things a starting place for new endeavors and a deeper commitment. So be it!

Hymn of Praise
   "Of the Father's Love Begotten" (Plainsong, Mode V. Aurelius Clemens Prudentius, 348-413; trans. John Mason Neale, 1854, and Henry Williams Baker, 1849; harm. C. Winfred Douglas, 1940). Consider using this as hymn of the month.

Facing Up To Ourselves

Introduction to Our Brokenness
A physician said to Charles L. Allen, author of *The Touch of the Master's Hand*, that half of his patients needed neither a drug nor an operation. They needed the forgiveness of God. Jesus was the greatest physician of all time; he saw this need in us. So, instead of saying, "Your paralysis be healed," he said instead, "Your sins be forgiven." Here is an opportunity to have our sins forgiven. Are you interested? If so, I invite you to pray this prayer: *(Pray either silently or in unison, while the organist/pianist plays a confessional hymn quietly.)* Lord, I'm uptight about so much these days. I wash my hands, my face, my body, because I want to be clean. But I'm still uptight and I want to be free. Free to live and love and rejoice. So, Lord, make my life holy. Purify the obscenities that disturb me and the people around me. Open us to each other; intensify relationships, create conversations. Help us to talk more to one another, do more, cry and laugh more, care more. Grant that we live full lives with our senses open, to complete our lives with purpose in what we do, freed of the weight of impatience. I want to be what you intend for me. Sanctify the sexes, the ages, relationships, each other. Give us awe and wonder. Give us freedom in the Christ who loves us all as brothers and sisters, and who does everything we allow him to do, and more, to make us holy and glad (source lost, slightly revised). *(Silent meditation for two minutes.)*

Invitation to Our Acceptance
We pray, "No longer remembering our sin and sins, O Lord," then we keep remembering them, recalling them, savoring them, letting them rummage around in our head. Intellectually, we believe that the past is forgiven; by your Spirit, integrate that belief into our guts (emotions, if you prefer).

Prayer of Acceptance
We thank you, God, for your forgiveness for our impatience, and for our entrance into your presence. Because of our thankfulness, grant that others may also have this same experience, through Jesus the Christ, who makes new life possible.

Response
"You Are the Lord, Giver of Mercy" *(sing it three times)*.

Looking Out To Others

Message with the Children of All Ages
Ask if they know what the words "persistence" or "perseverance" mean. You may want to use this *Peanuts* cartoon: Lucy is looking out of the window on a bitter cold, snowy day. She says, "He's so persistent, I'll say that for him. He just never gives up. Of course, I'm not so sure if that's always a good way to be ... Oh, oh, it looks like he's giving up ... He is! He's coming in! I'd better open the door for him ... He may need help ..." She opens the door and shivers. In comes Charlie Brown, dressed as warmly as possible. His kite string and kite are frozen solid. Charlie says, "You were right ... it's too cold out to fly a kite."

Response
Even though we may have difficulty understanding how God rewards us, we are called to respond out of thanksgiving for what we have received. So, let's sing the chorus only to "O Let's Get On" (words and music by Richard Avery and Don Marsh, *Folk Encounter*, Hope Publishing Company. See Appendix I for address).

Reading from the Newer Covenant

The text of Jesus' encounter with the Canaanite woman provides a powerful encounter of perseverance. The drama includes Jesus, the woman, and several of the disciples. If you have no drama group, as such, put it in dialogue form. Practice with the readers.

Proclamation of the Good News

Simeon Stylites, writing in *The Christian Century* years ago, titled his article "How to be Tiresome." The woman had a high "nuisance value." Contrast her results with this which appeared in the *Milwaukee Journal* (August 20, 1958). A suburb had denied the request of a Baptist congregation for a rezoning ordinance so it could build a new church building. Their attorneys assured the court that the church would do no damage to the community. (You may want to play with that for a while.) The brief read, "Evidence has been presented that the church would not affect the safety, health, or public morals of Bayside." Really now! Really?

Response

Meditational prayer, "Lord, I Have Time" (from *Prayers* by Michael Quoist, published by Sheed and Ward, New York. Library of Congress Catalog Card Number 63-17141).

Remembering Our Reason For Being The Church

Stewardship Challenge

Around the world for a pound of honey. To honeybees a pound of honey is worth traveling a distance equivalent to going around the world, not once, but three times. It is estimated that the average flight of a bee is about one mile to and from a flower, about 80,000 flights being necessary for one pound of honey. How's that for perseverance? And how does our perseverance stack up with the honeybee and the Canaanite woman?

Acting On Our Faith

Charge to the Congregation

"Nothing in the world can take the place of persistence. Talents will not! Nothing is more common than unsuccessful people with talent. Genius will not! Unrewarded genius is almost a proverb. Education will not! The world is full of educated derelicts. Persistence and determination alone are omnipotent. The slogan "press on' has solved and will always solve the problems of the human race" (from *Trained Men*).

Meditation

"Without any consecrated pesterers, a church may well go into such a spiritual coma that it has no effect on public morals ... These 'nuisances' for the sake of the Lord may be hard to take as neighbors. But they will have a high place in the Celestial City — right up there with the Shock Troops, all with Distinguished Service Medals on their chests. And I'd like to be of that number when the saints go marching in" (Simeon Stylites).

Music Possibilities In Addition To Those Already Suggested

Music for Preparation: Medley of perseverance hymns or "Reformation Symphony," Mendelssohn.

Hymn of Praise: "Lord Our God, With Praise We Come," Petter Dass, 1647-1707; trans. Peter A. Sveeggen, 1951; alt., 1972.

Response to the Prayer of Praise: (Choir) "All Glory, Praise and Majesty," J. S. Bach.

Response to the Message with the Children: "Reach Out to Your Neighbor," words and music by Roger Copeland, copyright 1971, in *A New Now*, by Hope Publishing Company.

Offertory: "O God, Thou Good God," Karg-Elert.

Hymn of Commitment: "God of Our Life, Through All the Circling Years," Hugh T. Kerr, 1916; alt., 1928, 1972.

Response to the Benediction: "Jubilate Chorus," from "Now on Land and Sea Descending," Samuel Longfellow, 1859 refrain added.

Music for Dismissal: Music on the theme of persevering faith, which is the only kind that the Bible encourages.

The Season Of The Holy Spirit

Proper 16, Pentecost 14, Ordinary Time 21

(Sunday between August 21 - 27, inclusive)

Liturgical Color: Green

Gospel: Matthew 16:13-20

Theme: *Peter's Declaration about Jesus.* What do you say and do when you hear the remark, "It doesn't matter what you believe, so long as you're sincere"?

Remembering Whose We Are

Invitation to the Celebration
   We come to worship in Christ's church, to celebrate, to declare, to affirm whose we are, who we are, what we do, where we go in the Name of the crucified, risen Lord. Welcome.
P: We continue to celebrate.
M: What? Ourselves? Others? Things? Objects? Success? Money?
P: No! We celebrate the Word made flesh.
M: Is that Word here today? If so, where? Can we see him? Hear him? Speak about him? How can worship help us find him?
P: Because celebration is a sign ... and in his signs, he is real. His presence is here!
M: Then we seek him in prayer, in the word, in our response, in our commitment, in our mission.
P: Come, Lord Jesus, we believe; help our unbelief!

Response
   "God Is! Rejoice!" (words and music by Avery and Marsh, from *Let the People Sing*, Hope Publishing Company. See Appendix I for address).

Prayer of Praise
   Center it around Peter's declaration of who Jesus was to him, and who he is to us, not some vague blur in the sky, but the unique Son of God who is Lord of lords, the one to whom every knee shall bow.

Hymn of Praise
   "God, You Spin the Whirling Planets" (Jane Parker Huber, 1978; Franz Joseph Haydn, 1797).

Facing Up To Ourselves

Introduction to Our Brokenness
   Where is your favorite hiding place from God? *(Silence for one minute.)* Anyone care to respond? Share your own. It may be your pastorate. For laypeople, it may be serving as a church officer, or a member of a committee, which does church business without seriously involving God in the decisions. It may be in becoming a "pillar of the church." *(Again, one minute of silence.)* Then offer this poem, written by Fran De Nardo, Grade 6: "I have a hiding place; it can be in a closet. Sometimes it is in the attic. Other times it is in the basement. But my favorite hiding place is in MYSELF."

Response

"I Don't Know How to Love Him" (lyrics by Tim Rice, music by Andrew Lloyd Webber, from *Jesus Christ, Superstar*, Leeds Music Corporation, MCA Music, 25 Deshon Drive, Melville, NY 11747). Ask one of your soloists to sing.

Invitation to Our Acceptance

Only God knows the extent of our dishonesty, our fear in proclaiming our declaration about who Christ is to us, our lack of obedience; for God alone has paid the supreme price for such knowledge. *(Two minutes of silence.)* Then say, "Nothing is so whole as a broken heart" (Rabbi Nachman of Bratslav). Conclude with this, or a similar prayer: O God, because we can hide nothing, including ourself, especially ourself, from you, we have confessed our cowardice and lack of obedience. We rejoice that you have forgiven us, even when we "feel" unforgiven and guilty. Remove from us the guilt which destroys our relationship with you and others, and the fear which betrays our trust in you and others. In the strong name of the Christ.

Response

(Choir) "You Are the Lord, Giver of Mercy" (any version).

Looking Out To Others

Message with the Children of All Ages

Focus on Peter. Sometimes he was "hot" and sometimes "cold" in his faith. Give some examples of Peter. Invite the children to give some examples from their lives when they made a decision and stuck by it, even when others made fun of them.

Reading from the Newer Covenant

Have the children remain while your actors dramatize Jesus' encounter with Peter.

Proclamation of the Good News

Consider this title, "Is Religion a Simple Matter of Sincerity?" Incorporate these ideas: Many of us believe in generalities when it comes to our faith; for example, "Everyone's going to the same place; even a sincere atheist goes to heaven; we're no different from other religions; God won't send everyone to hell; he/she is such a good person." Point out some differences between Christianity and other religions. Faith, however, is more than mouthing a word; more than saying "yes" to a church membership vow; more than joining the church. Faith is throwing your life in with the builders, not the destroyers; living on the growing edge of life, instead of hiding behind the bushes of security and comfort; living as though Christ is living *in* you, not *on* you, or *out there* somewhere. Add your own.

Response

"This Is the Good News" (*The Worshipbook*, 1972; based on Native American (Dakota) melody; arr. Richard D. Wetzel, b. 1935).

Remembering Our Reason For Being The Church

Stewardship Challenge

Consider the stewardship of our words. Our declaration of faith makes a difference, just as our daily speaking does. We have this idea that popular usage of words makes for correctness, as for example, "Winston tastes good, *like* ..." Or, "*who* do you trust?" used by politicians, and others who ought to know better. If it is *wrong*, it cannot be *right*, even though we all talk that way.

Acting On Our Faith

Charge to the Congregation
Live and speak as if Christ meant everything to us, everything!

Meditation
"How do we declare the name of Christ, in order to share the power of Christ, without becoming self-righteous and pompous? Take a cue from this: Our task is to show that Christ is not our possession, but that all of us, in every corner of the earth, and beyond, are his. We claim no finality or monopoly of truth for our version of a faith that came to us from the Middle East; but we claim that when anyone has met with the living Christ, there is no other Lord with whom his worship and ministry can be shared" (WHK).

Music Possibilities In Addition To Those Already Suggested

Music for Preparation: Medley of hymns which focus on God; or "Adante Tranquillo," Stickles.

Choral Introit: "You, Holy Father, We Adore," Calvin W. Laufer, 1931; alt., 1972.

Response to Our Acceptance: "Prayer of St. Francis of Assisi," Ron Nelson.

Response to the Message with the Children: "We Are Jesus' People," words and music by Shirley Whitecotton, copyright 1973, *Folk Encounter*, Hope Publishing Company. (See Appendix I for address.)

Offertory: "Berceuse," Stickles.

Hymn of Commitment: "Glorious Is Your Name, Most Holy," Ruth Elliot, 1960; alt., 1972.

Music for Dismissal: Medley of hymns which focus on the strong name of Jesus.

The Season Of The Holy Spirit

Proper 17, Pentecost 15, Ordinary Time 22

(Sunday between August 28 - September 3, inclusive)

Liturgical Color: Green

Gospel: Matthew 16:21-28

Theme: *Jesus Foretells his Death and Resurrection; The Cross and Self-denial.* Remember the posters in World War II in which Uncle Sam is pointing his finger and sternly says, "I want you"? Jesus does not demand; he invites. "I want you; and these are the conditions of my invitation."

Remembering Whose We Are

Invitation to the Celebration
    Have an alarm clock set to ring as the organist/pianist finishes the music for preparation. Then, wake up! We're here to celebrate life in the Presence/Power of God. We gather weekly (weakly?) in this sanctuary, not because God is more present here than anywhere else. We gather here to announce to each other and the world our experience of new life in Christ, our endurance in the midst of change, our enjoyments of God's presence everywhere. Worship is the celebration of God's activity in the world, all of the world, for Christ's sake.

P: Now that we're awake (we are awake, aren't we?), good morning! Who do you think you are?
M: Now that we're awake (we are awake!), good morning to you. We are the church of Jesus Christ. We have come here to remember what it means to be Christian, and to be the church in worship, so we will be the church in mission.
P: Will you be honest during this time? Will your hearts, minds, wills be open to God's truth?
M: We will be honest and open to God's truth!
P: Then we shall continue to praise God.
M: Amen. Let it be so in you and me!

Response
    Popular song: "Let it be; let it be; let it be; let it be; there will be an answer, let it be."

Prayer of Praise
    Focus on the theme that God awakens us to a new day and new opportunities, and that we, through God's Spirit, will be ready for them.

Hymn of Praise
    "God of Our Life" (Charles Henry Purday, 1860; Hugh Thompson Kerr, 1916; alt. 1928; harm. John Weaver, 1986).

Facing Up To Ourselves

Introduction to Our Brokenness
    Arthur Boers, in an article from *The Other Side* (May/June, 1989), titled "The Fullness of Christ and the Small Church," points out this sin of the church (you and me): Many want to know what they can get

out of the local congregation, so that churches are simply one more consumer commodity. Thus, worship is not a place for us to serve God and our neighbors and enemies, but a place where people expect to purchase the best: inspiring worship, which never deals with justice issues; good music which they "like"; moving sermons which comfort and never confront; and quality child care for every age. As if we could buy God ... *(Silence for two minutes, with the question, "Is this your expectation and experience?")*

Response
Soloist to sing "Both Sides Now" (words and music by Joni Mitchell, Siquomb Publishing Corporation). Or play the recording.

Invitation to Our Acceptance
(Sit down in silence for two minutes after the song.) Again, invite the people to write down their thoughts. Does the song fit their life? What does it say about their daily experiences? Offer a prayer which, while not summarizing their thoughts, may well summarize yours.
P: Christ has set us free to live responsibly.
M: The past is forgiven, every bit of it to this moment; the future is before us, every bit of it from now on.
P: I invite us to love life, and the people who share it with us.
M: We embrace life, and we live in Christ.

Response
"Lord, I Want to Be a Christian" (African-American Spiritual).

Looking Out To Others

Message with the Children of All Ages
Have you ever wanted something so badly that you think you will do anything to get it? Give examples of people who have, and then, who went to jail. Or, think of a swimmer who stays under water too long; he/she wants air more than anything. Tie this in with the second half of the Scripture.

Reading from the Newer Covenant
Have the children remain, as your actors dramatize Jesus' encounter with the disciples and Peter.

Proclamation of the Good News
Perhaps you can use this example: Following J.F.K.'s death, many people united with the church. Many of them tagged along for a short time and dropped out. After the immediate crisis, one family stopped participating, but sent a $500 check to "pay their way." The pastor asked the secretary to return it, with this note, "We want you, not just your money." Unfortunately, the family never returned.

Response
"Breathe on Me, Breath of God" (Edwin Hatch, 1886; Robert Jackson, 1894).

Remembering Our Reason For Being The Church

Stewardship Challenge
The real measure of our wealth and obedience is how much we would be worth if we lost all of our money. No one really trusts God until he/she trusts God with his/her money.

Acting On Our Faith

Charge to the Congregation
Read the second half of the text, and ask the people to charge themselves silently. Ask them to write down their charge when they get home, to bring that charge with them next week, and to place it in the offering plate, unsigned. Get their permission to use those charges in future worships, and in the church newsletter, anonymously.

Response
Hymn of Commitment: "O God, Our Faithful God" (Johann Heermann, 1630; trans. Catherine Winkworth, 1858; alt.; harm. J. S. Bach, 1685-1750; alt.).

Meditation
"Perfect obedience would be perfect joy if only we had perfect confidence in the power we were obeying" (author unknown, slightly revised).

Music Possibilities In Addition To Those Already Suggested

Music for Preparation: "My Heart Ever Faithful," Bach.

Choral Introit: (Choir) "Come, Let Us Worship God," Kettring.

Hymn of Praise: "Christ Is the World's True Light," George Wallace Briggs, 1931; alt., 1972. (Change "men" to "we.")

Response to the Newer Covenant: "The Lord's Prayer," Gates. Invite the people to pray as they sing.

Offertory: "Child's Prayer," Kerllak.

Hymn of Commitment: "Walk Tall, Christian," Miriam Drury, 1969.

Music for Dismissal: Medley of obedience hymns.

The Season Of The Holy Spirit

Proper 18, Pentecost 16, Ordinary Time 23

(Sunday between September 4 - 10, inclusive)

Liturgical Color: Green

Gospel: Matthew 18:15-20

Theme: *Reproving Another Who Sins.* "We cannot go against the grain of the universe without getting splinters" (H. H. Farmer).

Remembering Whose We Are

Invitation to the Celebration

Pastor begins: Alleluia! God created us within families because of the joys, despite the risks. God continues the creation through us, as biological families, as church families. God welcomes and pursues us as families; where two or three are gathered in God's Name, there God is in the midst. Therefore, good morning, in the Name of God, the Parent; God, the Child; God, the Spirit; as we celebrate together the Good News.

Response

"Come, Christians, Join to Sing" (Christian Henry Bateman; Spanish Hymn).

Prayer of Praise

Begin with words similar to these, as given by David Currie (slightly revised): "God, holy and loving, great beyond our understanding, wise beyond our imagining, powerful beyond our measuring, loving beyond our deserving, praise be to you." Continue with petitions that pertain to your local situation.

Hymn of Praise

"Immortal, Invisible, God" (Welsh Folk Melody; Walter Chalmers Smith, 1867; alt. 1987).

Facing Up To Ourselves

Introduction to Our Self-Righteousness

One of our favorite sins is to look for weaknesses in others. Sometimes we can hardly wait for people to disagree with us, so we can use our disagreement to discount them. Sometimes we can hardly wait for people to speak on certain issues, so we can use their ideas against them. We like to think that we are always right on the big issues. We like to think that people on the other side of the theological, social, economic, racial fence can't possibly be related to us, in the church, because of their beliefs and actions. We see this attitude around political campaigns. I invite us to recall that the religious leaders of Jesus' day, and other self-righteous folks of our day, have similar thoughts, feelings, ideas. Are you one of those? *(Three minutes of silence; ask people to write down their insights.)*

Response

"Lord, Have Mercy on Me" (any version).

Invitation to Our Acceptance

The Gospel lesson today speaks about our reproving another who sins. Response to that text has created all kinds of trouble throughout the church. Too often, the "reprovers" have acted self-righteously "We have the truth; we are the truth; and we're here to discipline you." Thus, we need, always, to begin where Isaiah began, with the confession of his own sin before the sin of his people. So, I invite us to pray this prayer. My life is filled with so many things that reveal my limits as a human being: my inability to communicate clearly with others; the hurt that I feel from broken relationships; the pain of knowing that I have failed at some task; the anguish of loneliness, self-pity, fear. There is so much that I hide within myself and think that I can reveal to no one. And yet, I also experience joy, the great surging feelings of wholeness that make life exciting and worth living. Sometimes they come from a new union with another human being. Sometimes it is the satisfaction of a job well done, an experience with beauty, the intangible but real knowledge that life is good. All of this is our humanity. We pray that we will treat it gently as a great gift, God, and that our reverence for life will grow.

P: So now, if we are in Christ, we are a new, not a revised, not a renovated, creation; the old has passed away, the new has come. The mercy of the Lord is from eternity to eternity. In the Name of the Christ, we are forgiven.

M: So be it!

P: O Lord, open our lips,

M: And our mouths shall express your praise; and our actions shall refract your will!

Response

"Into My Heart" (Harry D. Clarke, stanza 1; source unknown, stanzas 2 and 3).

Looking Out To Others

Message with the Children of All Ages

Make very clear what this Gospel reading means, in children's language and experience. Ask if any have ever tried it. If the immediate children haven't, then ask those people who remained in their seats. Give an example from your experience when the issue was resolved and when it was not. Much depends on how we approach the other.

Reading from the Newer Covenant

With the children still present, continue to explore the meaning of the Scripture and the importance of verse 20. This text is tough to make happen in which all are winners.

Proclamation of the Good News

Begin with two or three examples of how people have misused this text, both throughout history and presently. Present what Jesus was saying; and give two or three examples of a positive response. In your educational program, offer a course on active listening, developed by The Effective Training Associates, Thomas Gordan.

Response

If you are serving communion, use the hymn, "Draw Us in the Spirit's Tether" (Percy Dearmer, 1931; alt.; Harold Friedel, 1957).

Remembering Our Reason For Being The Church

Stewardship Challenge

As long as we want to change other people only to make ourselves feel better and superior, we're still playing power games. Are we willing to give up our superior-acting attitudes, in order to minister effectively on eye-level?

Acting On Our Faith

Charge to the Congregation
"The purpose of the covenant community of faith, hope, love, is to comfort and confront each other on our journey to the grave — and beyond" (WHK).

Hymn of Commitment
"Called as Partners in Christ's Service" (Jane Parker Huber, 1981; John Zundel, 1870).

Meditation
"If I am not for myself, who is for me? Yet, if I am only for myself, what am I?" (Pirke Abot).

Music Possibilities In Addition To Those Already Suggested

Music for Preparation: "Prelude on a Hymn Tune," T. Tertius Noble.

Hymn of Praise: "Jesus Shall Reign," based on Psalm 72; Isaac Watts, 1719.

Response to the Prayer of Praise: "O Be Joyful in the Lord," Don Muro.

Response to the Message with the Children: "Lo, I Am With You Always," words and music by Loretta Ellenberger, copyright 1973, *Folk Encounter*, Hope Publishing Company.

Offertory: "Aria," McKay.

Hymn of Commitment: "Reach Out to Your Neighbor," words and music by Roger Copeland, copyright 1971, in *A New Now*, Hope Publishing Company.

Music for Dismissal: "Festal March," Nordman.

The Season Of The Holy Spirit

Proper 19, Pentecost 17, Ordinary Time 24

(Sunday between September 11 - 17, inclusive)

Liturgical Color: Green

Gospel: Matthew 18:21-35

Theme: *Forgiveness and the Parable of the Unforgiving Servant.* "Is forgiveness only a word lodged somewhere in Webster's Dictionary; or, have we incorporated it deeply into our personal vocabulary?" (WHK).

Remembering Whose We Are

Invitation to the Celebration

In the Name of the vibrant Christ, welcome! What do we need more than anything to give us a refreshing and cleansing way to begin a new day, a day anew? A new relationship, a relationship anew? A new experience, an experience anew? Especially when the day, relationship, experience become broken and alienated? What do we need most when that happens in our home, with close friends, in the church with people we thought were on our side? *(Wait a few seconds; ask if anyone wants to respond. If no one responds, invite them to think about forgiveness for a few moments in silence.)* Offer to them your guess: What we need is forgiveness, the greatest healer of all time.

Response

"Great God, We Sing That Mighty Hand" (Philip Dodridge, 1702-1751; William Knapp, 1738).

Prayer of Praise

Gracious and Holy God, we thank you for creating us as your children, with all its joys, despite its risks. We praise you that you are here with us, and were here long before we arrived today, with love and justice and forgiveness, so that we may draw near to you with childlike openness to receive you. Today, give us some new insights and resolve into forgiveness.

Hymn of Praise

"God Created Heaven and Earth" (Taiwanese hymn, Pi-po melody; trans. Boris and Clare Anderson, 1981; harm. I-to Loh, 1963; rev. 1982).

Facing Up To Ourselves

Introduction to Our Reluctance to Forgive

Slowly and deliberately: Where and with whom do we experience our "living off-center"? Between us and someone in the congregation/sanctuary? *(Pause.)* In our home? *(Pause.)* In our job or at school? *(Pause.)* In our neighborhood? *(Pause.)* Name those persons silently. (Pause.) Notice if we picked someone on whom we lay the blame; or, do we recognize the barrier in ourself? *(Pause.)* La Rochefoucauld has said, "Almost all your faults are more pardonable than the methods you think up to hide them."

Response

"Lord, Have Mercy" (harm. Richard Proulx, 1984).

The Act of Receiving Forgiveness

Only God knows the extent of our dishonesty; for God alone has paid the price for such knowledge. God has done what God can do about the broken relationship; what will we do about it? Forgiveness begins with ourself, not the other.

P: The Word of Christ is Good News!

M: God's love never changes. Against all who oppose God, or ignore God, or patronize God, God expresses love in wrath. In that same love, God took on judgment and death in Jesus the Christ, to bring forgiveness, liberation, and new life.

P: I declare to you who mean business with God, that in the Name of Jesus the Christ, you are forgiven. Do you hear that? Do you believe that? Do you practice that?

M: We hear you; help us when we forget. We receive your gift; help us to keep receiving it.

Response

"Day By Day" (Stephen Schwartz; alt., Richard of Chichester, copyright 1971 by Valando Music, Inc., and New Cadenza Music Corp.; found in *The Genesis Songbook*, published by Hope Publishing Company).

Looking Out To Others

Message with the Children of All Ages

Perhaps you can use a story similar to this: One day my son, looking very sad, came home from school. I asked him what happened. "My best friends wouldn't let me play football with them at lunchtime today, and I had to sit alone." "No wonder you feel sad," I empathized. Steve went off to do his thing. I boiled, "How could those rotten kids treat my son that way?" The next day, I dropped him off at school; then I sat in my car and wept, and wondered how I could get even. I wrote an article for the local newspaper telling of my experience. Several weeks later, I asked Steve about the episode. "Do you remember?" He did not remember. I reminded him. "Oh, yes," he said, "we solved that the next day." You children often do better about forgiveness than we adults.

Response

Say, we bring death to our spirits when we refuse to forgive. So, let's sing this stanza to the tune, "I'm Gonna Sing": "I'm gonna live when the Spirit says live." Sing it several times; sing it as a round, as different age groups.

Reading from the Newer Covenant

Divide the scripture into two parts: the conversation between Jesus and Peter, and the parable of the unforgiving servant.

Proclamation of the Good News

This may in some ways appear as bad news. I invite you to take two extreme cautions: Never counsel a physically and sexually abused spouse to go back into that home and act "more Christian," thinking that will resolve the problem. It will not! Never ask or expect a person who has been raped, especially by a counselor or clergyperson, to forgive without repentance on part of the perpetrator. Remember that Jesus did not forgive from the Cross; he asked his Father in heaven to do so. Before speaking on this theme, write for information from the Center for the Prevention of Sexual and Domestic Violence, 936 North 34th St., Suite 200, Seattle, WA 98103; 206-634-1903. E-mail: cpsdv@cpsdv.Seanet.com

Response

Introduce the hymn with the biblical idea that justice needs to occur before forgiveness is possible for some people, especially for those who have been physically and sexually brutalized. Then sing "Forgive Our Sins as We Forgive" (Rosamond E. Herklots, 1969, 1983; harm. Margaret W. Mealy, b. 1922).

Remembering Our Reason For Being The Church

Stewardship Challenge

Stewardship of Forgiveness: "Pride and fear, which keep us from forgiving, are the same pride and fear which keep us from accepting forgiveness; and will you, God, please help us to do something about it? What are we willing to let God do about it, before and after we offer our gifts this morning?" (WHK).

Acting On Our Faith

Charge to the Congregation

The only way that we can even begin to think about forgiving some of our choicer enemies is to think about how God must see them, and us. So, in Christ we are free to live! In Christ, we are free to forgive! Therefore, if you know someone who needs your forgiveness, go to him/her today. If you need to ask for forgiveness from someone, go to that person today. If you know someone who no longer believes that forgiveness is even an option, spend some time with that individual.

Meditation

"Forgiveness means that I will not get even, in word, thought, or deed." And, as George Herbert reflects the New Testament truth, "The person who cannot (will not) forgive breaks the bridge over which he/she must pass."

Music Possibilities In Addition To Those Already Suggested

Music for Preparation: "All Beautiful the March of Days," Frances Whitman Wile, 1911; alt., 1972.

Response to the Prayer of Praise: "Heaven and Earth and Sea and Air," Joachim Neander, 1680.

Response to the Assurance of Pardon: "Lord Jesus, Think on Me," Synesius of Cyrene (375-430); para. Allen W. Chatfield, 1876.

Offertory: "Be Thou But Near," Bach.

Hymn of Commitment: "O Lord of Every Shining Constellation," Albert F. Bayly, 1950; alt.; Vicar Earle Copes, 1963.

Music for Dismissal: "Fairest Lord Jesus," Crusader's hymn.

The Season Of The Holy Spirit

Proper 20, Pentecost 18, Ordinary Time 25

(Sunday between September 18-24, inclusive)

Liturgical Color: Green

Gospel: Matthew 20:1-16

Theme: *The Laborers in the Vineyard.* How many times, and in how many ways, have we said, "It's not fair"? And, when we said that, with whom were we comparing ourselves? (WHK).

Remembering Whose We Are

Invitation to the Celebration
  Begin with words similar to those: Who are you? Who am I? Who are we in relation to God and each other? We are many things. We have many differences. Some of us are "big shots" in the world's eyes; some of us are "small shots." In the eyes of God, we are all on the same level, absolutely dependent on the grace and mercy and justice of God. As Sheldon Kopp says in his book, *If You Meet the Buddha on the Road, Kill Him,* "No one is any stronger or any weaker than anyone else."

Response
  Have the choir chant its response, while the congregation speaks its response. (Choir - C; People - P)
C: Come, come with open hearts and minds.
P: O Lord, we come.
C: Come into community, communion with one another, and with God.
P: O Lord, we come, we come.
C: Come then, awake, awake hearts and hopes waiting.
P: O Lord, we come, we come, we come.
C: Come to meet the reality of today and the vision of tomorrow.
P: O Lord, we come, we come, we come, we come. We are here!

Prayer of Praise
  Incorporate these ideas: Eternal Christ, who has called your church into being to witness to your reconciling power, we thank you, and rejoice in you for this high calling. O God, we pray for a continuous reawakening and renewal among your people. We pray for a new recognition of the presence of your Spirit which will gird us for the task. We pray for our acceptance of the power of your Spirit which will make us bold without our being obnoxious.

Hymn of Praise
  "God Created Heaven and Earth" (Taiwanese hymn, Pi-po melody; trans. Boris and Clare Anderson, 1981; harm. I-to Loh, 1963; rev. 1982).

Facing Up To Ourselves

Introduction to Our Brokenness
  Some questions to consider: "Lord, do I try to do your will, and end up trying your patience? If so, how? *(Pause.)* Do I make promises I know that I will not keep? Name a few. *(Pause.)* Does the conflict

between what I say and what I do startle you but not me? How? *(Pause.)* Do I envy those who have more than I, and lord it over those who have less? In what ways?" Invite the people to repeat this prayer after you: "Lord, help me, *(your name)* to prepare a place for you, before tempting you to think twice before preparing a place for me." *(Two minutes of silence.)*

Response

"Look All Around You" (words and music by John Fischer, from the recording *Cold Cathedral*, copyright 1969 by F.E.L. Publishing, Ltd.; found in *New Wine*, editors, Jim Strathdee and Nelson Stringer. See address in Appendix I). As people sing, have them look around at each other; and have them ask, "Whom do I envy and whom do I not envy — and why?"

The Act of Receiving Forgiveness

Robert West has said that "nothing is easier than faultfinding; no talent, no self-denial, no brain, no character are required to set up in the grumbling business." In the eyes of God, we are all on the same level. Our danger is to think that those who commit the more obvious sins are greater sinners than we are. Our greatest sin, of course, is to think that we do not need forgiveness for our spiritual sins.

P: In Christ we are willing to admit our humanity.
M: There is no need for us to hide. We can be ourselves.
P: Our lives have been accepted. We have been set free.
M: We give thanks now, and live now.

Looking Out To Others

Message with the Children of All Ages

Focus on the theme of envy. Do you wish you were someone else? Do you wish that you had what others have? Some steal to get what they want. Some of us "grouse around" for what we do not have. Who needs the greatest forgiveness?

Reading from the Newer Covenant

With the children present, act out the text between Jesus and the laborers. Update the unfair labor practices in a contemporary setting.

Proclamation of the Good News

Title the sermon "It's Not Fair!" Life is not fair. Who said it would be? Really? Who did? It wasn't fair that Jesus died at age 33. Cancer, heart attacks, disease aren't fair either. If we're in it for the reward, then our reward is only the hope of getting a reward. If we're in it for the joy of serving, that joy is our reward.

Remembering Our Reason For Being The Church

Stewardship Challenge

We can give in three ways: Grudge giving, duty giving, thanks giving. Which of these, do you think, avoids envy?

Acting On Our Faith

Charge to the Congregation

Seniority doesn't mean diddly in the eyes and in the response of God to us. Our reward will be, not according to our length of service, or notoriety of service, or popularity of service, but only according to God's grace, and our response to it (WHK).

Response

"The Strife Is O'er," insists God. (From anonymous Latin text, music by James Minchin; found in *New Wine*.) After singing, say, "God has won the victory; God calls us to celebrate the victory. We can give up our envy."

Meditation

Socrates called envy "the ulcer of the soul." Have we experienced it gnawing within us? If so, then we need to integrate what Epictetus said: "Fortify yourself with contentment, for this is an impregnable fortress."

Music Possibilities In Addition To Those Already Suggested

Music for Preparation: "Let Us With a Gladsome Mind," from Psalm 136; John Milton, 1623, alt.

Hymn of Praise: "God Is Our Strong Salvation," from Psalm 27, James Montgomery, para. 1822; alt., 1972.

Response to the Newer Covenant: Could also be used for the offertory. "What Shall I Render to the Lord?" from Psalm 116; *The Psalter*, 1912.

Response to the Proclamation: "Jesus, Lover of My Soul," Charles Wesley.

Music for Dismissal: "There's a Wideness in God's Mercy," Frederick Faber, 1854.

The Season Of The Holy Spirit

Proper 21, Pentecost 19, Ordinary Time 26

(Sunday between September 25 - October 1, inclusive)

Liturgical Color: Green

Gospel: Matthew 21:23-32

Theme: *The Authority of Jesus Questioned; the Parable of the Two Sons.* "We Christians are expected not to defend Christ, but to proclaim him Lord of all; so in which category do we fit: the group whose profession of faith is better than our practice, or the group whose practice is better than our profession?" (WHK).

Remembering Whose We Are

Invitation to the Celebration

Who are you? Who am I? A girl, a boy; a man, a woman? A husband, wife, child, parent, single, married? Employee, student, dropout? An entity, a nonentity? A child of God, a self-made person? A saint, a sinner? Who are we, according to our understanding? Who are we according to Christ's understanding? *(Review this list slowly; give people a chance to respond internally.)*

P: In and through the events of our lives, Christ, the Sovereign, invites, calls us to follow him, preferably closely behind.
M: His is a call to freedom. His is a call to responsibility. His is a call to new life, a new life of faith, hope, love, justice, peace.
P: I invite us to renew our lives together under his Lordship.
M: We celebrate life together under his Lordship — in the Name of the Living God. Indeed we do!

Response

"Eightfold Alleluia" (*Folk Encounter*, Hope Publishing Company).

Prayer of Praise

Consider using these ideas: Holy and Loving God, Maker of all that is good; Sustainer of that which You have created; Liberator of those who call upon You in truth, we ask You not to enter our presence, but to continue in our presence. By Your Spirit, cause us to walk in the light, to flavor the earth with the salt of Christ, to produce fruit in Your vineyard, and to quit making excuses. As You already have found us, even as we seek You, draw us even nearer to vital, vibrant, vigorous, and victorious living. And all the people said, *(your favorite affirmation).*

Hymn of Praise

"Joyful, Joyful, We Adore Thee" (Henry van Dyke, 1907; alt.; Ludwig von Beethoven, 1824; adapt. Edward Hodges, 1796-1867; alt.). *(If the congregation sings halfheartedly, point it out, and repeat it.)*

Facing Up To Ourselves

Introduction to Our Fractured Lives

Heard over a call-in counseling program: "We can always find ways to justify breaking our word. If our word is only as good as our comfort-level, we can rationalize our way out of it." How good is our word, in the light of the sons in today's parable? Review their statements; and give the people two minutes of silence. Invite them to write down their insights.

Response
Unison Prayer: God, we share a common humanity, but it is so hard to get down to it. We have so many games to play. We have difficulty understanding our own motivations. No wonder we are often so cut off from each other, and therefore, cut off from you. Lord, we pray for the grace and the courage to get in touch with ourselves, our justification and rationalizations, and at the same time, to reach out to each other. Grant that we shall discover the sense of community and personhood to renew your world. *(Silence.)*

The Act of God's Putting Our Lives Back Together
Someone has said that "only God knows the extent of our dishonesty; for God alone has paid the price for such knowledge." Ask the people to write down what that means to them today. Ask if anyone would share his/her insight. Share yours.

P: Christ declares a new humanity for each of us.
M: He accepts our lives, forgiving the past if we want it forgiven, and opening up the future, if we want it opened.
P: He calls us to face life, instead of playing games, and to see it through, instead of justifying our behavior.
M: He even calls us to celebrate our life in him and in each other.

Response
"Create in Me a Clean Heart" (Psalm 51:10-12, from *The Hymnbook*. See Appendix I for address).

Looking Out To Others

Message with the Children of All Ages
(Caution again: Wait until all of the children arrive before beginning the message.) Ask if they have had any experience being either or both of the two sons, and how. Offer your own experiences. Point out that the "ideal" son would have been the one who accepted his father's orders with obedience and respect, and who would carry them out without playing games.

Reading from the Newer Covenant
(Two parts) While the children are present, act out the parable of the two sons. After dismissing the children, dramatize the first half of the text.

Proclamation of the Good News
The parable tells us that the world has two classes of people: People whose profession of faith is much better than their practice; their words are better than their actions. (Does that fit anyone here?) People whose practice of faith is better than their profession; their actions outperform their words. (Does that fit anyone here?) Give illustrations of each. Conclusion: While the second class is infinitely preferred to the first class, neither class approaches perfection. Our goal is to let the Holy Spirit put our profession and practice together.

Response
Invite the people to pray in silence; then invite them to offer sentence prayers of commitment.

Remembering Our Reason For Being The Church

Stewardship Challenge

Is Christ our primary authority? If so, then we need to know that the more we have, the more is required of us in ministry to the neediest and oppressed in our world, and to causes such as justice and peace. No more wishy-washy behavior, as experienced by the two sons.

Dedication Prayer

Give us such commitment, God, that we shall willingly, gladly, and yes, even hilariously, turn our pocketbooks over to you to let you do with them what you want.

Acting On Our Faith

Charge to the Congregation

Too often we determine the effectiveness of worship by asking the wrong questions, instead of the right ones. The wrong ones are these: "Did I like it? What did I get out of it?" These put the emphasis on our emotions, and our response to the aesthetic. The right ones are these: "Is it true? How will I glorify God in my life, and reach out to my neighbor from this day forward?" How did we worship today? How will we minister this week?

Meditation

Here is a summary of today's message: The religious leaders and people said that they would obey God and didn't; the tax collectors and prostitutes said that they would not obey and did. Into which group do you fit? (Perhaps some of you wish that I had quit after that statement.)

Music Possibilities In Addition To Those Already Suggested

Music for Preparation: "Be Thou My Vision," ancient Irish song; Mary Byrne, trans. 1905; versified by Eleanor Hull, 1912; alt.

Hymn of Praise: "God Our Father, You Our Maker," Robert W. McClelland, 1950, 1969.

Response to the Proclamation: "All Hail the Power of Jesus' Name!" Stanzas 1, 2, Edward Perronet, 1779, 1780; alt. Stanzas 3, 4, John Rippon, 1787.

Hymn of Commitment: "All Praise Be Yours; for You, O King Divine," F. Bland Tucker, 1938, 1972.

Music for Dismissal: Medley of Holy Spirit hymns used this year. Make the congregation aware of what you are doing; list the pages; and invite the people to remain for five extra minutes to review what they have learned.

The Season Of The Holy Spirit

Proper 22, Pentecost 20, Ordinary Time 27

(Sunday between October 2 - 8, inclusive)

Liturgical Color: Green

Gospel: Matthew 21:33-46

Theme: *The Parable of the Wicked Tenants.* "Our entrance into Heaven, which occurs when we accept God's acceptance of us, and our living in the presence of God, isn't cheap; it's free" (WHK).

Alleluia! Alleluia!

Invitation to the Celebration

In the Name of the Living God, good morning. How are you doing? Even more importantly, how are you being? We often judge our own and other people's Christianity on what we, and they, do or don't do. God judges us mostly on our being, which, of course, leads to our doing, as we discover in today's Gospel lesson. Who we are in our relationship to God leads us directly into our behavior. We may try to kid ourselves, as did the wicked tenants; but we will never fool God. God invites us to find out what that means — now!

P: I remind you that this day is beautiful and sacred, because God is alive!
M: But we see little beauty and sacredness outside of these cozy walls!
P: I remind you that God is beauty ... God is love. That which is ugly we have made.
M: Does God love us amidst our ugliness? Even amidst our lives that betray God and each other?
P: Look again at the cross ... it says that God loves us as we are ... do you understand that?
M: We understand. We understand that we are important creations of a concerned God! Now, we express our thanks to God for such awesome confidence in us! LEAD ON!

Prayer of Praise

Holy and Loving God, thank You for inviting us to worship, for leading us in worship, and for directing our lives following worship. Sometimes we hide the joy of our faith under a bundle of excuses; yet we know that all the excuses in the world will not stop Your pursuit of us. Keep reminding us of the cross and resurrection, that life is beautiful, and that You have given us time in order to celebrate the gift of life. Keep us from getting so involved in the crude pettiness and ugliness of life that we miss the big picture that You are in control ... *(conclude with your own praises).*

Hymn of Praise

(Keep on inviting people to bring their instruments to worship; encourage those who cannot sing to hum or whistle.) "Praise to the Lord, the Almighty."

We Seek Forgiveness

Introduction to Our Enmity, Hidden or Obvious

A woman said to her priest after worship, "I'm tired of hearing about love and peace and friendly 'rubbish.' All I want is the mass." She represents a contemporary version of the wicked tenants. We do, in fact, hate others to the same degree that we hate ourself. Our enemy becomes the enemy of God. We refuse to recognize that in our hatred and hostility, we are the enemy of God. *(Three minutes of silence.)* Invite people to write down their thoughts. Invite a courageous person to respond; take the risk of responding yourself.

Response
"Look All Around You" (words and music by John Fischer; found in *New Wine*, Hope Publishing Company. See Appendix I for address).

Introduction to Newness in Christ
God's love never changes. Against all who oppose or ignore God, God exposes love in wrath, a word we seldom hear in the church. In that same love, God took on judgment and death in Jesus the Christ, to bring us liberation and new life. I declare to you who mean business with God, that in the name of the Christ, you are forgiven.
M: God, we thank you for your promise. We believe you, and we receive your gift. And now, we are better equipped to seek forgiveness, and to offer forgiveness, each day, each hour.

Response
"Lord, I Want to Be a Christian in My Heart" (stanzas 1, 2, 3).

We Are Listening!

Message with the Children of All Ages
Tell the story of the text using a contemporary setting for children and young people. Then, ask them to remain while your actors dramatize the Gospel lesson.

Reading from the Newer Covenant
Before presenting the passage, ask, "What is your usual reason for reading the Bible — comfort for yourself, or simply passages which you can use against those who disagree with you?"

Proclamation of the Good News
This may sound like bad news: In light of the passage, deal with the idea expressed in Bob Dylan's "God's On Our Side." It is so easy to see the wickedness of others and the purity of ourselves. God will have none of that! If we had been present on Jesus' death day, we would have reacted no differently from the crowd. When we choose to disobey, to live off-center, to justify our behavior, we are no different from the crowd or the wicked tenants.

Response
Include in the prayer the fact that it's easy for us to criticize the crowd, the wicked tenants, and decide that we are the "good ones." All of us need forgiveness, over and over, for our thoughts, words, feelings, behavior.

We Are Accountable!

Stewardship Challenge
"The Holy Spirit makes generosity a matter of the heart, not of the pocketbook, though the Holy Spirit never excludes the pocketbook, checkbook, ATM, or charge card" (WHK).

Prayer Following the Offering
We have received the greatest gift in the world. Thank you. Grant that our response in thanks may exceed our speaking about thanks, for the sake of your world.

We Leave For Ministry!

Charge to the Congregation
Who's who in the Kingdom of God? Only those who produce the fruits of the Kingdom. And Jesus warns us, "Many who think that they are first may well be last; and the last may actually come in first." Instead of our deciding about others, I invite us, in the Spirit of God, to evaluate ourselves.

Response
Sing again, "Lord, I Want to Be A Christian."

Meditation
"Verbal commitment to Christ, membership in the local congregation, being pillars of the church, giving to keep the institution open, these guarantee no special favors. These do place on us grave responsibilities toward others. How well do we respond?" (WHK).

Music Possibilities In Addition To Those Already Suggested

Music for Preparation: "Praise to the Lord," Joachim Neander; trans. Catherine Winkworth. (Order from Hope Publishing Company. See Appendix I for address.)

Hymn of Praise: "Joyful, Joyful, We Adore Thee," Henry Van Dyke, 1907.

Response to the Confession: "Judge Eternal, Throned in Splendor," Henry Scott Holland, 1902; alt.

Response to the Forgiveness: "Christ Is Made the Sure Foundation," Latin hymn, c. seventh century.

Hymn of Commitment: "How Firm a Foundation," Rippon's *A Selection of Hymns*, 1787; alt.

Response to the Benediction: (Choir) "Proclaim the Glory of the Lord," choral setting by Jack Schrader; words and music by Dwight Liles and Niles Borop. (Order from Bug and Bear Music/Word Music, LCS Music Group, Inc., P.O. Box 202406, Dallas, TX 75220.)

Music for Dismissal: "I To the Hills Will Lift My Eyes," from Psalm 121, *The Psalter*, 1912; alt., 1972.

The Season Of The Holy Spirit

Proper 23, Pentecost 21, Ordinary Time 28

(Sunday between October 9 - 15 inclusive)

Liturgical Color: Green

Gospel: Matthew 22:1-14

Theme: *The Parable of the Wedding Banquet. "Live! Live! Life is a banquet...!" (from Auntie Mame).*

Alleluia! Alleluia!

Invitation to the Celebration

Have all of your musicians begin with banquet music, which invites people to a party. Then, with much enthusiasm, reverently shout, "Ring the bells! Throw confetti from the rooftops! Deck the city with banners! Cover one another with flowers! Clap your hands and shout for joy! Christ is risen! Christ is here! Celebrate the feast of life!"

P: God in Christ invites us to the party!
M: We come to celebrate the Spirit's Presence and Power!
P: What a privilege! What a joy! What an honor!
M: We come with expectations! We come to experience what God can do with lives receptive to the living Christ!
P: We open ourselves, our own needs, the needs of others, our relationships, and the world to Christ's Spirit.

Response

"Rejoice, You Pure in Heart!" Stanza 1 only. Sing it until the people sing it as if they were attending a party.

Prayer of Praise

Center it around the theme that God has invited us to a banquet, a party, in which God is Host, that Jesus enjoys a good laugh, and that the Holy Spirit inspires a joyful worshiping people. (Well in advance, order from The Fellowship of Merry Christians one of the new portraits of the "Laughing Christ." You probably will be unable to find autographed portraits which a radio station from Texas advertised a few years ago. FMC address: P.O. Box 895, Portage, MI 49081-0895; 616-324-0990.)

Hymn of Praise

"The Lord of the Dance" (Sydney Carter, 1963; American Shaker Melody).

We Seek Forgiveness

Introduction to the Act of Self-awareness

If we could choose whom we would invite to God's banquet, whom would we choose; to whom would we send no invitation? *(Two minutes of silence.)* Write down the names of those whom you would and would not invite. Now, in another two minutes of silence, write down the names of those who, you think, would and would not invite you, and why. Write down their names also. Conclude the confession with these words of Walter Wink, in the February, 1987 issue of *Sojourners*: "It is not out there, but in me, that the oppressor must die." Our calling, of course, is to let God make the decisions about who is, and who is not, invited to the banquet.

Invitation to the Act of Healthy Self-awareness

Frederick Buechner, in his book *Telling the Truth: Gospel as Tragedy, Comedy, and Fairy Tale*, says that "if we want to make a fool of ourselves, we can most effectively do that by telling the truth," and I add, "Recognizing and telling the truth about oneself." What truth about yourself do you need to face today? God offers us a new invitation now to share in the banquet of life. Do we really want to attend, or do we only say that we want to attend, so long as we get to send out the invitations?

P: Listen folks! Here is the Good News! Jesus the Christ came into the world to liberate us from our I-centeredness. In him, the Lord of Life, we are forgiven, made whole, and free to be responsible.

M: I hear! We hear! This is Good news indeed! Jesus the Christ came into the world to liberate me, us. In him, I am, we are, forgiven, made whole, free to be responsible. What a deal!

Response

"Thank You, Lord!" (Avery and Marsh, from *The Avery and Marsh Sonbgook*, Hope Publishing Company. See Appendix I for address).

We Are Listening!

Message with the Children of All Ages

Probably most children have never attended a banquet; they have attended parties. Discuss whom they invited and whom they did not invite and their reasons. Refer to the banquet in this parable. Have them remain while the Scripture is dramatized.

Reading from the Newer Covenant

Again, this parable lends itself to an easy, though painful, dramatization. Let the passage speak for itself; interpretation and application come in the sermon. Offer this prayer after the reading of the biblical passages for the day: "Lord, we have heard the biblical words; teach us to respond to your biblical truths."

Proclamation of the Good News

Indeed, this may sound like bad news. Point out the surprise about who gets invited, who rejects the invitation at their own expense, and then who gets invited. This whole business of who's in, who's out is not ours to decide. On whose side are we?

Response

"God of Justice, God of Mercy" (Jane Parker Huber, 1983; Rowland Hugh Prichard, 1855; from *Joy in Singing*. See Appendix I for address). Sing the first two stanzas only.

We Are Accountable!

Stewardship Challenge

Jacque Ellul has said that "if we feel too much sadness in giving, if we feel torn or irritated, it is better not to give." However we need to know what this means: it means that our money still controls us, that we love our resources more than we love God, and that we still fail to understand and receive forgiveness and grace.

Prayer Following the Offering

Forgive us, Lord, if these gifts of money represent only the leftovers of our lives. If so, commit us to a renewal of, a recommitment of, ourselves to you.

We Leave For Ministry!

Charge to the Congregation

Auntie Mame speaks to us once again. "Live! Live! Life is a banquet ... and there are so many fools starving to death." What a sad commentary on us, if we profess to be followers of the Way, the Truth, and the Life. How will we allow the Spirit of the living Christ to transform our sadness into gladness?

Response

Sing the last three stanzas of "God of Justice, God of Mercy."

Meditation

"People (you? I?) love to label. If we didn't label, we might discover that we know next to nothing" (Lukas Foss).

"The Christian church has all the language of a party, but hasn't been able to pull it off" (Floyd Shaffer).

Music Possibilities In Addition To Those Already Suggested

Music for Preparation: Use some of the hymns the congregation has learned this year. Put the page numbers in the bulletin, and invite the congregation to read, sing, hum, or whistle them as they prepare for worship.

Hymn of Praise: "Rejoice, the Lord is King," Charles Wesley, 1746; alt.

Response to the Assurance of Pardon: "My Shepherd Will Supply My Need," Psalm 23, Isaac Watts, para. 1719; alt., 1972.

Hymn of Commitment: "The Lord's My Shepherd," Psalm 23, para. in *The Scottish Psalter*, 1650; tunes Chrimond C.M. and Evan C.M.

Music for Dismissal: See Music for Preparation.

The Season Of The Holy Spirit

Proper 24, Pentecost 22, Ordinary Time 29

(Sunday between October 16-22, inclusive)

Liturgical Color: Green

Gospel: Matthew 22:15-22

Theme: *The Question about Paying Taxes.* "Christianity should be (is) the alternative to Caesar, and so intent in its virtue that Caesar will not be able to stand in the strength of its light" (author unknown).

Alleluia! Alleluia!

Invitation to the Celebration
    In the Name of God the Creator, Liberator, Sustainer, Energizer, we're here, for whatever reason. Are we ready for a God-event, even though, especially because, we will wrestle with a difficult theme today? We can let it divide us or give us some new insights into the life of the church. Yes, we're here! Now what?

P: Fact: God owns the world — of nature, of persons — even when we think that we own it, even when we think that we are the only ones who know what God's will is, even when we think that we are the "true" Christians, even when we think that we have the "right" answers, even when we think that we are the only obedient ones left in the world.

M: We know that the earth is the Lord's, even when we act as though it belongs to us, even when we cry out, "I, only I am left to do God's will."

All: Lord, put our thoughts, words, feelings by Your Spirit, in proper perspective. Teach us the difference between obeying You and Caesar, whatever form Caesar happens to take.

Response
    "Holy, Holy, Holy Lord" (John Weaver, 1984).

Prayer of Praise
    Focus on the God of Scripture, who is Lord of the Universe, and God's power over the lesser gods of Caesar, whatever form they happen to take.

Hymn of Praise
    "Praise, My Soul, the King of Heaven" (Henry Francis Lyte, 1834; alt.; John Goss, 1869; notice also the alternate harmony; and other words. See *The Presbyterian Hymnbook*).

We Seek Forgiveness

The Act of Recognizing our Humanity
    For all practical purposes, for some of us, God is dead, especially around the issues of church and state, God and Caesar. Think about where we put our primary obedience, especially when we debate religion and politics. Our sin often is that we refuse to listen to those who disagree with us, especially when we need to hear that they're confronting our biases. In silence consider whose voice you need to hear. Write down the names of those voices. *(Two minutes of silence.)* Pray the prayer silently first; then we will pray it together.

All: O God, You love the world of persons, even when we do not. You love those who differ from us, for whatever reason. We confess that our greatest sin, our greatest source of estrangement, our brokenness and alienation lie in our lack of love for all people. Forgive us, Lord, for our lack of love.

Response
"Truth Shall Make You Free" (based on John 8:31-32; John F. Wilson).

The Act of Receiving New Life
Henry Longfellow once said, "If we could read the secret history of our 'enemies,' we should find in each one's life, sorrow and suffering enough to disarm all hostility." *(Repeat two or three times.)*

All: God, cleanse us from any desire for revenge, as tempting as the thought is; any desire to get even with those who disagree with us, who seek to destroy us physically, emotionally, spiritually, verbally or silently, obviously or subtly; any desire to say, "I told you so!" By Your Spirit, grant that we may seek to overpower through love those who seek to destroy, to silence Your witness and Your church through hatred, indifference, indecision, laziness, and the misuse of power.

Response
"God of Compassion, in Mercy Befriend Us" (John J. Moment, 1933; Paris *Antiphoner*, 1681; as in *La Feillé's Methode du plain-chant*, 1808).

We Are Listening!

Message with the Children of All Ages
Explain to the children what Jesus meant when he said, "Give to Caesar the things that are Caesar's, and to God the things that are God's."

Reading from the Newer Covenant
Have a group of "Pharisees" sitting around plotting some way, any way, to trap and thus to embarrass Jesus. Follow with the interaction between Jesus and the religious leaders. Then have them slink away.

Proclamation of the Good News
If you are like me, you might announce to the congregation that you would prefer not to preach this sermon, which may cause more heat than light. Basically, governments have two attitudes toward the church: supportive of those who agree; hostile and repressive toward those who disagree. Point out the impact of Jesus' response. This illustration may clarify (for some only): Vice President Spiro Agnew attacked what he called "the glib, activist element who would tell us our values are lies." He, of course, failed to understand that criticizing the state can be a way of honoring it; and that, without the honest and creative practice of dissent, the republic suffers, sometimes beyond repair.

Response
"God of the Ages, Whose Almighty Hand" (Daniel Crane Roberts, 1867; alt.; George William Warren, 1892). Stanza 2 only.

We Are Accountable!

Stewardship Challenge
Would you give if your gift were not tax-deductible? If so, how much? Compare what you give, which is deductible, with what you would give if it were not.

Prayer of Dedication

Forgive us, Lord, when our standard of living for self exceeds our standard of giving to others, in the name of him who gave everything he had, so that we might learn how to give and live.

We Leave For Ministry!

Charge to the Congregation

Whenever anything comes between God and us, including demands of the state which go against our own conscience, that is sin. The Christian puts his/her obedience to God above obedience to anything or anyone else in the world.

Meditation

Would you worship if the state ruled that you were breaking the law? If you did worship, how would you do it?

Music Possibilities In Addition To Those Already Suggested

Music for Preparation: "Toccata," Frescobaldi.

Hymn of Praise: "O Sing a New Song to the Lord," Psalm 96, para. in *The Scottish Psalter*, 1650; alt.

Offertory: "Chorale," Purvis.

Hymn of Commitment: "God of Grace and God of Glory," Harry Emerson Fosdick, 1930; alt., 1972. Note: Ask the people to read it in silence and to select which of stanzas 2, 3, or 4 they will sing. Invite everyone to sing stanza 1; then those who will sing stanza 2 stand and sing; then stanza 3; then stanza 4. Everyone will sing stanza 5. (Idea suggested by Doug Adams, Pacific School of Religion, Berkeley, California.)

Response to the Benediction: Jubilate chorus, only, to "Now on Land and Sea Descending."

Music for Dismissal: Medley of dedication hymns.

The Season Of The Holy Spirit

Proper 25, Pentecost 23, Ordinary Time 30

(Sunday between October 23 - 29, inclusive)

Liturgical Color: Green

Gospel: Matthew 22:34-46

Theme: *The Greatest Commandment; the Question about David's Son.* It is much easier to talk about God's love for us than to talk about our love for God, which, of course, is expressed through our love for friends, acquaintances, and enemies.

Alleluia! Alleluia!

Invitation to the Celebration
We come to worship to celebrate Good News, to declare our allegiance, to affirm whose we are, who we are, what we do, where we go, in the name and power of the risen Christ. So, let's do that! Here! Now! And, all the people said, "Amen! Be It So! Let's Do It! Tah-dah!" *(Keep repeating the response until the congregation responds with enthusiasm.)*
P: We are here today, for whatever reason.
M: We are here because God called, invited us, as God does every week. Today, we said "yes," for whatever reason.
P: Now that we're here, Lord, heal us and free us to be persons who love You, our friends and enemies.
M: In order to do that, Lord, we're going to need all the help that You can give us. Thanks for Your loving us, so that we will love those whom You have placed in our personal histories.

Response
"We Thank You, Lord, for You Are Good" (Severus Gastorius, 1681; John G. Dunn, 1985; harm. *Common Service Book*, 1917).

Prayer of Praise
Center it around the heighth, depth, width, breadth of God's love to and for the world, a love which exceeds our comprehension; a love which is extended to those whom we do not know, and some whom we do not like; and wonder how God can possibly love them, when to us they are so unlovable.

Hymn of Praise
"Holy, Holy, Holy, Lord God Almighty!" (See Appendix I for address).

We Seek Forgiveness

The Act of Seeing How Poorly We Love
C. S. Lewis, in his book *The Four Loves*, says, "If you want to make sure of keeping your heart intact, you must give it to no one, not even to a cat or a dog." *(One minute of silence with no comment.)* Now, silently consider your potential for love, and for your actual practice of loving, those in your home *(pause)*; those in your neighborhood *(pause)*; those with whom you work or attend school *(pause)*; those whom you do not like *(pause)*; those who actually have set out to do you in *(pause)*. Consider your

thoughts, silently, about Jesus' commandment. *(Two minutes.)* Invite the people to offer sentence prayers of confession. After each prayer, ask the people to respond, "Lord, have mercy on us."

The Act of Receiving New Power to Love

John Thompson, in a sermon titled "A Christian 'Love-In,' " says, "Love unites [I add, hate unties], for to love another is to accept unlimited responsibility for his good. In other words, love is being fully responsible in our relationships." I put it this way, "We are responsible *for* ourself; we are responsible *to* another, to listen, to affirm, to be available to comfort, to confront." Ask if the people have any response to these comments.

Prayer

"O God of love, may the light of your love dawn in our lives and through us, shine into our world, which first and foremost is your world. Dispel the gloomy cloud of night, and death's dark shadow put to flight by your loving presence and your awesome power. Come now, O Christ, and prepare us to receive you when you come to us in the person of the homeless one, the hungry one, the enemy, or the stranger. By your great love, rule in our hearts and our heads, and let your light shine in us and through us forever" (author unknown, slightly revised).

Response

"Open My Eyes That I May See" (Clara H. Scott, 1895).

We Are Listening!

Message with the Children of All Ages

Do you have an easy time, or a hard time, loving people, especially brothers or sisters, or even parents, when you don't get what you want? Distinguish between loving and liking. We can love others without liking many of the things they do; just as they may not like many of the things we do. Our parents do not throw us into the street because of certain things we do or say. Not true of all parents, as we read about in the daily newspaper. *(Be careful about not making this a legalistic message; that is, "you should ... you have to ... you must because I say so....")* We love others for one reason only; because God loves us, even when we have no idea how to love ourselves.

Reading from the Newer Covenant

Include the children in the first half of today's gospel. The passage makes for great drama. Then dismiss the children and continue the drama.

Proclamation of the Good News

Perhaps you can use these or similar events from your own life:

1. My son, when he was quite young, said to me one day, "Daddy, I'm rich." I asked, "Why do you think you're rich?" Steve responded, "Because I have a lot of love."

2. A patient in the hospital said to the chaplain one day, "Chaplain, tell me something important, the most important thing you can." The chaplain responded, "God loves you." The patient shot back, "Phttttt!"

Response

"Pass My Love Around" (words and music by David Yantis and Gio Sgarlata, found in *New Wine*. See Appendix I for address). Eliminate the sexist words as you sing.

We Are Accountable!

Stewardship Challenge

We are stewards of God's love, either positive or negative stewards. Probably I would be smart not to say this; however, Jesus told us that if our brother or sister has a grudge against us, we are, first, to go to that person and get squared away before bringing our offering. That may cut down on the offering today; but it might transform our church and community. *(One minute of silence before receiving the offering.)* After the offering, did anyone made a decision to reach out to someone from whom he/she is alienated?

Prayer of Dedication

There is no use in our pretending, God, that we can repay all of the damage that our lack of loving has done to ourselves, others, and you. We offer these gifts as partial payment, not because we *must* do so to win your love, but because we *choose* to do so to thank you for your love.

We Leave For Ministry!

Charge to the Congregation

"How shockingly indiscriminate is the love of God" (author unknown). "How shockingly discriminate is the love of *(our name)*" (WHK).

Meditation

"The world is not through with the Cross, but it will be through without it" (Phillips Brooks). "To be out of love is to be in hell" (author unknown).

Music Possibilities In Addition To Those Already Suggested

Music for Preparation: "Andante," C.P.E. Bach.

Hymn of Praise: "Sing to the Lord of Harvest," John S. B. Bonsell, 1866; alt.

Response to the Act of New Life: "He Comes to Us," Jane Marshall.

Response to the Message with the Children: "Magic Penny," Malvina Reynolds, copyright 1965, by Blue Seas Music, Inc., JAC Music Co., Inc., New York, NY; found in *Singing the Lord's Song* published by Discipleship Resources. (See Appendix I for address.)

Offertory: "What the World Needs Now is Love, Sweet Love," lyrics by Hal David; music by Burt Bacharach, copyright 1965, by Blue Seas Music, Inc., JAC Music Co., Inc., New York, NY.

Hymn of Praise: "Take Thou Our Minds, Dear Lord," William H. Foulkes, stanzas 1-3, 1918; stanza 4, 1920.

Music for Dismissal: "Love One Another," Natalie Sleeth, copyright 1975, Hope Publishing Company.

The Season Of The Holy Spirit

All Saints' Sunday

Liturgical Color: White

Gospel: Matthew 5:1-12

Theme: *The Communion of the Saints with the Beatitudes.* Are you one of the saints in communion? If so, how do you make your decision? If not, how do you make your decision?

The Source Of Our Sainthood

Invitation to the Celebration

In the Name of the Living God who calls us to our sainthood, welcome. Continue by welcoming some of the saints by name; for example, "Welcome to saint Bill, saint Carol, saint Joseph, saint Julie, and so forth." Select people whom you know could accept such a designation. Then, ask the rest of the saints to stand. You may need to invite them several times before everyone is standing.

P: The Lord be with you saints.
M: And the Lord be with you, also, saint *(pastor's name)*.
P: Praise the Lord for his gift of sainthood.
M: The Lord's Name be praised for his gift of sainthood to us.

Response

"Glory to God" (words and music by Jim Strathdee, from *New Wine*. See Appendix I for address). Update the sexist language as you sing.

Prayer of Praise

Center it around the fact that God is the Author of our sainthood. Many church members continue to believe that saints are special people who have done something special to achieve their sainthood. Refrain from giving the whole story away this early in worship.

Hymn of Praise

"Rejoice, the Lord Is King" (Charles Wesley, 1746; John Darwell, 1770; desc. Sidney Hugo Nicholson, 1875-1947).

The Source Of Our Joylessness And Our Joy

The Source of Our Joylessness

When we live "off-center," one New Testament definition of sin, we miss the joy of our relationship with God, others, and our best self. And when we live "off-center," demanding our own way, we discover the pain of the human condition. How do you see yourself living off-center; and what does that do to your relationships? *(Two minutes of silence; write down what you learn about yourself.)*

Prayer

Make us uncomfortable, Lord. Make us uncomfortable about what we do with our sainthood. Disturb us, God, until we sense that our true calling is to grow into the broadest, deepest, most vital person possible; to seize now this awesome opportunity for searching out wisdom; to find joy in reading and grappling and growing; to live richly and responsibly; to do our part to help create a better world; to be constantly grateful for the capacity, creativity, and courage that are given to us saints ... freely ... by you.

Response

"It's Me, O Lord" (Traditional Spiritual).

The Source of Our Joy

Where do you experience joy? *(Ask for responses. Then after a few moments ask:)* Are you aware that the saints of God experience the joy of Christ? Malcolm Muggeridge, in his book *Jesus Rediscovered*, points out that when Dietrich Bonhoeffer was led away by the Nazi guards to be executed, his face was shining with joy, to the point that even the guards noticed it. In that place of darkest evil, he was the joyful one, he the executed.

P: Jesus said, "Be of good cheer, (you saints), your living off-center is forgiven. Did you hear that? Forgiven! Forgiven! Forgiven! Breathe more easily, you saints!

M: Lord, we believe. Help us when we have a hard time believing that we are forgiven, when we fall into the trap of thinking that we must earn our sainthood, rather than receiving it as your gift to us.

Response

"Blessed Be the Name," Ralph E. Hudson, from *Let the People Sing*, published by Hope Publishing Company.

We Learn About Joy

Message with the Children of All Ages

If you could have anything in the world to "make you happy," what would you choose? Ask the same of the adults who did not come forward. If they say something similar to "Jesus in my heart," ask them if they are only trying to impress the rest of us. Today we will look at the Beatitudes, which often are translated "blessed" or "happy." One day, Linus said to Charlie Brown, "What would you say you want most out of life, Charlie Brown, to be happy?" Charlie responds, "Oh, no ... I don't really expect happiness; I really don't. I just don't want to be unhappy." No wonder C.B. dreads only one day at a time. I want you to understand that having a good time, or getting what you want, does not bring happiness. The Beatitudes tell us that serving God brings true joy. Sometimes, even parents think that their main goal in life is to make their children happy. Not so!

Reading from the Newer Covenant

With the children still present, have two people read the Gospel, from two versions. One person will stand in the chancel; the other will be at the rear of the sanctuary. Take turns reading slowly and deliberately. Read from *Phillips* and *The Cotton Patch* translations for some new insights into the passage.

Proclamation of the Good News

Incorporate these ideas: L. P. Jacks said that "I regard the quest for happiness as the most unfortunate enterprise upon which the human race has ever embarked. Most of the miseries of humanity are attributed to it." And Thomas Carlyle was even more emphatic. "Happiness! Bah, that's for pigs." Literally, the word "blessed" means "how fulfilled, how complete, how satisfied are ..." Because of the connotations of the word "happiness," I prefer the word "joy." The Beatitudes reflect and refract the life of the saint.

Response

"What Signs Has God Revealed to Us" (Jane Parker Huber, 1982; English melody, probably sixteenth century).

We Respond As Saints

Stewardship Challenge
According to William Barclay, "A saint is someone whose life makes it easier to believe in God." How will that happen through what we give and how we live?

Dedication Prayer
God, we are mindful that you ask all from us; we are grateful that you give all to us. Lord, now that you've given so much, give us two more things, a grateful heart and an obedient body.

We Take Our Sainthood Into The World

Charge to the Congregation
As the saints of God, the saints in communion, our joy comes from the capacity to feel deeply, to enjoy simply, to think freely, to risk openly, to be needed intimately ... and all the people said, "Tah-dah!" (Storm Jameson, slightly revised).

Meditation
Jack Paar once said that "happiness can be found in the yellow pages of your telephone book, under saloon." What a contrast with a statement by William A. Ward, *Meadowbrook* (Texas) *Herald*: "Happiness [though I would use the word "joy"] comes not from having much to live on but from having much to live for."

Music Possibilities In Addition To Those Already Suggested

Music for Preparation: "From God I Ne'er Will Turn," Bach.

Hymn of Praise: "You Servants of God, Your Master Proclaim," Charles Wesley, 1744; alt.

Response to the Act of Forgiveness: (Choir) "Now Sing We Joyfully Unto God," Gordon Young.

Response to the Proclamation: "O Love That Will Not Let Me Go," George Matheson, 1882.

Offertory: "In Thee I Trust," Peeters.

Hymn of Commitment: "There Is a New Wind Blowin'," words and music by David Yantis, from *New Wine*, Hope Publishing Company.

Music for Dismissal: Version of the Beatitudes, for all of the instruments.

The Season Of The Holy Spirit

Proper 26, Pentecost 24, Ordinary Time 31

(Sunday between October 30 - November 5, inclusive)

Liturgical Color: Green

Gospel: Matthew 23:1-12

Theme: *Jesus Denounces Scribes and Pharisees.* Do you know anyone who has all of the answers for everyone else, and few or none for him or herself? And who goes around insisting that his/her answers are for all of us? Who are the humbled and who are the exalted ones of this world?

Alleluia! Alleluia!

Invitation to the Celebration

At the end of the Music for Preparation, bang a gavel on the lectern. Then say something similar to this: "Theoretically, we're awake; and we're ready for a God-event, not only for ourself, but also for the community of faith. So, let's worship, in the Name of God, the Creator, Liberator, Sustainer, Energizer! And, all the people said, 'Tah-dah!'"

P: The call of Christ is not an easy one.
M: It is an invitation to self-giving humility.
P: It requires hard work in the face of disappointment.
M: It means going on when it seems as though everyone else has given up.
P: We will need to stop judging each other's faith and to support each other if we are to follow Christ.
M: We offer this support as we celebrate the life of faith, hope, love, together.

Response

Chorus only to "Allelu!" (words and music by Ray Repp, *Folk Encounter*, Hope Publishing Company. See Appendix I for address).

Prayer of Praise

O Christ, the life, keep on waking us up; that we, confronted by your majesty, the nearness of your Kingdom, and the power of your truth, may rise, ashamed from dreaming about ourself, enter into life, serve your purpose, and celebrate your truth anew, in spirit and in reality, not only with our words, not only with our emotions, but with our whole life.

Hymn of Praise

"O Lord, Our God, How Excellent" (Fred R. Anderson, 1986; *Este's Psalmes*, 1592).

We Seek Forgiveness

The Act of Recognizing Our Self-Righteousness

Where did we ever get the idea that we're not supposed to be disturbed? The Gospel disturbs us before healing us. If we read the Scripture carefully, and let God's Spirit interpret it for us, we will discover that all of us have the spirit of the scribes and Pharisees. *(Two minutes of silence, with the suggestion that we write down how we see the spirit of the religious leaders of Jesus' day living in us today.)*

Prayer of Confession

O God of grace and power, you come to us in surprising ways with surprising messages, some of which we want to hear, and some of which we want to ignore. You call us to live in unexpected ways, performing unexpected tasks. We confess that we do not always welcome your surprises, or greet you with joy. We prefer the familiar, the comfortable, the usual; we prefer to think that we have the answers for others. From our resistance to your bringing to birth within us any new visions; for our attempts to reject your truth about ourself, because we prefer self-denial; for our desire to create you in our image, rather than to give ourselves to your new creation, forgive us. Forgive us, God, and bring to birth in us a new openness to your expected presence, and your surprising direction for our lives.

Response

"Standing in the Need of Prayer" (Black Spiritual from *Singing the Lord's Song*, Discipleship Resources. See Appendix I for address).

The Act of Pardon for Our Self-Righteousness

We have a choice: We can refuse to recognize that in our own self-righteousness, which leads to hatred and hostility, we are God's enemy. Or we can choose to recognize that in our loving and accepting, we are God's friend. We make that choice in every decision, every relationship, every event of our life.
P: God in Christ accepts our humanity, every bit of it.
M: Despite our brokenness and I-centeredness and self-righteousness, we embrace our humanity, and the One who redeems and renews it.
P: God in Christ has set us free.
M: We are free! And we are responsible!
P: God in Christ allows us to experience newness, a new person, a new day, a new song.
M: We celebrate life in the risen, living Christ.
P: So be it!

Response

"Oh, Freedom!" (Black Spiritual, found in *Singing the Lord's Song*, Discipleship Resources. See Appendix I for address).

We Are Listening!

Message with the Children of All Ages

Jesus was not always a nice man. He said some tough things to the religious leaders of his day. His motto for life was not "don't worry; be happy." What do you think of that? *(Pause.)* One day a young boy said to his friends, "I don't like Jesus; he makes me brush my teeth every night." It's easy to use Jesus, or to use what we believe about Jesus, against others. Jesus will have none of that. Explain in children's words the meaning of the last two verses of the Gospel.

Reading from the Newer Covenant

With the children still present, have one of your actors present the Scripture in language that speaks to us today. You may want to refer to *The Cotton Patch Version*, by Clarence Jordan, and revise it for your congregation.

Proclamation of the Good News

John Fife, in the January/February, 1997 issue of *The Other Side*, points out clearly that the early church understood its mission. It stood against the corrupt powers of the church and state. They knew why they were being killed, just as Jesus knew. The church, when it takes the biblical mandate seriously, will suffer persecution, both by the state, and the church which is indebted to the state. (Order from *The Other Side*, 300 West Apsley St., Philadelphia, PA 119144-4221; 215-849-2178.)
Response

"Song of Hope"   (Alvin Schutmaat, 1984 Argentine Folk Melody).

We Are Accountable!

Stewardship Challenge

Stewardship of Humility and Servanthood. How slick and weasel-like is self-righteousness! Humility is a quality we often question in others, but assume in ourselves. As Walter B. Knight says in the *Gospel Herald*, "Humility is elusive. It is such a fragile plant that the slightest reference to it causes it to wilt and die."

Prayer of Dedication

We pray, Lord, that these gifts of money represent our humble, rather than our self-righteous, relationship with You and toward Your world.

We Leave For Ministry!

Charge to the Congregation

How will we avoid the religion of the scribes and Pharisees this week, as we remember that a critic is one who points out how imperfectly other people do that which the critic does not do at all? Any suggestions?

Meditation

"The Florentines flattered Savonarola until they found he meant business; then, they burnt him" (Dean Inge).

Music Possibilities In Addition To Those Already Suggested

Music for Preparation: "Carillon for a Joyful Day," McKay.

Hymn of Praise: "O Lord, Our God, Most Earnestly," *The Psalter*, 1912; alt., 1972.

Response to the Prayer of Praise: "Let Us Sing to the Lord," Psalm 95, Moyer.

Response to the Act of Receiving New Life: "The Lord's Prayer," West Indies Version; melody set down by Olive Pattison, 1945; harmony by Richard D. Wetzel, 1972.

Offertory: "A Prayer for the Innocent,"   McKay

Hymn of Commitment: "O Master, Let Me Walk with Thee," Washington Gladden, 1879.

Music for Dismissal: "Benedictions," McKay.

The Season Of The Holy Spirit

Proper 27, Pentecost 25, Ordinary Time 32

(Sunday between November 6 - 12, inclusive)

Liturgical Color: Green

Gospel: Matthew 25:1-13

Theme: *The Parable of the Ten Bridesmaids.* "Do we prefer the immediate security and safety of our personal Egyptian slavery, knowing that we have 'plenty' of time to prepare later for our end; or the fear and excitement of our personal wilderness journey, knowing that we have no idea when the end will come?" (WHK).

Alleluia! Alleluia!

Invitation to the Celebration
 Walk out into the middle of the sanctuary, and say, "In the Name of the Living God, welcome to the celebration. How (not why) have you come today? Ready? With expectations? Alert? Mark Twain said, 'Blessed are those who expect nothing (and I add, those who expect the wrong things); for they will not be disappointed.' And I say again, 'Blessed are those who come, not as observers, but as participants, ready and ripe, responsive and responsible to God, others, self — for they shall be filled!' However we have come, we are here — to celebrate the Presence and Power of the living God."

Response
 "Morning Has Broken" (Gaelic Melody, adapted by Cat Stevens; words by Eleanor Farjeon).

Prayer of Praise
 God of the awesome vision, Who imagined the universe, and it became; Who thought a people, and we lived; grant to us the courage to dream dreams, and to make plans, worthy of Your catholic church, and to see visions of what Your people may be/do when obedient to the Holy Spirit; so that we may dare great things for You, venture everything for the sake of Your Kingdom and glory; and Your church, indeed, be the force that the world dare not ignore, through Jesus the Christ, the sovereign one and our Lord (author unknown, revised).

Hymn of Praise
 "O God of Earth and Space" (Hebrew Melody; Jane Parker Huber, 1980; adapt. Thomas Olivers and Meyer Lyon, 1770).

We Seek Forgiveness

The Act of Confession
 Some of us have developed the art of procrastination into a science. "I have plenty of time — for whatever." Identify some aspects of your life in which you procrastinate. Write them down. *(Three minutes of silence.)* Yes, this will be uncomfortable for some; better now than later, when we have no more time. Offer this idea: Procrastination usually means internalized anger. "I'll show you; I'll get around to it when I get around to it, so buzz off!" We see and experience this in our homes, at school, in our jobs. Nobody is going to tell us what to do and when to do it! So there! *(One minute of silence.)*

Response

"Sleepers, Awake" (Richard Avery and Don Marsh, from *The Second Avery and Marsh Songbook*, Hope Publishing Company). Though, technically, this is a Christmas hymn, it can be used here to encourage people to get ready for that event which comes in a few weeks. The idea is to wake us up, and to be prepared for the Christ-event.

The Act of Receiving Pardon for Our Procrastination

You may find this example helpful: One day a young man just beginning in the banking business came to his pastor. "I'm about to get fired; I always come to work twenty minutes late. My boss is tired of it." During a one-hour counseling session, the young man discovered his anger toward his father; his boss reminded him of his father; so he was going to "show" his father by taking it out on his boss. The insight cleared up the problem. Obviously, not all problems are solved that easily. However, what will we do to solve our problem delays? *(Two minutes of silence; write down your new decision about readiness.)* Anyone want to take the risk of sharing? If you dare, you, the pastor, share one of your favorites.

Response

"Rejoice! Rejoice! Believers" (Welsh Folk Melody; Laurentius Laurenti, 1700; trans. Sarah Borthwick Findlater, 1854; alt. *The Hymnal*, 1982).

We Are Listening!

Message with the Children of All Ages

With the children present, act out the Scripture. Afterward, ask them what it means, and if it has anything to do with them. Do they always do their homework before watching television? Do they always do their chores without fifty reminders? Remind them of the importance of readiness, in ways that pertain to your situation.

Reading from the Newer Covenant

See Message with the Children of All Ages.

Proclamation of the Good News

Continue to make the comparison between readiness and procrastination. Many of us have said something similar to this: "Later, Lord, later, I'll become a Christian when I'm older; I want to have my fun first. Then, just before I conk out, I'll make a deal with you." Of course, the trouble with this attitude is that our indecision is one of the things that will keep us from the Kingdom of God. The disease of indecision infected the foolish maidens. It infects many of us who like to believe that we are on God's side, never questioning if God is on our side. It infects those of us who cry out "Lord, Lord," but who do not do God's will. It infects those who want the benefits of the Kingdom, without obeying the Lord of the Kingdom. It infects the fence-sitters, the spiritual sponges, the passive onlookers.

Response

" 'Sleepers, Wake!' A Voice Astounds Us" (Philip Nicolai, 1599; trans. Carl P. Daw, Jr., 1982; harm. Johann Sebastian Bach, 1731).

We Are Accountable!

Stewardship Challenge

What kind of a life-story are we writing each day, one of readiness, or one of waiting until a "more opportune time"? Ask the people to write down their thoughts before receiving the offering.

Prayer of Commitment

God, possess us by your power; illuminate us by your truth; fire us by your flame; enable us by your presence; be made visible in us by your fruits....

We Leave For Ministry!

Charge to the Congregation

I do hope not, but perhaps some of us have missed the point. At this moment, we still have time to make a decision, or a re-decision, for a life in Christ. What shall we do with this *kairos* moment? Waste it, destroy it, rationalize it, sluff it off, and then hear Christ say, "Away with you, fools"? Or instead, shall we use it, cherish it, redeem it, and then hear Christ's words, "Enter with me into the joy of life, and death, and eternity, beginning now!"?

Meditation

"It's the set of the sail, and not the gale, that determines the way we go" (from the cover of *Quote* magazine).

Music Possibilities In Addition To Those Already Suggested

Music for Preparation: "Fantasie Chorale," Whitlock.

Hymn of Praise: "God of the Living, in Whose Eyes," John Ellerton, 1859, 1862; alt., 1972.

Response to the Act of Confession: "For These Blessings," source unknown, from *Folk Encounter*, copyright 1972, *Music for Young Voices*, Hope Publishing Company.

Response to the Newer Covenant: "All Good Gifts," Schwartz.

Offertory: "Andante," Franck.

Hymn of Commitment: "Wake, Awake, for Night is Flying," Philip Nicolai, 1599; trans. Catherine Winkworth, 1958, 1863; alt., 1972.

Music for Dismissal: A version of the passage, "Seek the Lord while he may be found; call upon him while he is near."

The Season Of The Holy Spirit

Proper 28, Pentecost 26, Ordinary Time 33

(Sunday between November 13 - 19, inclusive)

Liturgical Color: Green

Gospel: Matthew 25:14-30

Theme: *The Parable of the Talents.* A literary critic once said that he begins every day with the belief that he is on trial for his life, and probably will not be acquitted. How do we begin every day of our life? Daydreaming? Wishing? Hoping? Trusting?

Alleluia! Alleluia!

Invitation to the Celebration

In the Name of God the Creator, the Liberator, the Sustainer, the Energizer, welcome. God invites us, calls us to worship. Today, we said, "Yes." So, we are here today *(pause)* because we are not somewhere else. We are here because, today, we have accepted God's invitation. Now what?

P: God owns the world — of nature (think about that for a few moments); of animals (think about that for a few moments); of persons (think about that for a few moments).
M: We realize that the earth is the Lord's, even when we ravage and rape it.
P: God has provided all that we need for the good life and the God life.
M: In God's Presence and Power, we think and speak and respond.
P: Present yourself before God, ready to learn new lessons.
M: We present all that we are, and all that we have before God.

Response

"He Is Lord" (source unknown, found in *Folk Encounter*, Hope Publishing Company).

Prayer of Praise

Focus on the reality that God is involved, enmeshed in all of life; that God is Sovereign, even when we act as though we are in charge; that God is with us on the mountaintops, in the valleys, in the pits, with us, claiming lordship over all of our life.

Hymn of Praise

"God Reigns O'er All the Earth" (Jane Parker Huber, 1981; Franklin L. Sheppard, 1915).

We Seek Forgiveness

The Act of *Reviewing* Our Stewardship

How do we describe ourself as the steward of God? As a faithful Christian or an ambivalent self? Which of these would describe our qualities: doubt, forgetfulness, worry, laziness, anger, lust, prayerlessness, talkativeness, overbearing, self-centeredness, pride, unreasonableness, resentment, hypocrisy, racism, timidity, *(add your own)*? *(Two minutes of silence; write down your self-discovery.)*

The Act of Renewing Our Stewardship
Keep your paper and pen handy.

1. If you could rewrite your past in order to make yourself and your stewardship more creative today, how could you change what has happened to you? *(One minute of silence).*

2. If you could revive any portion of your life, any situation, or any relationship, all of which has to do with your stewardship of life, what would you do differently? *(One minute of silence.)*

3. If you could change what any person has said about, or done to, you, or what you have said or done to another, what would you change? *(One minute of silence).*

Obviously, we cannot change the past; we can let God forgive it; we can choose to live our lives differently, beginning NOW!

P: I invite us to remember the good news of our liberation.
M: In Christ, our self-worth has been declared.
P: We have been forgiven, accepted, received.
M: The past is forgiven, all of it, up to this moment. The present has been given new meaning, beginning this moment; the future, beginning now, is full of new visions, dreams, possibilities, commitments.
P: In the name of the living Christ, I invite us, I urge us, to live freely and responsibly.
M: Indeed we shall! So be it! Let it happen, Lord!

Response
"When I Had Not Yet Learned of Jesus" (Dngchul Chung, 1967; Yoosun Lee, 1967; para. Jane Parker Huber).

We Are Listening!

Message with the Children of All Ages
Again, with the children present, act out the parable. Ask them if they have any idea what it means. Put the story in a contemporary setting. We may envy the ten- and five-talent people; that's no help. God asks us to use what we have, not complain about what we do not have.

Reading from the Newer Covenant
See the Message with the Children above.

Proclamation of the Good News
The source of this story is lost: A woman from Paris was poor and blind. One day she put 27 francs into the offering plate. "But you can't afford so much," said her friend. "Yes, I can," she answered. When pressed to explain, she said, "I am blind and I asked my fellow straw workers how much they would spend in a year for oil for their lamps when it is too dark to work. They told me 27 francs. So I found out that I save that much in a year, because I am blind and do not need a lamp to work. I give it to shed light in the dark lands."

Response
"Lord of Light, Your Name Outshining" (Howell Elvet Lewis, 1916; alt.; Cyr Vincent Taylor, 1941).

We Are Accountable!

Stewardship Challenge
Noah Webster of dictionary fame was asked, "What is the greatest thought that has ever entered your mind?" Ask the congregation if anyone knows. After a pause, Webster answered, "The thought of my accountability to God." Is that our response?

Prayer Following the Offering

Forgive us, Lord, when we live "responsibly" on the millions of dollars we do not have, and fail to live responsibly on the thousands of dollars we do have. Make us responsible managers, stewards, of what you have given us freely.

We Leave For Ministry!

Charge to the Congregation

Every day is crisis (opportunity) day; for every day is our call to commitment, to responsible stewardship. We build a life, earthly and eternal, not by an emergency call at the end, but by a perpetual connection all along the way.

Meditation

"Unless there is within us that which is above us, we shall soon yield to that which is around us" (P. T. Forsythe).

P.S.

By the way, did you get the humor in the conclusion of the parable? You didn't? Read it until you do.

Music Possibilities In Addition To Those Already Suggested

Music for Preparation: "Chaconne," Buxtehude.

Hymn of Praise: "Heaven and Earth and Sea and Air," Joachim Neander, 1680 trans. composite; *Church Book*, 1868.

Response to Reviewing our Stewardship: "O Holy God, Whose Gracious Power Redeems Us," Jane Parker Huber, 1978; Alfred Scott-Gatty, 1902, from *Joy in Singing*.

Response to Renewing our Stewardship: "Called as Partners in Christ's Service," Jane Parker Huber 1981; John Zundel, 1870, from *Joy in Singing*.

Offertory: "Prayer for Peace," Jean Baptiste Lully

Hymn of Commitment: "Join Hearts and Voices as We Lift," Jane Parker Huber, 1982; John Hatton, d. 1793; from *Joy in Singing*.

Response to the Charge: "Reach Out to Your Neighbor," words and music by Roger Copeland, from *A New Hope*, Hope Publishing Company.

Music for Dismissal: "Prelude and Fugue in D-Minor," J. S. Bach.

The Season Of The Holy Spirit

Pentecost 27

(Lutheran Only)

Liturgical Color: Green

Gospel: Matthew 24:1-14

Theme: *Destruction of the Temple Foretold; Signs of the End of the Age; Persecutions Foretold.* Where did we ever get the idea that Christians are not to be disturbed?

Alleluia! Alleluia!

Invitation to the Celebration
    If we had to make a choice between the comforting words of Jesus, and the confronting words of Jesus, which would we choose? God gives us no choice: We get both! The Gospel not only is love *(agape)*, it is also justice, righteousness, holiness. We cannot have one without the other.
P: You have heard it said that God is dead, or absent, or always forgiving no matter how we behave. I say to you that God is living, actively comforting and confronting us, here and now.
M: Praise to the living God.
P: God is here! Do you hear God's truths?
M: We know God through the word, spoken and sung; in the Scriptures and hymns; in laughter and sadness; in joy and in hurt.
P: God is here! Do you experience God's realities?
M: We experience God through Holy Spirit, in support and challenge from God's word, in common unity of purpose and mission, in persons who love as God taught us to love.
P: I invite us to celebrate God's Presence and Power, God's comforting and confronting us.
M: So be it! (source unknown, revised)

Prayer of Praise
    Our Father/Mother, we wait, sometimes patiently, sometimes impatiently, in Your Presence; because we know that You are Creator, Sustainer, Liberator, Energizer of life. We wander aimlessly, and complain continually; we refuse to listen to You, because we think that we have life all figured out. Silence the unnecessary things that take our attention away from you. Open our ears to hear Your word, our hearts to respond to Your invitation, and our wills to obey Your will.

Hymn of Praise
    "God, Give Us Eyes and Hearts to See" (Jane Parker Huber 1982; *Geistliche Kirchengesand*, Cologne, 1623; from *Joy in Singing*).

We Seek Forgiveness

The Act of Reading the Signs
    Are we always looking for the signs of the end of time, rather than God's signs to us along the way? Many writers seem to know more about the end of the world than Jesus knew. It is possible to spend so much energy trying to "psych out" God's timetable that we miss the essence of the "precious present"

moment. Now, I invite you to take out paper and pen (pencil if you prefer; it's easier to erase our decisions). Write down a "yes, no, maybe, later, never" after each statement.
1. I freely choose to believe that I am personally responsible for my decisions and actions, rather than looking for scapegoats. *(Pause.)*
2. I reject the notion that someone else is responsible for my decisions and actions. *(Pause.)*
3. I choose to accept responsibility for my own way of life as I live it; and I accept the consequences for my own decisions. *(Pause.)*
4. I am pleased with myself in that I am willing to take personal responsibility for the commitments I make to myself, others, and God. *(Pause.)*
5. I am prepared to make my position clear to others when they ask me to do so. *(Pause.)*
6. I will make at least two commitments and will keep them. *(Pause.)*
7. I consistently uphold the commitments I have made to God, others, self. *(Two minutes of silence; after which, ask for a response from the people.)*

The Act of Responding to the Right Signs

We can play the game of trying to "psych out" God's timetable forever; or we can make a new decision to live to our fullest in the here-and-now moment. If we choose, we will look for the wrong signs, which will keep us anxious or self-righteous. It's our choice.

Response

"God Is Working His Purpose Out" (words by A.C. Ainger; v. 3 Jim Strathdee; music by Jim Strathdee, from *New Wine*).

We Are Listening!

Message with the Children of All Ages

While driving across the U.S., I decided to look for signs. My favorites were the "Burma Shave" signs. After returning home, I presented a sermon, "Sermonettes from Signboards." You can find a variety of ways to interest the children in signs, probably now on television or the Internet. Tie the signs with the signs that Jesus was giving to the disciples and to us. Always be ready!

Reading from the Newer Covenant

Ask someone who reads well to sit on a stool in the middle of the chancel and read these hard sayings of Jesus, slowly and deliberately.

Proclamation of the Good News

Invite the people to stop playing games around the signs of Jesus, and to focus upon their readiness to enter eternity. You may want to use this quote of John Henry Newman: "To take up the Cross of Christ [which is radically different from our burdens, WHK] is no great action done once for all time; it consists in the continual practice of small duties [some of] which are distasteful to us [and some of which bring extreme joy] (Source unknown; bracketed material, mine).

Response

"God's Law is Perfect and Gives Life" (George Frederick Handel, 1748; harm. C. Winfred Douglas, 1941; Christopher L. Webber, 1986).

We Are Accountable!

Stewardship Challenge

What kind of a sign does our giving represent?

Prayer Following the Offering
Lord, by your Spirit, show us how to look for the right signs.

We Leave For Ministry!

Charge to the Congregation
"If we believe that we have life in Christ, if we lay claim to reality in Christ — and refuse to share this with others, with *all* others, with *any* others, this signifies a subconscious hatred for the other" (Justin Morrill). So, instead of our arguing about the coming of the end, I invite us, instead, to share the good news along the way (WHK).

Meditation
"Look for the signs of God's Presence, rather than for the signs of God's coming" (WHK).

Music Possibilities In Addition To Those Already Suggested

Music for Preparation: "Before Thy Throne," Bach.

Hymn of Praise: "We Praise You, O God, Our Redeemer, Creator," Julia Cady Cory 1902, 1956; alt., 1972.

Response to the Assurance of Pardon: "Send Out Thy Light," Gounod.

Response to the Newer Covenant: "He Comes to Us," Jane Marshall; text, A. Schweitzer.

Offertory: "Geneva," to the tune of "Not Alone for Mighty Empire," William Pierson Merrill, 1909, 1910; alt., 1972.

Hymn of Commitment: "You Servants of God, Your Master Proclaim," Charles Wesley, 1744; alt.

Music for Dismissal: "Tallis' Canon," to the tune of "All Praise to Thee, Our God, This Night," Thomas Ken, 1693, 1709; alt., 1972.

The Season Of The Holy Spirit

Christ The King

Liturgical Color: Green

Gospel: Matthew 25:31-46

Theme: *The Judgment of the Nations.* If Christ is sovereign in our lives, how does his presence direct and empower our thoughts, words, feelings, actions?

Alleluia! Alleluia!

Invitation to the Celebration

Are we ready for the final judgment, which, of course, takes place every day? If we are not ready, what are we willing to do to get ready? How are we getting ready? The living God provides all of the resources we need to prepare. The living God provides our model for living. The living Spirit provides the energy we need to be the community of faith, hope, love.

(Just before the response, have the musicians play, "A Mighty Fortress Is Our God." The musicians continue to play during the litany.)

P: God owns the world of nature, of animals, of people.
M: The earth belongs to the Lord; and so do those who dwell in it.
P: God has established it from the beginning.
M: By God, we exist. In God, we live.
P: Lift up your heart, mind, will.
M: We lift them up, and offer them, to the Lord of Creation.

Response

"A Mighty Fortress Is Our God" (Martin Luther, 1529; trans. Frederick Henry Hedge, 1852). Use one tune during the litany; and the other tune for congregational singing.

Prayer of Praise

God, thank You for Your presence and power which invite, urge, call us to be Your people. Show us again today what You want from us, as persons appointed to specific tasks in Your world. Continue with us that we may keep on learning that You so loved the world, the whole world, the world of races and peoples and tribes and tongues; the world of nations; the world of families; the world of men and women; the world of little children, that You gave Your unique, one-of-a-kind son, that whoever believes in him shall not perish but have life eternal.

Hymn of Praise

"O God of Earth and Space" (Jane Parker Huber, 1980; adapted from a Hebrew melody). If this hymn is unknown, invite the choir to sing stanza 1, the people to read stanza 2, to hum or whistle stanza 3, and all to sing stanza 4. Use all of your musical instruments.

We Seek Forgiveness

The Act of Judgment

While the organist plays some somber music, have someone read from a loudspeaker the verses 25:40-46. Follow the reading with two minutes of silence. Ask the people to write down their thoughts. Invite them to share their awareness. Share a couple of your own.

Response

"Jesus the Man (Confession)" (words and music by David Farley, found in *New Wine*). If this is too difficult for the congregation, have a soloist, quartet, or choir sing it.

The Act of Hope

Now, while the musicians play some energetic, hopeful music, have a second reader, on the loudspeaker from outside of the sanctuary, read with much enthusiasm verses 34-40. Again, ask the people to write down their thoughts. Invite them to share their awarenesses. Share a couple of yours.

Response

"When a Poor One" (J. A. Oliver and Miguel Manzano, 1976; English trans. George Lockwood, 1989; alt., arr. Alvin Schutmaat).

We Are Listening!

Message with the Children of All Ages

(Bring a teddy bear with you.) How many of you wish that you were a teddy bear? Point out the advantages of being one: never have to eat; sit in the corner all day; people pick you up and play with you once in a while; no pain when ignored. A country-western song says, "I wish I was (were) a teddy bear, not living or loving, not going no where ... a wooden head and sawdust brains." Nice, huh? No feelings of any kind. Those folks at the end of Jesus' words seemed to have no feelings either; they ignored, never thought about, the people in need. They cared only about themselves. And, now, notice the other group. How can you be a part of that group?

Reading from the Newer Covenant

With the children still present, enact the passage.

Proclamation of the Good News

Perhaps you will want to begin as I do, with words similar to these: "I speak about this passage because it's a part of the Scripture which I would rather avoid. I come, mostly, with tears, rather than answers, with frustration, rather than solutions." As you begin, hand around to the congregation pictures which depict the latter part of the passage. Ask the people to write down their thoughts as they look at the scenes. Give them an opportunity to share their insights. Point out that the church has the power and resources to change that part of the world in which it resides; the church is you and I. Offer some specific ways for the church, corporately and individually, to involve itself in the healing part of Jesus' statement.

Response

Sing, once again, "When a Poor One."

We Are Accountable!

Stewardship Challenge

Christians are saved, that is, made whole, not by feeling guilty about what we do not do. We are made whole/saved by receiving God's love. Then we respond to that love in whatever capacity God calls us to share it, not because we *must*, but because we *choose* to do so.

Dedication Prayer

Freely we have received; freely we now give of our money, time, energy, resources, our being — because we have these to give; and because the world needs these gifts.

We Leave For Ministry!

Charge to the Congregation

Worship is something that happens, not between the church (we are the church) and God (because if worship stops here, we have not worshiped); rather, worship is something that happens between the world and God. "God loved the world so much that God gave ... and God gave *us* to minister to the world, the whole world in our space."

Response

Once more, sing, "When a Poor One."

Meditation

A church member, on an evaluation sheet of the church's program, said, "The church will survive only if it sells its property and helps the poor. A rich church is a contradiction in New Testament terms." Catholic layman Matthew Ahman puts the question this way: "When is the church going to stop playing games and really put its wealth to the service of the poor?"

Music Possibilities In Addition To Those Already Suggested

Music for Preparation: "Now Thank We All Our God," Bach.

Hymn of Praise: "O Come and Sing Unto the Lord," *The Psalter*, 1912; alt., 1955; or "For the Beauty of the Earth," stanzas 1-4, Folliott S. Pierpoint, 1864; alt. stanza 5, composite.

Response to the Newer Covenant: "Sing to the Lord of Harvest," S. Drummond Wolff.

Response to the Proclamation: "Come, You Thankful People, Come," Henry Alford, 1844, 1865; alt., 1972.

Response to the Newer Covenant: "He Comes to Us," Jane Marshall; text, A. Schweitzer.

Offertory: "Thanks Be to Thee," Handel; or "Song of Joy," Wesley.

Hymn of Commitment and Thanksgiving: "Now Thank We All Our God," Martin Rinkart, 1636; trans. by Catherine Winkworth, 1858; alt., 1972.

Charge to the Congregation: "He Ain't Heavy; He's My Brother," words by Bob Russell, Harrison Music Corp., 39 West 55th Street, New York, NY 10019. If you sing this, include "sister, mother, father."

Music for Dismissal: Medley of Thanksgiving music.

The Season Of The Holy Spirit

Thanksgiving Eve/Day

Liturgical Color: White/Red

Gospel: Luke 17:11-19

Theme: *Ten Healed of Leprosy.* Of what kind of leprosy do you need healing?

Celebrating God's Presence And Power

Invitation to the Celebration

As grateful people, welcome to the last worship in Pentecost. Identify how you came to worship today. *(Pause.)* Who would be willing to express *how* you came into the sanctuary? *(Give time for responses; we need not rush through worship.)* Let them know, honestly, how you came. It's okay not to be perfect and always in control.

Response

Everyone: Thanks for creating us, Lord. Your creation of us amazes us. You acted out of your love in Jesus, and that gives us hope forever. Thanksgiving means choice; and choice is made freely. Thanksgiving means life, life pulsating with courage. Thanksliving means acting out our faith; for our faith is seen in our actions. We celebrate with thanks.

Hymn of Praise

"We Gather Together" (Netherlands Folk Hymn, 1625; trans. Theodore Baker, 1894; harm. Eduard Kremser, 1877).

Prayer of Praise and Thanksgiving

In this prayer, avoid self-aggrandizement, and the notion that we are superior because we have so much more than others.

Celebrating Our Forgiveness

Call to Confession

We have used or heard the phrase, "God, thank you for our many blessings" hundreds of times. Do we ever consider the impact of our prayer?

1. If God is the provider, why are so many without even the necessities, while we thank God for our luxuries? *(One minute of silence.)*
2. Today, in the confession, I invite us to use this time to repent, rather than to thank. Think about those things/that stuff we had to have, which in a short time appeared in our garage sales or garbage bags. *(Pause until the people feel uncomfortable.)* Perhaps our "many blessings" are actually "many cursings." Because the more we have, the more we want. Perhaps we are the rich young ruler who chooses to turn away. We may turn away by saying that we really deserve all that we have. To turn to God, we will need to give up our self-righteous attitude, which insists that we have all of this stuff, because God, somehow, favors us above all the rest of the creation. NOT! If we read the Scriptures carefully, God seems to favor the poor and powerless, those at the bottom of the economic and social ladder. *(Silence for two minutes.)*

P: Lord, have mercy on us.

M: Christ, have mercy on us.
P: I invite us to keep taking a look at ourselves in light of the Gospel.
M: We seek forgiveness for turning our backs to others, for claiming superiority over others, for living out our God-given freedom without taking responsibility.
P: We confess to you, Lord, who we are, what we believe, where we go apart from you, and there is no health in us.
M: By your Spirit, make us thankful people, who live grateful lives — with less.

Response
"Lord, Have Mercy Upon Us" (*The Worshipbook*, 1972; arr. David N. Johnson, 1972).

Call to Pardon
God forgives only those who repent, that is, those who change their attitude and behavior. How could it be any other way? So, today, this week, examine your blessings. Check off which ones may or have become cursings. Write them down, and make them a part of your daily prayers. Identify one of them now; write it down. *(One minute of silence.)* No, Jesus never said that the rich will *not* enter the Kingdom. It's more difficult, he said, because we spend more time with our riches, and what they can buy, than with God. We too easily depend on our riches, whatever form they take, to save us, rather than Christ. So, what are you willing to let go, and let God take over? *(One minute of silence.)*
P: Christ's spirit has set us free and made us responsible to express thanks, to live thanks.
M: We express thanks, we live thanks because we know that the past is forgiven, that the future is before us.
P: I invite us to love life, and the people who share it with us.
M: We embrace life in Christ; we live life in Christ.

Response
Chorus only to popular song, "Let It Be."

Celebrating the Word

Message with the Children of All Ages
Edward Spencer was a student at Northwestern University in 1850. One day, while walking along the shore of one of the Great Lakes, he noticed a boat sinking. For the next several hours, he swam out to the survivors, bringing them to shore one by one. He saved seventeen lives. But the ordeal broke his health. He could not pursue his intended career. As an old man, he acknowledged that not one of those people ever thanked him. Now, that sounds similar to today's Scripture. I invite you to remain while the drama group enacts this story.

Reading from the Newer Covenant
(Plan well in advance.) Have ten people carry signs identifying some of today's "lepers." Suggestions: viral infections, MS, cerebral palsy, AIDS, cancer, deaf, blind, deformed, lame, leper. Have them dress the part if possible. As Jesus "heals" them, they throw their signs on the ground, and run out of the sanctuary. In a while, one returns. Jesus asks, "Weren't ten healed; where are the other nine? Isn't anyone going to turn and praise God for what's been done, except this stranger?" Jesus then touches the person and says, "Go on your way. Your faith has made you whole." And the person replies, "Thanks, Jesus."

Proclamation of the Good News
Consider these ideas:
1. Gratitude is the "memory of the heart."
2. If you lost everything, except your life, for 24 hours, and then, at the end of the 24 hours, you were able to have returned to you the five most important things, what would they be?
3. It was left to the Samaritan, the hated enemy of the Jews, the one who had no business being with them in the first place, to return and reply, "By the way ... thanks." Which of the ten are you? And you? And you? Am I?

Response

"I Will Give Thanks With My Whole Heart" (Christopher L. Webber, 1986, 1988; arr. Johann Sebastian Bach, c. 1708).

Celebrating Our Obedience

Stewardship Challenge

What if you lost everything, except your life, for 24 hours? At the end of the 24 hours, you were able to have returned to you the five most important things. What would they be? *(One minute of silence; write down your responses.)* Then ask, how many of you included "God" on your list? *(Pause before receiving the offering.)*

Prayer Following the Offering

By your Spirit, Lord, teach us how to use our money, checkbooks, credit cards for the building of your Kingdom, rather than ours.

Hymn of Commitment

"The World Abounds with God's Free Grace" (David G. Mehrtens, 1980; George Frederick Handel, 1749; harm. C. Winfred Douglas, 1941).

Charge to the Congregation

"If we cannot or will not give thanks to God for what we receive, then I invite us to give thanks for what we have escaped" (author unknown, slightly revised).

Meditation

"Poverty does not prohibit gratitude; prosperity does not produce it" (author unknown).

Music Possibilities In Addition To Those Already Suggested

Music for Preparation: "Prelude to Caprice #3," E. Nanny.

Hymn of Praise: "O Be Joyful in the Lord," based on Psalm 100; Curtis Beach, 1958; alt., 1972.

Response to the Newer Covenant: (Choir) "The Guiding Christ, Our Shepherd," Lloyd Pfautsch.

Response to the Stewardship Challenge: "Adagio," Vierne.

Hymn of Commitment and Thanksgiving: "Now Thank We All Our God," Martin Rinkart, 1636; trans. by Catherine Winkworth, 1858; alt., 1972. Lindell Sawyers has written a revision of this hymn, which appeared in *Monday Morning*, September 12, 1988. This magazine is a publication of the Presbyterian Church (U.S.A.). See address in Appendix I.

Response to the Benediction: Tune: "Kum Ba Ya,"
   "We are thankful, Lord. We give thanks.
   We are thankful, Lord. We give thanks.
   We are thankful, Lord. We give thanks.
   O Lord, we give thanks." (repeat for as long as you want)

Music for Dismissal: "Gigue from 1st Suite," J. S. Bach.

Introduction To The Appendices

Additional Insights for Cycle A
1. To plan creative worship requires at least six to eight weeks. In my entire ministry, I made this happen. No procrastination allowed.
2. Vary the placement of the reading and dramatizing of the Scripture — before, during, and after the proclamation; and sometimes, use it in all three places.
3. I make no apology for repeating certain acts of worship. Remember that only about one-fourth to one-third of your members attend any given Sunday.
4. Remember that God calls us to an impossible task; God expects of us only one thing: faithfulness, not success (a non-biblical word), or popularity, or acceptance, not even the appreciation of our members.
5. In all of your worship planning, use your imagination to create a powerful worship, in which God's primary qualities of love and justice are honored. We cannot have one without the other.

Contents Of The Appendices

Appendix I
Music Resources

Appendix II
Worship Resources (Because some of these are classics, in my opinion, send me a SASE for further information.)

Appendix III
Ways to use the Senses in Worship as Celebration.

Appendix IV
An Order of Worship Based on the Concepts in this Workbook, with Suggested Pastoral Responses.

Appendix V
A — Sermon Evaluation Form for Members of the Congregation.
B — Worship Evaluation Form for Members of the Congregation.

Occasionally, you may want to give these to the whole congregation at one time. Most of the time, I suggest that you give it to about ten or twelve selected people, people whom you know support you, and some who do not. Remember that these represent opinions; nevertheless, you may learn some things about your theology, your clarity or confusion, your presentation, your enthusiasm or boredom, your life, that you need to learn. After all, the liturgy is "the work and the play of the people," even the ones who give you a bad time.

Appendix I

Music Resources

Richard Avery and Donald Marsh Songbook, The Second Avery and Marsh Songbook, Folk Encounter, Let the People Sing, A New Now, Folk Songs For Choirs, The Genesis Songbook: Songs for Getting It All Together, compiled by Carlton R. Young, published by Agape. All of these are published by Hope Publishing Company, 380 South Main Street, Carol Stream, Illinois 60187.

The Hymbook, published by the Presbyterian Church in the United States, The United Presbyterian Church in the U.S.A., The Reformed Church in America, Richmond, Philadelphia, New York.

Discovery In Song, published by Paulist Press, editorial office, 304 W. 58th Street, New York, New York 10019.

Joy In Singing, published as a joint project of The Office of Women, General Assembly, Mission Board, 341 Ponce de Leon Avenue, N.E., Atlanta, Georgia 30365, and The Joint Office of Worship, 1044 Alta Vista Road, Louisville, Kentucky 40205.

The Presbyterian Hymnal, published by Westminster/John Knox Press, 100 Witherspoon Street, Louisville, Kentucky 40204-1396.

Singing the Lord's Song, published by and copyrighted by World Around Songs, Burnsville, North Carolina 28714; and distributed by Discipleship Resources, P. O. Box 189, 1908 Grand Avenue, Nashville, Tennessee 37202 (615-340-7284).

Songs by Paul Simon, published by Charing Cross Music, 40 East 54th Street, New York, New York 10022; sales and shipping, 8th Floor, 17 West 60th Street, New York, New York 10023.

Workers Quarterly: A Portfolio for Good, Bad, or Rotten Times, July, 1967; Volume 39, number 1 and *Hymns For Now*, published by the Walther League, 875 North Dearborn Street, Chicago, Illinois 60610.

New Wine, editors: Jim Strathdee and Nelson Stringer, copyright 1973 by Board of Education of the Southern California/Arizona Conference of the United Methodist Church, 5250 Santa Monica Boulevard, Los Angeles, California 90029.

Appendix II

Additional Worship Resources

Some books become classics. Some music becomes identified as classical music. In my opinion, the following worship resources also are classics. Some are out of print. Perhaps you can find them in a used book store.

Aesop's Fables for Modern Readers. Illustrated by Eric Carle, Peter Pauper Press, 202 Mamaroneck Avenue, White Plains, New York 10601 (800-833-2311).

Bird Life in Wington. J. Calvin Reid, Pubished by William B. Eerdmans Publishing Company, 255 Jefferson Avenue S.E., Grand Rapids, Michigan 49503 (800-253-7521). Orders only: 616-459-4591. Try Baker's Book Store (used book section) 616-957-3110; or Kregel's Books, 616-459-9444.

A Book of Hugs. Dave Ross, Thomas Y. Crowell, New York, merged with HarperCollins, 10 E. 53rd Street, New York, New York 10022 (212-207-7000).

A Coney Island of the Mind. Poems by Lawrence Ferlinghetti, New Directions Publishing Corporation, 80 Eighth Avenue, New York, New York 10011 (800-223-2584).

Creative Brooding. Robert Raines, Macmillan Reference, 60 5th Avenue, New York, New York 10010; or 200 Old Tappen Road, Old Tappen, New Jersey 07675 (800-223-2336).

Discovery in Word. Discovery in Prayer. Robert Heyer and Richard Payne, Paulist Press, 997 MacArthur Boulevard, Mahwah, New Jersey 07446 (201-825-7300).

Footnotes and Headlines. To Believe in God. Sister Corita and Joseph Pintauro. Rights controlled by the authors, c/o Curtis Brown, Ltd., 575 Madison Avenue, New York, New York 10022.

Games Christians Play. Judi Culbertson and Patti Bard. HarperCollins Publishing, 1000 Keystone Industrial Park, Scranton, Pennsylvania 18512-4621 (717-941-1500).

Garfield. Jim Davis, published by Ballentine Books, Division of Random House, 201 E. 50th Street, New York, New York 10022 (800-733-3000). And the daily newspaper.

"George" and Other Parables. Patricia Ryan, published originally by Argus Communications, now Tabor Publishing, 200 E. Bethany Drive, Allen, Texas 75002 (800-822-6701). Author's address unknown; check with Tabor Publishing.

He Sent Leanness. David Head, the Macmillan Publishing Company, Division of Crowell-Collier Publishing Company, 866 Third Avenue, New York, New York 10022.

I-Openers: 80 Parables. Herbert Brokering, Concordia Publishing House, 3558 South Jefferson Avenue, St. Louis, Missouri 63118 (314-268-1000).

The Joyful Noiseletter, a newsletter; and new portraits with Jesus laughing are two of many resources of the Fellowship of Merry Christians (open to anyone). Cal and Rose Samra, P. O. Box 895, Portage, Michigan 49081-0895 (616-324-0990).

Knots. R. D. Laing, Vintage Books, Division of Random House, 201 E. 50th Street, 22nd floor, New York, New York 10022 (800-726-0600).

Kudzu. Doug Marlette, Creators Syndicate, Inc., Sepulveda Boulevard, Suite 103, Los Angeles, California 90025 (213-477-2776).

The Old Testament Made Easy. Consider the Lemming. Jeanne and William Steig, Michael Dicapua Books, Farrar, Straus, Giroux, Inc., 19 Union Square, W. New York, New York 10003 (800-788-6262).

On Edge. Parables. Jim Crane, published originally by John Knox Press; now Westminster/John Knox Press, 100 Witherspoon Street, Louisville, Kentucky 40202-1396 (502-569-5043).

Peanuts. Charles Schulz, United Features Syndicate, Inc., 200 Park Avenue, 6th floor, New York, New York 10166-0190 (212-692-3700). And the daily newspaper.

Politically Correct Parables. Robert Martin Walker, Andrews and McMeel, a Universal Press Syndicate Company, 4900 Main Street, 9th floor, Kansas City, Missouri 64112 (800-826-4216).

Prayers. Michel Quoist, Sheed and Ward, 115 East Armour Boulevard, Kansas City, Missouri (816-531-0538).

The Prophets on Main Street. J. Elliott Corbett, Westminster/John Knox Press, 100 Witherspoon Street, Louisville, Kentucky 40202-1396 (502-569-5043).

Sound Effects. Ampex Media Corporation, 401 Broadway Street, Redwood City, California 94063-3126 (415-367-2012).

The Story of the Christian Year. George Gibson, Abingdon Press, 201 8th Avenue S., Nashville, Tennessee (615-749-6000).

Twelve Baskets Full. Margaret T. Applegarth, HarperCollins Publishing, 1000 Keystone Industrial Park, Scranton, Pennsylvania 18512-4621 (717-941-1500).

The Velveteen Rabbit. Margery Williams, Camelot Books, published by Avon Books, 1350 Avenue of the Americas, 2nd floor, New York, New York 10019 (800-223-0690).

Worship and the Arts Series, multi-media, filmstrips, and cassettes, published by The Joint Office of Worship, 1044 Alta Vista Road, Louisville, Kentucky 40205. This series included the following: Psalm 150; Sounding Praise; Architecture; Drama; Liturgical Dance; Sharing the Spirit in Music. (For a one-time use, send me $10.00.)

Resources for the History of Many Hymns

My Life and the Story of the Gospel Hymns, Ira D. Sankey, The Sunday School Times Company, Philadelphia, Pennsylvania 1906-1907.

Lost in Wonder, Charles Wesley: The Meaning of His Hymns Today, S.T. Kimbrough, Jr., The Upper Room, United Methodist Church, 1908 Grand Avenue, P.O. Box 189, Nashville, Tennessee 37202-0189 (615-340-7256).

The Presbyterian Hymnal Companion, Lindajo H. McKim, Westminster/John Knox Press, Louisville, Kentucky. (Perhaps your denomination has a similar companion.)

Use worship, classes, and your church newsletter to educate your people about the hymns they sing.

Appendix III

Ways To Use The Senses In Worship As Celebration

I. **Touch** — opens communication.
   1. Shake hands
   2. Laying on of hands
   3. Hugging those close
   4. Join hands
   5. Grabbing of arm
   6. Arms around a person
   7. Share hymnbook
   8. Accidental touching, as at offering time
   9. Keep hands free and empty; hands outstretched
   10. Natural expression
   11. Hold hands when singing (slide projector)
   12. Hold hands when praying, give squeeze at end
   13. Sanctuary in the round
   14. Everyone turn around and greet people
   15. Create more involvement to build community — through mission
   16. Keep awareness of who we are
   17. Do not become exclusive with feelings
   18. Move around — dance
   19. Holy kiss
   20. Serve communion to each other
   21. Be aware of spontaneous possibilities
   22. Create sense of freedom
   23. Greet people as we come to worship
   24. People move around sanctuary during prelude
   25. Sit next to new people — take hand
   26. Invite people and pick them up
   27. Need to be sensitive to people's feelings

II. **Smell** — opens communication.
   1. Myrrh and incense
   2. Flowers; handing out flowers
   3. Fresh-baked bread for communion aroma
   4. Coffee aroma
   5. Odors in sanctuary: polish and wax
   6. Room fresheners
   7. Unpleasant odors: sulphur, garbage, pollution
   8. Hay and grass
   9. Apples and farm produce
   10. Stable odor at Christmas
   11. Spices: on drops of blotter or cotton to take home
   12. Beach odors
   13. Creosote or tar
   14. Medical: alcohol, ether
   15. Moth balls
   16. Wet wool
   17. Passing envelope with odor (to recall memories)

III. **Taste** — opens communication.
   1. Passion/Holy Week — Passover meal (ask Rabbi to describe meal)
   2. Birthday cake — Christmas (sharing)
   3. Candy Easter egg — "Legend of Easter Egg" — greeting "Jesus Christ is Risen! Yes, He is Risen Indeed!"
   4. Communion — Various elements; seated at table
   5. Extending church fellowship night into communion
   6. Sacrificial meal: duplicate poverty meal (one great hour)
   7. Live on food stamps for a week
   8. Fast as a congregation
   9. Challenge families to put themselves on welfare budget means; close cupboards with masking tape — "Any milk today"/"Got milk?"
   10. Pentecost breakfast
   11. Sunrise breakfast
   12. Family potlucks — put name of person who brought food beside food
   13. Food from other lands

IV. **Sight** — opens communication.
   1. Posters, banners
   2. Filmstrips, slides, colored lights
   3. Architecture: shape of room, windows
   4. Good paintings
   5. Pews and communion table — change positions
   6. Opaque or overhead projectors
   7. Bulletin covers
   8. Bibles
   9. Colors of walls and carpet
   10. Open windows, bright lights
   11. Faces and gestures of people
   12. Upkeep of building
   13. Cross, candles
   14. Where pastor stands
   15. Ushers' and greeters' attitudes
   16. Proximity of people
   17. Children present: crying rooms, nursery, child seats (car seats), restaurant seats, sit on chancel
   18. Ushers wear buttons, rather than flowers: "Smile, God loves you"
   19. Clock
   20. Hymnbook
   21. Flags, posters
   22. Sermon notes, notes about sermon
   23. Palm Sunday: palm leaf or floral procession
   24. Blindfolds for blind
   25. Children around baptismal font; family to baptismal font
   26. Choir robes: necessary or not
   27. What is appropriate dress: "If the kids come dressed up, then it isn't important." Want to wear grubbies; should we have a "grubby Sunday"? Shoes off in narthex; come in your labor clothes.

V. **Sound** — opens communication.
   1. Tape recordings
   2. Key words/phrases repeated often
   3. Instruments
   4. Silence
   5. Use sounds around us
   6. Dialogue service and laypeople
   7. Congregational anthems — joys
   8. Clapping, stomping, whistling, laughing
   9. Conversations
   10. Recording of news during sermon
   11. Children's noises —   accepting them
   12. Sound — with Scripture reading
   13. Choir in pews
   14. Contrasting sounds
   15. Creating a new language. "Snow falling off roof — okay. Boys throwing rocks on roof —   not okay."
   16. Human sounds: moans, grumbling stomachs, etc.
   17. Sounds causing feelings/emotions
   18. Sounds causing us to hear God
   19. Give out rhythm instruments to anyone who wants them
   20. Hawaiian music with theme
   21. Sounds of world with human heartbeat
   22. Reading of the newspaper
   23. Write some new music

Appendix IV

**An Order of Worship Based on the Concepts In This Workbook
with
Suggested Pastoral Responses**

The Congregation of _____ Gathers Together
occasionally
To Celebrate the Good News
that Christ is Alive and Living Among and Through Us.
We Celebrate Good News This Day
in Order to Recall
Whose We Are   What We Do
Who We Are   Where We Go
Because
God in Christ has Prepared the Way — God in Christ is the Way

"Christ comes, Christ is here, Christ will come to make new persons of us,
and the world."

The Community Gathers To Celebrate
"We offer ourselves in the Spirit of the Living Christ."

Music for Preparation   Medley of Praise Hymns
(Invite the People to bring Musical Instruments.)

Adoration
Invitation to the Celebration   Isaiah 6:1-4
Response to the Invitation: "He Is Jehovah."
(Soloist with Congregation Standing)
(God is Nonsexist/Listen for the Biblical Names of God)

Declaration of Joy   Pastors and Ministers
P: We are here because God has invited, called us from whatever bushes we hide behind.
M: We rejoice that God has taken the initiative to say YES! to us. We rejoice that we, finally, have said *yes* to God.
P: Now, I invite us to say *yes* to one another until everyone has experienced a *yes* from one of God's people.

Prayer Response   "The Lord's Prayer" (Malotte)
Choirs, People, Instruments

The Community Faces Up To Itself
"We Receive New Life"

Confession
Introduction to the Act of Recognizing Our Humanity   Isaiah 6:5

The Act of Recognizing Our Humanity

Everyone: *(Pray only that part of the prayer which you believe.)* "You've said to us, Lord, that we have perfect freedom in your services. Well, I don't feel perfectly free. I don't feel free at all. I'm a captive to myself. I've created my own prison. I'm bound by self-pity, by my lack of honest involvement with people — the young and the old, the disenfranchised, the powerless, the lonely, the dying. My fears chain me. I am no different from my neighbor, or my enemy, about whom I constantly complain. I'm no different from Mary Magdalene ..."

"I Don't Know How to Love Him"
From *Jesus Christ, Superstar*
(Interpretive Dancer and Powerful Soloist)

(Silence for One Full Minute)

Forgiveness

Introduction to the Act of Receiving New Life   Isaiah 6:6-7
"Christ was more of an artist than all the others.
He worked in the living flesh." (Van Gogh)

The Act of Receiving New Life

P: In Christ we have listened to the Good News. Have you heard it?

M: Yes, we hear, we know that the past is forgiven, all of it, up to this moment. We hear, we know that Christ has accepted us, all of us, up to this moment.

P: The Spirit of the living, reigning Christ has set us free to live. The future, all of it, is before us.

M: We give thanks for the past and the future, as we learn how to live in the precious present moment. We live, in the Spirit of Christ, with courage and commitment to a new humanity. "The glory of God is man/woman fully alive." (Iranaeus, about 200 A.D.)

P: So be it! And all the people said (*your favorite praise word*).

Ministers with All Instruments Respond with "Let It Be"
(popular song, chorus only)
"Let it be, let it be, let it be.
There will be an answer, let it be." *(Repeat)*

The Community Learns of Christ's Mission

"We Are Listening"

Reading from the Older Covenant	Isaiah 6:1-8 (His Call)
Response	"How Clear Is Our Vocation, Lord"
Dramatizing the Newer Covenant	John 4:1-26
Proclamation of the Good News	"No Spectators Allowed: Worship as Drama, Celebration, Play"
Response to the Proclamation	"Holy God, We Praise Your Name"

The Community Becomes Responsible To (Not For) God's World

"We Respond in Faith"

Stewardship Challenge — Isaiah 6:8

Doxology by Richard Avery and Don Marsh

Prayer of Commitment with Congregational Amen

Hymn of Commitment — "Here Am I, Lord"

Charge to the Congregation — Benediction

Choral Response — "Up and Get us Gone"
Ed Seabough; William Reynolds

The Community Scatters For Ministry

Music for Dismissal — Medley of Dedication Hymns

Meditation
"Only the disciplined change the world" (Socrates). How will you and I change the world of our home, neighborhood, school, job, recreation, shopping. living, being?

Possible Pastoral Responses to Each Act of Worship

Invitation to the Celebration

In the Name of God the Creator, Liberator, Sustainer, Energizer, welcome to this celebration of Good News. In the tradition of Isaiah the Prophet, we celebrate the Presence and Power of God. In a powerful vision during worship, Isaiah envisioned the Sovereignty of God. He saw the seraphs calling to each other, "Holy, Holy, Holy is the Lord of Hosts, the whole earth is full of God's glory." We know that God is neither male nor female — for God is Spirit (Holy Spirit) — and those who celebrate God's Presence and Power, do so in spirit and reality. So, I invite us to focus on the Cross, and to listen to some of the biblical words for God in "He Is Jehovah."

Introduction to the Act of Recognizing Our Humanity

When Isaiah saw God for who God is, he began to see himself — his brokenness, alienations, I-centeredness — he had the good sense to begin with himself. "I am finished; I am a foulmouthed man." He began with his own confession. I prefer to begin with yours — then I will have no time left for mine. *(One minute of silence.)* Now, I invite you to take out paper and pencil/pen. Please write down the names of all the people you wish would confess their sins *(Pause.)* Now, please write down the names of the sins you wish that they would confess. *(Pause.)* Isaiah began with himself, and only after, confessed the sins of his people. "I live among a foulmouthed people." We're in it together, friends. *(One minute of silence.)* So, now, I invite us to pray only the parts of the prayer which we believe.

Introduction to the Act of Receiving New Life

All true confession leads to forgiveness. "The red-hot coal touched his mouth. The Seraph said, 'Your guilt shall go and your sin is forgiven.'" "The only thing that we contribute to our salvation is our sin." We have only one legitimate response for our new life: Gratitude — thanksgiving and thanksliving. Rejoice! Rejoice! Amen! Amen!

Stewardship Challenge

(1) If we gave no money today, what of ourself would we give; what would we keep for ourself? (2) Some years ago, a woman wanting tickets to the Sonics' playoff game affirmed, "I'll do *anything* for two tickets; and I mean *anything*." Isaiah said, "Here I am, Lord, send me. I'll do anything you want! You name it! Send me!"

Charge to the Congregation

The question to ask ourselves, as individuals, as the church, is not, "Did I like/dislike the worship, music, sermon?" That has nothing to do with anything. Rather, God calls us to respond, "Here I am, Lord! What do you want me to be, to do, not so much for the sake of the church, but for the sake of the world?"

Response to the Benediction (in the tradition of Bill Cosby*):

Pastor will say:	Congregation will respond:
1. That's right	1. Amen
2. You said it	2. Amen
3. It's true	3. Amen
4. Count on it	4. Amen
5. Sure	5. Amen
6. It can be done	6. Amen
7. It's a promise	7. Amen
8. Let's go	8. Amen
9. Okay, Lord	9. Amen
10. I'm counting on it	10. Amen
11. Make it so, Lord, make it so	11. Amen
12. So be it	12. Amen
13. Yes	13. Amen
14. Yeah! Yeah!	14. Amen
15. Tah-Dah!	15. Tah-Dah

*Source Unknown

Appendix V-A

Sermon Evaluation by the Congregation

_____
Worship Leader   Date _____

	Very Good	Good	Average	Poor	Very Poor
1. Voice					
Range and Quality	( )	( )	( )	( )	( )
Inflection and Enunciation	( )	( )	( )	( )	( )
Natural and Commanding	( )	( )	( )	( )	( )
2. Delivery					
Posture and Gestures	( )	( )	( )	( )	( )
Eye Contact	( )	( )	( )	( )	( )
Use of Notes	( )	( )	( )	( )	( )
3. Style					
Terse and Vigorous	( )	( )	( )	( )	( )
Clear and Plain	( )	( )	( )	( )	( )
Concise	( )	( )	( )	( )	( )
4. Construction					
Structure and Logic	( )	( )	( )	( )	( )
Quotations/Illustrations	( )	( )	( )	( )	( )
Introduction	( )	( )	( )	( )	( )
Conclusion	( )	( )	( )	( )	( )
5. Content					
Theological					
a. Grace — God's Love for Us	( )	( )	( )	( )	( )
b. Judgment — Strip Away Pretense	( )	( )	( )	( )	( )
Ethical					
a. Obedience — Our Love for God	( )	( )	( )	( )	( )
b. Commitment — Our Love for the World	( )	( )	( )	( )	( )
Significance	( )	( )	( )	( )	( )
Biblical	( )	( )	( )	( )	( )

6. Did the Sermon   Decisively   Slightly   Not At All
   Prompt a Response   ( )   ( )   ( )
   Require a Yes or No   ( )   ( )   ( )
   Lead to Action   ( )   ( )   ( )

Sermon was strong in: _____
_____
_____
_____
_____

Suggestions for strengthening: _____
_____
_____
_____
_____

_____

Signed (optional)

Appendix V-B

Worship Evaluation

Name (optional) _____   Date _____

1. Is the music, in general, integrated with today's theme?   Yes ____   No ____
   Suggestions _____
   _____

2. Is the music, specifically, integrated with each part of worship?
   Praise/Adoration (Focusing on God)   Yes ____   No ____
   Confession of Sin/Assurance of Pardon   Yes ____   No ____
   Thanksgiving/Intercession   Yes ____   No ____
   Dedication/Commitment (Response to God)   Yes ____   No ____
   Suggestions _____
   _____

3. Are the prayers integrated with each part of worship?   Yes ____   No ____
   Suggestions _____
   _____

4. Is the message with the children integrated with the scripture or worship theme?
   Yes ____   No ____
   Suggestions _____
   _____

5. How did/would drama,   Comments: _____

   liturgical dance,   _____

   pictures,   _____

   banners, for today, for each season,   _____

   enhance, empower, enliven worship as celebration, as Good News?

6. How did you experience today's worship? (Check all that apply)
   Inspiration ____   Education ____   Comfort ____   Challenge ____   Other ____
   God's love ____   God's holiness/justice ____

7. Did worship command a change in your thinking ____ and actions ____ ?

8. Comments: _____
   _____
   _____
   _____